1994

Medieval Literature

Texts and Interpretation

medieval & renaissance texts & studies

VOLUME 79

Medieval Literature

Texts and Interpretation

Edited by

TIM WILLIAM MACHAN

Medieval & Renaissance texts & studies
Binghamton, New York
1991

© Copyright 1991
Center for Medieval and Early Renaissance Studies
State University of New York at Binghamton

Library of Congress Cataloging-in-Publication Data

Medieval literature : texts and interpretation / edited and with an introduction by
Tim William Machan.
    p. cm. — (Medieval & renaissance texts & studies : v. 79)
    Includes index.
    ISBN 0-86698-090-3
    1. English literature—Middle English, 1100-1500—Criticism, Textual.
2. Manuscripts, Latin (Medieval and modern)—England. 3. Manuscripts, English
(Middle) I. Machan, Tim William. II. Series.
PR275.T45M4 1991
820.9'001—dc20   90-48431
                                 CIP

This book is made to last.
It is set in Garamond, smythe-sewn
and printed on acid-free paper
to library specifications.

Printed in the United States of America

Table of Contents

Medieval Literature

Texts and Interpretation

Late Middle English Texts
and the Higher and Lower Criticisms

TIM WILLIAM MACHAN

One of the most basic divisions in the labors of literary critics has been that between textual and interpretive studies. Today, of course, a label such as "textual criticism" or "literary interpretation" scarcely designates something monolithic and static, for the theoretical diversity of both can be almost overwhelming. "Textual criticism" conjures images of recension, best-text editing, eclecticism, various kinds of bibliography, and the "socialization" of the text. "Interpretive studies," on the other hand, implies Marxism, feminism, deconstruction, historicism, and old-fashioned New Criticism. And all of these approaches, in turn, admit a variety of refinements and specializations. But as diverse as each of these disciplines is, they are nonetheless often perceived and enacted as if different from each other in at least one very general way: textual critics construct texts which literary critics then interpret. And to this extent their essential objectives and methods have often seemed to be distinct.

The perception of these disciplines as distinct is, however, changing, as an awareness of the complementary nature of textual and interpretive studies continues to grow in the scholarly community. The work of such critics as Jerome McGann on literary production as "a social and an institutional event," D. F. McKenzie on "bibliography as the study of the sociology of texts," and Hershel Parker on the editorial consequences of New Critical aesthetics has underscored the fact that just as there can be no value-free literary interpretation, so there can be no value-free textual criticism.[1] This work indicates that textual and interpretive studies of any orientation are not in fact *potentially* complementary but *necessarily* so.

In theory many critics would happily accept such a proposition, but in practice much criticism continues to be resolutely textual or interpre-

---

[1] *A Critique of Modern Textual Criticism* (Chicago: University of Chicago Press, 1983), 100; *Bibliography and the Sociology of Texts* (London: The British Library, 1986), 5; *Flawed Texts and Verbal Icons, Literary Authority in American Fiction* (Evanston: Northwestern University Press, 1984). I would like to thank my colleagues Michael McCanles and Russell J. Reising for their very helpful comments on early drafts of this paper.

tive; it isn't often, for instance, that an article in *New Literary History* contains a reference to one in *Studies in Bibliography* and vice versa. Indeed, it is not always clear whether apparently disparate procedures—text-editing and Marxist hermeneutics, for example, or enumerative bibliography and feminism—should or even can be meaningfully integrated. But for medievalists in particular, the interrelations between textual and literary study, especially when unacknowledged, are in any case as far-reaching as they are unavoidable. As we become increasingly dependent on the edited text rather than the medieval manuscript we are concommittantly dependent on (and limited by) editors' hermeneutic decisions for our own sense of medieval literature and literary history; it is in part through these decisions that we arrive at definitions of such terms as author, text, genre, and literary tradition. Yet an editor must already have some such definitions in mind in order to edit any medieval text. And as both manuscript studies and literary theory grow increasingly specialized, they necessarily risk moving even farther apart and working towards separate if not incompatible goals.

Briefly stated, the following essays on late Middle English literature explore the practical consequences of the interrelations between textual criticism and literary interpretation. In this introduction, therefore, I want to elaborate on these interrelations on a theoretical level. My intention is not at all to attempt a definitive answer to the questions this interdependence raises; they have, indeed, already been explored by a variety of critics, and I shall for the most part use "textual criticism" and "literary interpretation" in reference not to any of their particular permutations but to the broad distinction I noted at the outset. Rather, I want to sketch out, with special reference to Middle English literature, some of the theoretical overlaps between these disciplines and the very conception of them as distinct disciplines. I hope, thereby, to provide a theoretical rationale for the following practical illustrations.

I begin with a longstanding and well-entrenched framework. Even if not always articulated or recognized as such, there has been in literary studies of English literature since the early nineteenth century a theoretical and practical distinction between the "Lower" and "Higher" criticisms. The former is the establishment of literary, social, and cultural contexts and thus subsumes biography, bibliography, and textual criticism. The Higher Criticism, conversely, embraces what is commonly called literary interpretation and theory. Of the two, the Lower Criticism is perhaps commonly viewed as the more factual or "scientific": it provides numerical, analytical, and categorical information which is used to define historical realities—that which was said, or written, or done. These realities, of course, may be refined or even redefined, but that they are realities—of texts or lives—is the hermeneutic essence of the Lower Criticism as it is commonly practiced and more commonly perceived. In

Paul Oskar Kristeller's observation on textual and interpretive studies in particular,

> [T]here are two layers of historical scholarship, the textual scholarship which we pursue and which is more modest but more certain, and the general theory of history and of literature which is more ambitious but also more conjectural. I see no reason why the two should not coexist. Social history, the general theory of literature and of its place in society, the changing reception of a work of literature in later criticism, these are very interesting topics worthy of much study and investigation. But they are no substitute for the groundwork of textual scholarship which should be pursued by other scholars and perhaps even by the same scholars who are interested in general theories, for they cannot succeed in establishing their general theories unless they are in agreement with the method and results of textual scholarship.[2]

Though Kristeller's formulation involves a base/superstructure model, his rhetoric implies that there is something grudging in his acceptance both of "the general theory of literature" as a "very interesting" topic "worthy of much study" and of the efforts of "even" literary scholars on the "groundwork of textual scholarship." The values underlying this view, in other words, in a way seem to champion the tortoise of textual criticism over the hare of literary interpretation and thereby reflect a widely held view.[3] An equally common view in which a value judgment is also quite clear sees the Higher Criticism as the spirit which gives life to the letters established by the Lower Criticism; it is the intellectual and aesthetic activity which, depending on one's critical viewpoint, reveals, constitutes, or disassembles the meanings of a text. Thus, in Wolfgang Iser's view, it is the aesthetic response of a reader which in a sense completes a literary work:

> In literary works . . . the meaning is transmitted in two ways, in that the reader "receives" it by composing it. . . . Practically every discernible structure in fiction has this two-sidedness: it is verbal and affective. The verbal aspect guides the reaction and prevents it from being arbitrary; the affective aspect is the fulfilment of that which has been prestructured by the language of the text.[4]

---

[2] "Textual Scholarship and General Theories of History and Literature," *Text* 3 (1987): 8.

[3] See, for example, Fredson Bowers, "Textual Criticism and the Literary Critic," in *Textual and Literary Criticism* (Cambridge: Cambridge University Press, 1959), 1–34.

[4] *The Act of Reading, A Theory of Aesthetic Response* (Baltimore: The Johns Hopkins Press, 1978), 21.

Both pedagogically and professionally, it is the Higher Criticism which of late has been most frequently valorized; at least since the New Criticism approached the text as a phenomenon separate from social and cultural contexts, the question "What does it mean" (rather than, for instance, "Where does it mean," or "To whom does it mean," or "What does it do") has dominated the discussions of both students and scholars. Indeed, as the vertical metaphor which relates the two criticisms suggests, the Lower Criticism, from either common view, can be perceived as only a stepping stone to the Higher, and sometimes more important, one.

There are two issues in this framework which merit further examination: the objectivity of the Lower Criticism and the Lower Criticism's contradistinction from the Higher. The former, again, is often considered as necessarily an objective assessment and arrangement of objective facts and phenomena. But studies in other areas have increasingly demonstrated the illusory character of such objectivity; the perspective of the linguist shapes linguistic phenomena as much as that of the historian shapes historical events or that of the literary interpreter shapes literature.[5] It has in fact become commonplace to say that the observer always has an influence on the nature of what is being observed, in part because, as Terry Eagleton wittily suggests,

> Anyone who is not "interested" will never "see the object as it really is," if only because he or she, superbly untainted by all whiff of interest, would see no point in looking in the first place.[6]

Unless it is a hermeneutic aberration, textual criticism, it would seem, must also be subject to such constraints. Indeed, the objectivity of textual criticism in particular is rendered suspect in a variety of ways. On the broadest level it might be noted that the "objectivity" of the Lower Criticism is foremost a cognitive concomitant of the "subjectivity" of the Higher Criticism. That is, as modes of analysis one cannot exist without

---

[5] Two especially noteworthy studies are R. G. Collingwood, *The Idea of History* (Oxford: Clarendon, 1946); and Roger Lass, *On Explaining Language Change* (Cambridge: Cambridge University Press, 1980). As Jerome McGann has recently put the matter: "We have come to see that all of the discourses of knowledge—even the discourses of the so-called 'hard sciences'—are socially and historically determined; that the ideal of scientific 'objectivity' and the quest for universal statements are at best a heuristic and enabling mechanism for a certain kind of knowledge-discourse and at worst an ideology—an illusion—of truth; that knowledge, in short, is a function of the particular lexicon, grammar, and usage in which it is pursued and framed." *Social Values and Poetic Acts, The Historical Judgment of Literary Work* (Cambridge: Harvard University Press, 1988), 96.

[6] "Ideology and Scholarship," in *Historical Studies and Literary Criticism*, ed. Jerome J. McGann (Madison: University of Wisconsin Press, 1985), 117.

the other, inasmuch as the Lower Criticism provides the facts which the Higher Criticism interprets; without the traditional Lower Criticism's construction of texts, for instance, there can be no focus for the theorizing of the Higher Criticism, just as without the traditional Higher Criticism's interpretation of texts there can be no contexts within which the Lower Criticism can identify facts.

It is also worth considering here whether the "objectivity" of textual criticism is not in fact informed in general by the "subjectivity" of literary interpretation. In considering such matters, one must invariably address the superlative work of George Kane, who is one of a very few scholars to have offered explicit theorizing about the editing of Middle English texts and who thus by default must often speak for the profession at large.[7] Kane observes that "the data for making grammars of Chaucer's style in his various poems are actually abundant" and that an editor can recover Chaucer's or Langland's actual texts with a remarkable degree of certainty. He also suggests that the the difference between the literary critic's "grammar of the style" of a work and the textual critic's *usus scribendi* "is in the objective:

> the critic of style analyzes the poet's language in order to account for its effects; the textual critic applies the results of such analysis to identification of damage sustained by the poem, of unauthorial, that is, uncharacteristic, elements in the received text.[8]

These points about objectivity are certainly true within the framework of textual criticism as it is commonly perceived. But this perception seems to be as much literary and subjective as it is textual and objective, inasmuch as it is predicated on notions of the aesthetic superiority and hence desirability of a creative writer's words. For instance, in his early discussion of the evidence for William Langland's authorship of *Piers Plowman*, Kane notes, "We . . . are concerned with three poems each a great work of art, and with a situation where creative abilities of a major order were applied to a major theme";[9] the differences Kane and E. Talbot Donaldson draw between authorial and scribal *usus scribendi* are

---

[7] Kane himself, however, has always insisted that he meant to speak only about the editing of *Piers Plowman*. Of his introduction to the *A* text he observes,"[T]his was not a do-it-yourself kit for theorizing about editing but an account of a single editor's predicament and his attempts to resolve it." " 'Good' and 'Bad' Manuscripts: Texts and Critics," in *Studies in the Age of Chaucer, Proceedings No. 2, 1986 Fifth International Congress 20–23 March 1986 Philadelphia, Pennsylvania*, ed. John V. Fleming and Thomas J. Heffernan (Knoxville: The New Chaucer Society, 1987), 137.

[8] " 'Good' and 'Bad' Manuscripts," 143.

[9] *Piers Plowman, The Evidence for Authorship* (London: The Athlone Press, 1965), 24.

essentially qualitative not quantitative, as they are in St. Bonaventure's famous classification;[10] and it is Langland's "greatness" as a rationale for the distinctiveness and exclusive validity of his text which Kane in part relies upon in his review of A. G. Rigg and Charlotte Brewer's edition of the so-called *Z* text and again in recent general restatements of his positions.[11] But the very act of defining and valuing the "major" themes of the "great" works of a great vernacular writer is itself, it might well be argued, literary and subjective in nature and bespeaks Romantic and New Critical aesthetics. In the Middle English period, it should be recalled, truly "great" literature was for the most part that written by classical and patristic *auctores*. And, even within the vernacular corpus, Lydgate's poetry was surely considered stylistically superior to Langland's, while in terms of the number of surviving manuscripts, Chaucer's *Astrolabe* was more popular than his *Troilus*. When Kane notes, furthermore, that he has "yet to come upon an instance of ["a high level of intellectual and even creative engagement" on the part of scribes] in the case of a great work," he makes an impressionistic and self-validating literary judgment in the guise of an objective textual assessment: he is really saying, in a circular manner, that according to standards derived from the behavior of certain writers as distinct from other writers, the latter writers fail to attain the standards of the former.[12]

In other words, the conceptual validity of the "grammars" of Chaucer's style and of his actual texts depends on the following assumptions: that the distinctiveness of his style in and of itself merits isolation from that of the "scribes"; and that the actual texts he wrote are by definition correct and worthy (if not obligate) of recovery. Theoretically, of course, such assumptions may well be valid. But the ability to isolate a writer's style or words does not *ipso facto* validate the isolation. And as Kane's own formulation indicates, the objective "damage" which a poem sustains in transmission can be predicated on the literary critic's subjective analysis of a poet's (or poem's) "style." The "authority" which Kane imputes to some writers and denies to others, like all authority and power, is thus not a transcendent, unimpeachable quality. As Peter L. Shillingsburg has put the matter:

---

[10] See, for example, *Piers Plowman: The 'B' Version* (London: Athlone, 1975), 130.

[11] "The 'Z Version' of *Piers Plowman*," (*Speculum* 60 [1985]: 910-30) and " 'Good' and 'Bad' Manuscripts." This position and all of the other positions outlined here are also briefly stated in "The Text," in *A Companion to "Piers Plowman,"* ed. John A. Alford (Berkeley: University of California Press, 1988), 175-200.

[12] " 'Good' and 'Bad' Manuscripts," 139. The incorporated observation with which Kane is disagreeing is from Derek Pearsall, "Editing Medieval Texts: Some Developments and Some Problems," in *Textual Criticism and Literary Interpretation*, ed. Jerome J. McGann (Chicago: University of Chicago Press, 1985), 103.

It is important for critic and editor alike to see that "authority" is a concept about which there is legitimate disagreement and that it is not an inherent quality of works of art but is instead an attribute granted by the critic or editor and located variously or denied entirely depending on the critical orientation of the perceiver.[13]

The characterizations of the Higher and Lower Criticisms may in fact be largely conventional in nature; if textual criticism is objective and preliminary to interpretation, for instance, it is so because of a literary critical framework which considers—requires—it to be so. What can then be said in this regard about the overall goals of textual criticism and literary interpretation and the types of evidence these disciplines consider? Perhaps the most explicit advocate of traditional views on these issues is, again, Kane, for whom textual criticism is concerned only with the author, so that to "think of a manuscript as 'good' in that it provides evidence of 'how the poem was first read' is not a primarily editorial consideration; it might be of interest to literary historians if the evidence were not almost invariably so jejune."[14] For Kane, experience is authority, inasmuch as the final demonstration of the validity of traditional positions is editorial experience. He observes, for example, that "Knowledgeable editors use" the term scribal "sophistication" cautiously.[15] According to Kane, Rigg and Brewer's belief that differences between readings which are not manifest errors "are as likely to be authorial as scribal in origin" is "held in defiance of five centuries of textual criticism," and in producing their edition they "take no account of even the most elementary indications of textual criticism."[16] And Kane doubts whether scribal alteration can offer insight into the expectations and tastes of medieval readers: he himself "was not vouchsafed such insight in ten years and more of reading manuscript variations."[17]

In order to evaluate these traditional critical positions more thoroughly, I will refer to some specific examples and lay open the ways in which they reflect the interdependence of textual and literary study. When Walter Skeat asserted that the manuscripts of *Piers Plowman* embody three authorially determined textual states, he was articulating not only

---

[13] *Scholarly Editing in the Computer Age* (Athens: University of Georgia Press, 1986), 17.

[14] " 'Good' and 'Bad' Manuscripts," 138–39. The quoted material is from B. A. Windeatt, *Troilus and Criseyde* (London: Longman, 1984), 33.

[15] "John M. Manly and Edith Rickert," in *Editing Chaucer, The Great Tradition*, ed. Paul G. Ruggiers (Norman: Pilgrim Books, 1984), 182.

[16] "The 'Z Version' of *Piers Plowman*," 917 n. 16 and 927.

[17] " 'Good' and 'Bad' Manuscripts," 139 n. 3.

a solution but a fact and a problem as well: the fact was that though the fifty-odd manuscripts containing the "Visio" and the "Vita" of Dowel, Dobet, and Dobest are not lexically and physically identical, they nonetheless do contain in some significant way the same poem; the problem was the nature of the relationship between these substantively different manuscripts; the solution was that Langland wrote and then twice revised his poem.[18] Skeat's analysis, based on the comparison of parallel passages in the manuscripts, would thus generally be considered an exercise in textual criticism, as would Kane and Donaldson's inconclusive attempts to classify the *Piers* manuscripts according to scribal error and to identify among the divergent readings an authorial *usus scribendi* by means of which Langland's *A* and *B* texts could be recovered.[19] Textual criticism would also embrace both Rigg and Brewer's attempt to demonstrate that the peculiarities of the so-called *Z* text result from Langland's compositional techniques,[20] as well as Kane's attempt to demonstrate that Rigg and Brewer are wrong in almost every conceivable way.[21] Kane and Donaldson and Rigg and Brewer all agree with Skeat's conception of the fact and the problem of the *Piers* manuscripts: all the critics attempt to present the "original" or "authoritative" text, and this attempt, according to a recent handbook, "is precisely the point of textual criticism."[22] It is only the solution on which opinions vary.

R. K. Root's argument about the *Troilus* similarly involves a fact—sixteen manuscripts and two printed editions of independent authority which preserve the same poem, though they disagree in a number of substantive ways; a problem—the relationship between the texts preserved in these manuscripts; and a solution—Chaucer wrote and then twice revised the poem.[23] In refuting Root's position, Barry Windeatt and Ralph Hanna accept the fact and the problem but disagree on the solution,[24] a position parallel to that of Charles Owen in his attempt to

---

[18] *Parallel Extracts from Forty-Five Manuscripts of "Piers Plowman,"* E. E. T. S., o. s. 17, 2d ed. (London: N. Trübner, 1886).

[19] *Piers Plowman: The 'A' Version* (London: Athlone, 1960), and *Piers Plowman: The 'B' Version*.

[20] *Piers Plowman: The 'Z' Version*, Studies and Texts 59 (Toronto: Pontifical Institute of Medieval Studies, 1983).

[21] "The 'Z Version' of *Piers Plowman*."

[22] William Proctor Williams and Craig S. Abbott, *An Introduction to Bibliographical and Textual Studies* (New York: The Modern Language Association of America, 1985), 10.

[23] *The Textual Tradition of Chaucer's Troilus* (London: Kegan Paul, Trench, Trübner, 1916).

[24] Windeatt, "The Text of the *Troilus*," in *Essays on Troilus and Criseyde*, ed. Mary Salu (Cambridge: D. S. Brewer, 1979), 1–22; Windeatt, *Troilus and Criseyde*

refute Windeatt and Hanna and thus to vindicate Root.[25] Again, inasmuch as each scholar is concerned with the identification of an authorial text, each approach would commonly be considered the business of textual criticism.

It is worth considering, however, to what extent the "point" of traditional textual criticism—the recovery of an authoritative text—suits the surviving medieval manuscripts. The problem which all the *Piers* critics have attempted to solve is predicated on a perception of the textual evidence in which the manuscripts are considered to represent the creative endeavors of a single individual. But there are no textual or contextual features in the manuscripts which imply the exclusive right of Langland's text, for example, to be authorial; which identify various manuscripts as containing the versions known now as *A*, *B*, and *C*; or even which indicate, like a modern title page replete with bibliographical information, that the various manuscripts of *Piers* (or the *Troilus*) contain in some significant and absolute way the same poem. There is, in fact, only one rubric in all of the manuscripts which unequivocally ascribes *Piers Plowman* to "William Langland," who thus might arguably be considered at least simply a name, and at most a poetic persona irrespective of an actual identity, but in no case the sole legal and cultural determinant of the poem(s). Indeed, the manuscripts clearly embody the creative (here used descriptively rather than evaluatively) efforts of several other individuals in layout, in minor lexical alteration, and in larger structural rearrangement, as in the manuscripts which contain hybrids of the *A* and *C* texts. Such phenomena, like all phenomena, assume meaning—that is, they become facts—in relation to *a priori* definitions, and by the definitions of traditional textual criticism most of these phenomena are inconsequential facts because they do not in themselves facilitate recovery of an authoritative text.

Without denying that a William Langland may have been the efficient cause of the text, or that it is possible to recover the text he was responsible for, or that his own efforts may be superior to others' according to certain aesthetic standards, I am simply pointing out that the valorization of *his* text is necessarily an interpretive imposition on the manuscript evidence. That in the case of both *Piers Plowman* and the *Troilus* the various critics perceive the same facts and problems and differ essentially on the solution to the problems might indicate otherwise: the scholarly consensus seems to imply that the evidence—the

---

(London: Longman, 1984), 36–54; Hanna, "Robert K. Root," in *Editing Chaucer*, 191–205.

[25] "*Troilus and Criseyde*: The Question of Chaucer's Revisions," *Studies in the Age of Chaucer* 9 (1987): 155–72.

textual facts—precedes the analysis—textual criticism. But as I have suggested in my formulation of the examples and throughout the preceding discussion, the various critical approaches articulate not simply textual solutions but textual facts and problems as well; and the textual facts are what they are *because* they are being analyzed from a traditional textual critical perspective, which employs a particular definition of evidence and which recognizes the validity of particular analytical approaches. Moreover, this imposed perspective is again as much literary criticism as textual, for in privileging Langland's text, the critic is bringing to the manuscripts specific notions of authorship, aesthetics, and the nature of literature. To be sure, textual variation in the *Piers* manuscripts can be identified only against a presumed text which *de facto* has authoritative status. But this presumed authoritative text is Langland's "original" only for the modern scholar who has access to the entire extant manuscript tradition; for a medieval scribe, who had neither the means to evaluate this larger tradition nor a cultural context which would give meaning to such an evaluation, it was simply the exemplar which inherently had *ad hoc* authority.[26] In the *Troilus* example, similarly, critics' viewpoints help to characterize the textual evidence through certain assumptions about the nature of literary texts—namely, that texts have specific and fixed forms on which the meanings of the texts are predicated and that the nature and identity of these forms can be fixed only by an original writer. Again, while the facts, problems, and solutions of the *Troilus* manuscripts may seem to be the matter of textual criticism, the textual criticism itself is informed by certain literary judgments.

Both these examples affirm, then, that criticism, like other disciplines, does indeed very much determine the nature of the evidence it analyzes through the categories of interpretation it employs and the problems it consequently perceives. The issue is not that solutions to textual problems vary, but that, depending on the interpretive framework in which they are viewed, the facts and problems themselves and their identification as textual or literary phenomena vary. The *Piers* manuscripts might be approached, for instance, from a perspective which defines authorial intention as the ideology which informs each particular manuscript. And the *Troilus* manuscripts could be viewed from a perspective which accepts textual determinacy as another of the tem-

---

[26] For opposing views see Kane, "The Text," 183; and Karl D. Uitti and Alfred Foulet, "On Editing Chrétien de Troyes: Lancelot's Two Steps and Their Context," *Speculum* 63 (1988): 275. There is some evidence that Middle English manuscripts could be corrected from one another, but such manuscripts are decidely the exception. For one example see Ralph Hanna III, "The Scribe of Huntington HM 114," *Studies in Bibliography* 42 (1989): 120-33.

poral codes (like romantic love) which the poem shows finally to be inadequate in a Christian universe. In each case, the textual and literary facts and problems change in relation to the literary perspective.

This line of analysis can be carried even farther. If the categories and nature of textual criticism and literary interpretation are conventional, what one does with the evidence assembled from these perspectives must also be conventional. Consequently, to present critically an "authoritative" text is only one of the things, and perhaps the most historically problematic, which one can do with a medieval work. Thus, the variants recorded in Manly and Rickert's edition of the *Canterbury Tales* are not facts in any absolute sense but only in relation to a presumed text which represents Chaucer's authorial intention; the textual evidence might well be categorized as facts for the reconstruction of the hypothetical text underlying the *a* or *b* grouping. The evidence might even be identified and categorized in a way not designed to privilege a literary *text*—that is, one might privilege orthographic rather than lexical differences, or glossarial response in place of glossed text, or dialectal difference rather than textual constitution. The top of the page in volumes 3 and 4 of the Chicago edition, in other words, might contain a text reconstructed in a given dialect and the bottom only those lexical items which derived from dialectal difference; or irrespective of actual manuscripts the top might contain phonetic rather than lexical phenomena and the bottom phonetic variation; or the top might contain a given manuscript text and the bottom a record of the various contemporary responses to it; or there might be no bottom at all—there might be no attempt to identify "facts" suggesting that the various manuscripts all contain the same tales of Canterbury, inasmuch as this fact might exist only for the modern scholar with all the manuscripts in front of him. It is important to recognize here that every hermeneutic code—every interpretive category—limits the potential of other hermeneutic codes not simply to interpret the evidence but to recognize the evidence as evidence. Moreover, however many textual "facts" one accumulates, these facts can in no way demonstrate the validity of the overall interpretive code; they only confirm that the code regards them as facts. For example, Nicholas Jacobs's classification of scribal substitution is both thorough and valuable, but it does not (and does not attempt to) prove absolutely that the phenomena under discussion are "scribal substitutions" in an "authoritative" text; it must *assume* these categories in order to classify the evidence.[27] To maintain that other approaches are not textual critical and distort the evidence is to overlook that the

---

[27] "The Processes of Scribal Substitution and Redaction: A Study of the Cambridge Fragment of *Sir Degaré*," *Medium Ævum* 53 (1984): 26–48.

norm of analysis or presentation against which distortion is identified is rarely (and clearly not in the examples of *Piers Plowman* and the *Troilus*) in any way intrinsic to manuscript phenomena, but is rather the articulation of certain hermeneutic codes. The identification and presentation of any manuscript evidence is necessarily an identification and thus distortion of the *potential* evidence of the manuscript.

As I noted at the outset, for the study of late Middle English literature the theoretical overlaps between "textual criticism" and "literary interpetation," however individually constituted, are as far-reaching as they are unavoidable. But these overlaps invite—rather than preempt—analysis. Since interpretive codes determine the nature of the evidence to be interpreted, more inclusive codes, which define the evidence more broadly and which are self-conscious about the ways in which they shape the evidence, would thus seem to be desirable. The primary disadvantage for Middle English studies of the traditional definition of textual criticism in particular is that in valorizing primarily the recovery of an authoritative text one not only engages in a historically problematic activity but also, more importantly, assumes a viewpoint which precludes—pronounces "wrong" or "other"—other kinds of evidence and analysis which may in fact be less historically problematic and are, in any case, equally valid as aesthetic activities. This collection, accordingly, was organized to confront or transcend traditional distinctions between textual and interpretive study in a variety of approaches to a variety of texts and writers. Collectively, the essays survey some of the best-known and most widely read figures and genres of the late Middle English period and also explore the varied ways in which readers and critics, both medieval and modern, have responded to them. The essays do not attempt to preempt other modes of analysis or to prescribe a specific mode. Rather, they affirm, in an increasingly pluralized critical climate, the value of broadening interpretive options even more through what might be called a Middle Criticism—one which draws on the complementary potential of what is commonly considered textual criticism and literary interpretation. As these essays suggest, such a criticism is self-conscious about the historicity both of the evidence it examines and of its own examination, and this criticism recognizes the ways in which this historicity determines what constitutes evidence. Individually, the essays thus contribute to an expanding body of criticism of similar theoretical orientation, but collectively they represent the first attempt to demonstrate in one forum the applicability of these views to a diversity of texts. Consequently, I hope, this collection will help to define a coherent, cogent method and thereby reveal in practical use what is often only accepted in theory.

The first four papers concentrate on the interactions between medieval authors and modern editors in printed editions. Chaucer and Langland, the two writers whose works have been the focus of perhaps most textual and interpretive discussions of Middle English, are well represented here. In the opening essay, Ralph Hanna III considers how editing (of Chaucer in particular) can create its own self-validating literary history at the expense of cultural and manuscript evidence to the contrary. Derek Pearsall then provides a cogent illustration of this point in his examination of how theories about meter lead editors into obscuring "the freedom, variety and flexibility of Chaucer's meter" which are apparent in the manuscripts themselves. Charlotte Brewer examines the relations between Kane and Donaldson's textual practice in their editions of *Piers Plowman* and their theories about composition, revision, literary texts, and authorial and scribal *usus scribendi*; in making explicit what is often only implicit in the editions, she also confirms the need for self-conscious and forthcoming hermeneutics in general. In the final essay of this section, A. S. G. Edwards reveals the qualities and characteristics which both define the genre of verse romance and also render that genre resistant to the methods and objectives of much traditional textual or interpretive study. The last four essays address the manuscripts and contexts in which medieval texts were read and consider how these contexts can be used by the modern reader. In the opening essay of this section, Richard Beadle examines the unique manuscript of the York Cycle to show how literary history evolves from textual and interpretive observations and how when these observations change, so must literary history itself. Julia Boffey then discloses the wealth of information latent in a lyric's manuscript context and, in so doing, exposes the weakness of any hermeneutic endeavor which does not take account of this information. George R. Keiser also considers the manuscript context as well as one other context of Middle English poetry—the audience—in order to see what these contexts reveal about how these poems (specifically Lydgate's *Life of Our Lady*) were read and understood in the late Middle Ages. And in the final essay of this collection, Sherry L. Reames explores still another context—medieval literature in general—as she examines the transmission of the Latin legend of St. Cecilia and thereby provides a concrete illustration of how the authorial language compared to the vernacular with respect to some of the issues raised in the previous essays.

Presenting Chaucer as Author

RALPH HANNA III

As a sanctioned professional activity, textual criticism has conventional goals, indeed conventions, propagated by those handbooks from which
everyone begins to acquire the craft. For Paul Maas, "The business of
textual criticism is to reproduce a text as close as possible to the
original." And M. L. West specifies the nature of that original quite clearly
when he identifies "the immediate aims" of textual criticism as "ascer-
taining as exactly as possible what the authors wrote and defining the
areas of uncertainty."[1] Such views, not completely uncontested these
days, presuppose that the editorial act reduces that multiplicity found in
the varying witnesses in which the text survives; at its conclusion, the
editor's work arrives at a unific single version, purged of excrescences,
which can be identified as "the original" or an authorial product.

But one should recognize that these procedures are not universal or
eternal imperatives. Nor have they always preceded textual consumption.
As gestures toward received documents or, alternatively, toward an
author, such activities are historically placeable. Documentary correction,
the removal of *corruptela* deemed in some sense or another obvious, was
a central concern in the humanist rediscovery of the classics. And the
idea that such correction reproduces an "authorial" version is only two
centuries old, a part of a general Romantic concern with the sovereign
subject. The ability to place such methodological approaches undermines, of course, any argument for their claim to *a priori* transhistorical
validity. Because the editorial objective of arriving at a unific single
version is in fact informed by historically-bound presuppositions, certain
difficulties may manifest themselves when modern editorial method is
applied to materials whose historical origin and transmission are
inconsonant with these presuppositions.

The English vernacular origin for such a respect for the primacy of the
author occurs, perhaps unsurprisingly, in a proto-Renaissance context.
Chaucer created for our language and its literary heritage a conception

---

[1] Paul Maas, *Textual Criticism*, trans. Barbara Flower (Oxford: Clarendon, 1958),
3; M. L. West, *Textual Criticism and Editorial Technique* (Stuttgart: Teubner, 1973),
8.

of culturally significant authority, an authority which demands textual correctness. Perhaps to a degree unique among all Middle English poets,[2] yet nonetheless compelling, Chaucer asserts the value of the author's *ipsissima verba*:

> And for ther is so gret diversite
> In Englissh and in writyng of oure tonge,
> So prey I God that non myswrite the,
> Ne the mysmetre for the defaute of tonge. . . .
>
> *(Troilus* 5.1793-96)[3]

> Under thy long lokkes thou most have the scalle,
> But after my makyng thow wryte more trewe;
> So ofte adaye I mot thy werk renewe,
> It to correcte and eke to rubbe and scrape,
> And al is thorugh thy negligence and rape.
>
> ("Adam" 3-7)

"*My* makyng," but "*thy* negligence": Chaucer is oppressively conscious of the way in which literature physically subsists and thereby enters culture. And he retains a fastidious hope that he can arrest that process, apparently down to the level of insuring that words get written with the proper final -e's. His authorial self-consciousness makes his canon a provocative testing ground for presumptions about the status of texts.

Chaucer's awareness of the ways he might be misunderstood was not only fastidious, however; it was also prescient. He knew that he was *sui generis*, that he made demands of a unique sort on contemporary transmission procedures. These forms of transmission were geared to other kinds of textual production, for example, the varieties of active redaction which typify surviving versions of Auchinleck romances; and the literary world of circa 1400 was not ready for authorship as Chaucer perceived it. The only Middle English literary figure I know who expresses a similar scrupulousness about his text is, significantly, a learned author with learned goals, Henry Daniel, a Dominican probably of the Stamford convent. Near the end of the prologue to his *Liber uricrisiarum* (1379), he comments:

---

[2] Peter Nicholson's meticulous codicological studies dispell Macaulay and Fisher's notion that Gower exercised a considerably firmer, and perhaps more fastidious, control over his text than Chaucer; see "Gower's Revisions in the *Confessio Amantis*," *Chaucer Review* 19 (1984): 123-43; and "Poet and Scribe in the Manuscripts of Gower's *Confessio Amantis*," in Derek Pearsall, ed., *Manuscripts and Texts* (Cambridge: Brewer, 1987), 130-42.

[3] All citations and references to the poet are from Larry D. Benson et al., *The Riverside Chaucer* (Boston: Houghton, 1987).

Ouer þat I praye euery writer or compiler of þis þat [he] kepe my
writyng, but if he be of þe langage of anoþer contre, forwhie as for
þe langage of English tong as anentz a discrete man and hym þat
hath þe gift of tunge, trewe and parfite craft of orthographie is taugh
in þis boke. He þat vnderstondes noȝt, praie he þat he may inter-
pretate it, seiþ þe trompe of Criste, id est Seynt Poule.[4]

In the fifteenth century, textual deviation, which troubled both the poet
and the friar, was for many book-producers a matter of indifference; at
least some scribes seem to have behaved as if it didn't exist (although a
small but visible number of conflated manuscripts testifies that this view
was far from universal), or as if, if it existed, it was not of much import.
In the case of Chaucer, such deviation in transmission meant that
audience reception differed radically from explicit authorial statement.

Yet modern forms of reception differ from either Chaucerian holo-
graph or fifteenth-century manuscripts. We typically consume Chaucer
through a single-volume *The Works of* ... edition, and such a book
addresses a professional necessity which is ours and neither the author's
nor scribes'. For the evidence shows that, whatever Chaucer thought of
his own authoriality, he was remarkably negligent about "publishing"
and made no effort at collecting a "works." There is particularly minimal
evidence for any supervised publication (in this instance probably
meaning only "release to the poet's private coterie audience through
circulating drafts"): *Boece* was available (c. 1385) to the minor London
official Thomas Usk; the Lollard courtier and poet Sir John Clanvowe (d.
1391) quotes "The Knight's Tale" (perhaps in a pre-*Canterbury Tales*
form); and on the basis of the prologue to "The Legend of Good
Women," *Troilus* was greeted with some hostility by readers.[5]

Whatever Chaucer's actual behavior, modern readers perceive him
differently—as a part of literary history. Consequently, for us Chaucer
must be formed like other parts of that history, assimilated to a range of
texts transmitted through different mechanisms and in different situations. The signs of such assimilation are apparent everywhere in modern
editions. Chaucer, for instance, is the only medieval author routinely
consumed "normalized," with the signs of his medievalism expunged so
far as possible. His text, as usually read, contains nary a thorn (or yogh,

---

[4] I cite the English version from e Musaeo 187, fol. v[v], with one correction from
the only other copy in English, Royal 17D.i. Daniel's comments show him engaged in
a quite peculiar learned project, arresting vernacular dialecticism so as to render
English a "fixed" language like Latin.

[5] I survey some possible evidence, only inferential in nature, for lifetime circulation
of individual *Canterbury Tales* beyond that of the Knight in "The Hengwrt Manuscript
and the Canon of *The Canterbury Tales*," *English Manuscript Studies 1100–1700* 1
(1989): 64–84.

or even a consonantal *u*); it usually includes at least one non-medieval letter (*j*), and often, especially for non-*Canterbury Tales* works, appears in a synthetic spelling. Indeed, I have heard conference papers which argued that even this form of the text brings with it excess estrangement. Some, at least, would prefer a text completely assimilated to the canon—transliterated, so far as possible, into modern English forms, without even those final -e's whose omission may have constituted one of Adam's Scriveyn's negligences.

But I would fault this assimilation to the English canon for reasons beyond the superficial. Canonicity assumes a relatively fixed or closed text. This rule, as it were, has been perceived as a requirement for centuries and appears in perhaps the oldest statement of canonicity, Deut. 4:2. There the temple scribes (who in fact redacted, if not composed, the text) write an end to its composition and directions for its transmission: "Ye shall not add unto the word which I command you, neither shall ye diminish aught from it." Secular canon-formation follows, I think, such a model. Resistance to textual change, especially challenge to any *textus receptus*, is, typically, strenuous, and the strong attractions of "diplomatic editing" or "the tyranny of copy-text" indicate the desire for a unific textual version which may be construed as relatively persuasive and received, available without editorial interference.[6]

For the procedures of textual criticism always play against the demands of canonical fixity. Insofar as textual criticism operates openly and leaves detritus, it suggests that the text does not fit the canon, that it is in doubt, not fully assimilated and thus not fully known. Editors seek to still readerly disquiet precisely because they know their job is to mediate the text to readers who wish to discuss it as a fixed canonical object. And simultaneously, readers do not wish to be disconcerted by the possibility (signaled by anything other than one clean textual column) that they are not in touch with such an object.

As a consequence of this need for textual fixity, editions of Chaucer and other poets often encourage, if not prescribe, naive readings. A polite (and typically misleading) way of saying this is to argue that they endeavor to be "user-friendly." They facilitate unhindered textual consumption and generally gloss over difficulties, which they remove

---

[6] Modern Chaucer studies provide two examples. John M. Manly and Edith Rickert's *The Text of the Canterbury Tales*, 8 vols. (Chicago: University of Chicago Press, 1940) was so unsettling as to be suppressed from the editorial conversation for nearly forty years. When N. F. Blake made Manly and Rickert's work central to the discussion, and attempted to use its conclusions as a guide to re-editing *The Tales*, the response in some circles was agony. And Blake's solution to editorial problems, of course, proves to be thoroughly diplomatic: for him, the excellence of a single witness obviates editorial activity.

from the text pages—indeed hide away in inaccessible portions of the volume. The implication is that readers will surely want to "read the text" and that any further interest—any questions about how the text came about—are supererogatory. The enterprise demands a clean single column inescapably connected with authorial remains and including a minimal patina of visible editorial activity.

But the very presumption of "editing Chaucer" in this way is foreign to the form of the surviving (yet not clearly Chaucerian) evidence. For such an editor in pursuit of authorial readings must silently reduce much of the textual exuberance which comprises Chaucer's fifteenth-century reception. Thus, s/he may come to approximate something like Chaucer's interest in a stable text (as exemplified in "Adam"), however inexactly. But in so doing, the editor risks sheer reductiveness: the longing for a single Chaucerian text has often proceeded in such a way as to ignore uncomfortable evidence and to overfamiliarize the remaining evidence. At least one result of this behavior has been to substitute a certain modern neatness—partially driven by a sense of how canonized texts should work—for manuscript material which evinces a much more various author. But responsible editors might recall West's claim that the editor should "defin[e] the areas of uncertainty" and thus they might profitably consider what has often been suppressed. The manuscript sources for the text indicate that, whatever Chaucer's hope for textual fixity, he did not achieve it.

Consider a rather basic issue: how should one print the text of *The Canterbury Tales*? For over a century, this extremely intricate issue has been posed as a single question: where should the editor place Fragment B2/VII? Here Manly-Rickert, Robinson, Fisher, and Donaldson stand alone against virtually every other editor of the last century: they follow the order presented by El.[7] In doing so, they can be perceived as superior to their competitors (except for Blake, who follows Hg). All other editors—Skeat, the Globe, Baugh, and Pratt—perform "the Bradshaw shift," and move B2/VII to follow MLT, an ordering for the text which has no evidentiary support in any manuscript.[8]

This reduction of the problem represents an historical view of Chaucer's activity. As its origins suggest, moving B2/VII is a product of specifically Victorian perceptions about how Chaucer ought to fit into literary history. This editorial decision reflects two views, neither logically

---

[7] I use, for convenience, the standard manuscript sigla and abbreviations for poems from *The Riverside Chaucer*.

[8] One surviving copy (Se) juxtaposes B^1 and B^2; but Se can hardly be construed as direct evidence for "the Bradshaw shift," since the manuscript opens with the order A CIT D MchtT SqT B^1 B^2.

dependent on the other but exerted in tandem. First, adherents of such a view assume that *The Canterbury Tales* either resembles or ought to be made to resemble comparable pieces of the English canon. Like other medieval and Renaissance long poems, it should appear as a continuous and finished narrative: as a text, it is closed. Ignoring numerous signs of manifest incompleteness, Bradshaw and others assume that the poem must appear to a reader in a final form, one in which Chaucer's major thematic emphases have been fully articulated.

These emphases, at least as the problem of tale order was initially posed and resolved, were those provided by contemporary literary views: the approach to Chaucer as roadside dramatist. The Victorian editors who popularize these views find value in the frame narrative, conceive that the poem should therefore emphasize naturalistic detail, and, as a result, are most attentive to getting Rochester and Sittingbourne references in the right order. Editorial production gets driven by an historical pre-conception of how Chaucer should have behaved (he looks enough like a nineteenth-century realist to have had a similar interest in getting detail right).

But this insistence on the placement of B2/VII skews interest from and suppresses editorial awareness of better attested problems with ordering the poem. Some of these one may describe as internal difficulties; for example, excepting El-Gg-*a*, every copy of *Tales* places Fragment G/VIII after FranT and at mid-poem. Such placement almost certainly occurs in imitation of Hg (which, on codicological evidence, quite deliberately made this placement, but although deliberately, not for any reasons clear to anyone today). And similar evidence might be adduced to suggest that placement of MancT is far from certain. The Manciple's performance comprises an unlinked fragment, and, although the order MancT-ParsPro occurs in every extant copy, it again looks dependant upon Hg, which did not originally have that order, since the word "Manciple" in I/X 1 has been written over an erasure of another (now unrecoverable) name.[9]

In twentieth-century discussions of tale order, the legacies of Victorian itinerarism have lingered on to obscure the problems involved in the placement of Fragments G and H. Modern order, however different the critical climate it serves, derives from Victorian preoccupations and

---

[9] In Hg, SNT was deliberately added after FranT, the quire size being doubled to accommodate this mid-course change in plan. For discussions of the process (and of the erasure in I 1), see A. I. Doyle and M. B. Parkes, "Paleographical Introduction" to *A Variorum Edition of the Works of Geoffrey Chaucer, Volume I* (Norman: University of Oklahoma Press, 1979), esp. xxx–xxxii. Both features may reflect a shift from a stage of production in which the team planning the codex intended the large block of manuscript beginning at fol. 112 to end with FranT, as I suggest at "Hengwrt Manuscript," 81–82 n. 15.

follows the geographical directives in the text. Thus, G 556 (not in Hg) contains a reference to Boughton-under-Blean; one may couple this with a second reference (H 3-4) to Harbledown. Both places are near Canterbury and at the end of the journey down; hence the stories ought to occur near the end of a one-way pilgrimage poem. But the itinerary is so obvious a form of ordering that it could surely have occurred to manuscript editors circa 1400-1410 (those behind El-Gg-*a* seem to have understood the poem as Donald R. Howard's one-way trip), and they thus decided to place these particular tales appropriately. Hence modern orderings dependent upon El may only be following some version of Victorian map-reading, in this case exercised by early fifteenth-century production teams.

Such variation, of course, directs attention to the first of the assumptions behind ordering the tales noted above, that the poem resembles *The Faerie Queene* or *Paradise Lost* in its degree of finish. But given the evidence that circa 1400 substantial chunks of the poem appear to have been moveable, can one really be certain that there is an authorial order? And, if one finds no basis for one, how should one present the poem?

The difficulties these questions raise are compounded by the nature of modern editions themselves. An editor must present the text in some form, as if a fixed entity; consequently, as an editor, one must come to a decision on this issue, and the decision will make a difference to a reader's perception of the text. But such a decision should be made by considering what evidence one wishes to privilege and that, by privileging different sorts of evidence, one can produce different orderings and varying effects on the reader. For example, should one wish to follow Maas, West, and other manuals and to privilege the poem when it left authorial control and entered transmission, one might most properly try to reproduce the open situation in which early manuscript editors appear to have found it. As Derek Pearsall has suggested, an accurate representation of such authorial papers would necessitate a publishing experiment—a board-covered volume with only head and end actually bound in and the middle comprised of loose paper-bound pamphlets with separate paginations. And such pamphlets would correspond only partially to the familiar Fragments—some would contain more than one of these, some much less than a whole one.[10]

But it is equally possible to consider other alternatives. Pearsall's solution has much to recommend it, if one chooses to privilege the text as the author's artifact. If one decides to see the text from some other vantage, different organizations, equally foreign to many editions in

---

[10] See *The Canterbury Tales* (London: Allen and Unwin, 1985), 23; Pearsall's entire discussion of tale order, which concludes at this point, is relevant to my argument.

common use, might be more practicable. As I noted above, only four editions follow the order of any manuscript. Blake opts for Hg, a choice one might deprecate, since evidence, both codicological and textual, suggests that the producer of this codex lacked access to a full and revised version of the poem. On the other hand, if one wishes to privilege the form which the poem had in its earliest discernible moments of circulation, perhaps among members of the poet's coterie, Blake's choice has much to recommend it. But I would suggest that Blake in fact cosmeticizes even this least organized of versions. A more disrupted edition than the one he presents, one which takes into account all the palpable signs of Hengwrt's discontinuous access to Chaucerian materials, down to the changes in its ink and in the quality of its parchment, would be more fitting.

But one can equally fault Robinson, Donaldson, and Fisher's choice of the El order. This book stands near the end of a variety of experiments at ordering the poem, and by the time the El production team acquired its archetypes, a number of possibilities evident earlier in transmission had already been shut down. One can imagine editions in the form of those manuscripts the El team would have known and used as models—Cp or Ha⁴, for example. (As Doyle and Parkes show, the scribe responsible for these two copies may have known the scribe of El, and, at the very least, they shared book-trade acquaintances.)[11] From Jerome J. McGann's perspective, which privileges the collaboration between the author and those modes of literary propagation normal at his time, such an edition reproducing one of these orders might almost seem inevitable: books like Cp and Ha⁴ provide the best surviving evidence for what *The Tales* looked like in its initial public appearance, an appearance which would have exercised constraints on the production of El. And from a rather different possible perspective, one which privileged reception, the historical form in which early readers—including for example, Hoccleve, Lydgate, and Henryson—knew Chaucer, presentation from one of these manuscripts again would be difficult to impeach.[12] In any event, the possible presentations of the tale order are multiple, and those forms in

---

[11] See A. I. Doyle and Malcolm Parkes, "The Production of Copies of the Canterbury Tales and the Confessio Amantis in the Early Fifteenth Century," in Parkes and Andrew G. Watson, eds., *Medieval Scribes, Manuscripts, and Libraries: Essays Presented to N. R. Ker* (London: Scolar, 1978), 163–210.

[12] I should clarify that in this paragraph I address only the issue of tale order. The textual detail Cp and Ha⁴ present often is not Chaucer's, and most twentieth-century attention to the text has been concerned with rejecting this detail; as a result, a Cp or Ha⁴ edition would present a split copy-text, with order from one source, but lections and spellings from another, presumably El or Hg. In addition to these forms of the text, of course, El knew *a* or a derivative.

common use are among the less satisfactory of the alternatives.

Pearsall's projected edition—one which allows Chaucer's longest poem a variable, ad lib shape—adumbrates a second problematic area. A substantial amount of fifteenth-century evidence for Chaucer's text indicates that in transmission, the concept of "the poem" might well have been a variable one; thus, modern practice, with its insistence upon the unblemished single textual column, may misrepresent much of the canon. In presenting many of Chaucer's works, the act of editorial decision naturalizes the received evidence. Rather than a singular text, there are plural texts—not simply the expected rash of local variants but disparities between how much the manuscripts present and in what form. In reducing these to a single presented "work," editors recuperate Chaucer, by overleaping the variety of fifteenth-century evidence, to a modern conception of the great author's unitary work.[13] In using any edition, readers are allowed to presume that the text has been transmitted in a simplified modern form in which it exists without substantial alternatives.

Although such problems occur in *The Tales*, they are absolutely endemic to the "minor poems." This state of affairs certainly represents effects attributable to Chaucer's own negligence in not providing a "collected works": for many poems, whatever their date of composition, any evidence for a text is excessively belated and most likely the product of several generations of copying. To one degree or another such problems affect *Troilus*, LGWProl, Anel, Truth, Purse, BD, and PF.

Editors have usually "addressed" this difficulty by conflating discrete traditions into a composite text. Perhaps typical would be the usual handling of BD and PF, where portions of the poems known only from a minority of the witnesses (in the first case, in fact, from a sixteenth-century print), have, without appreciable defense, been intercalated into the other versions. But the model provided by recent studies of *King Lear* might suggest that such conflations simplify textual situations considerably more variable and fluid.[14] In these cases, the decision to present a unific text of Chaucer often seems an uneasy compromise, perhaps born of a certain slackness in analyzing the problem and a concomitant desperation. Such conflation may only serve a hope that the editor has got, whatever else s/he has done, all the genuine Chaucer in. Informatively, only one text in the canon, LGWProl, has ever

---

[13] I call these conceptions "modern" in allusion to the basic theoretical efforts one would associate with the name of Fredson Bowers. Obviously, post-modern views have tended to take a critical stance toward the notion of textual unity; I hope to examine these ideas, especially as enunciated by Jerome J. McGann, elsewhere.

[14] See the discussions in Gary Taylor and Michael Warren, eds., *The Division of the Kingdoms* (Oxford: Clarendon, 1983).

appeared in a parallel-text format.[15]

Yet not all textual alternatives in Chaucer were produced by the same mechanisms, and consequently, they may reflect a gamut of possibilities demanding disjunct treatments. One might wish to add to the loose-leaf *Canterbury Tales* an edition which includes other works in appropriately shifting and multiple formats. Simply to outline a few of the possibilities: in some cases (LGWProl and NPProl are probably noncontroversial examples) the varying forms of the *textus receptus* represent different moments of authorial composition. In this situation, some editors may wish to achieve closure and a fixed single text by invoking the rule of final intentions; assuming that some clear temporal priority can be demonstrated, an earlier state of the text might be relegated to the *corpus lectionum*. (In doing so, however, editors might well leave some tracks on the text pages to indicate to readers how the evidence has been handled—not a normal feature of Chaucer editions.)[16]

But a range of other examples admits no solution so simple as the determination of temporal priority. With other poems, as A. S. G. Edwards has suggested recently of Anel, we may receive fragments, not all certainly Chaucerian in origin. In others, to my mind (but not Pace's) Truth, the majority of the manuscripts conveys a non-authorial recension of the text; in yet others, in my reckoning (but not Root's or Owen's) *Troilus*, we have been left mixtures of authorial and scribal variation not easily susceptible of any single presentation.[17] The conflationist approach, to which editors have subjected all these texts without any particular discrimination, produces the fixed author desirable in a canonical edition; but it does so by ignoring the various author to whom the manuscript evidence points.

Moreover, each of the poems I have mentioned demands a different handling, a different kind of edition. Edwards's reading of Anel transmission presupposes a complete overhaul of what has been printed: at a minimum, the narrative and the complaint should be re-edited as separate fragments with at least partially separate histories of transmission. (Some might wish to go further and place the unascribed portion of the poem

---

[15] The parallel presentation of the many Chaucer Society volumes, e.g., the Six-(Eight-) Text *Canterbury Tales*, is not an exception: rather than editions, these volumes are preludes to collations.

[16] As an outstanding counter-example, one might note Pearsall's presentation of the two versions of NPProl in his *A Variorum Edition, Vol. II, Part 9* (Norman: University of Oklahoma Press, 1984), esp. 132 (3981n); cf. 85–87.

[17] See for Anel, *Studies in Bibliography* 41 (1988): 177–88; for Truth, *Studies in the Age of Chaucer* 10 (1988): 23–40; for *Troilus*, Paul G. Ruggiers, ed., *Editing Chaucer: The Great Tradition* (Norman: Pilgrim, 1984), 191–205, this study inspired by those which lie behind Barry Windeatt's recent edition (London: Macmillan, 1984).

completely apart from Anel, among what Robinson called "Short Poems of Doubtful Authorship.") In the case of Truth, all copies can be collated, and at five points must be, since the "authorial version" includes scribalisms only correctable from the "scribal recension." But the differences between versions are particularly extensive, and in its purposive rewriting, the scribal recension has an integrity collation only fragments; for full appreciation of the transmission one needs something approximating parallel presentation.[18] Moreover, from a perspective which would privilege the text as received, such presentation of Truth will seem an attractive alternative, since the scribal recension held the field as The Text for nearly half a millennium. And in contrast to both these editions, in the present rather unfocused state of research, a reputable *Troilus* can only be constructed on the basis of a free-floating eclecticism such as Stephen A. Barney's *The Riverside Chaucer*: until scrupulous re-examination of the variants, like Barney's, reveals what attestation means in the case of this text, other presentations appear to beg the question.

Given these possible varying editorial forms, the one piece of *The Works* traditionally presented in a deviant fashion may merit brief re-examination. The most recent editors of LGWProl in *The Riverside Chaucer* offer no real explanation for their parallel texts, beyond noting the existence of two versions; A. S. G. Edwards and M. C. E. Shaner do mention with approval John Livingstone Lowes's arguments that Gg contains the revised version, F the original. In this silence, the editors simply bow to Robinson's second edition and adopt his presentation. But Robinson offers a clear—and different—rationale for what he does: he prints both versions because he is *not* thoroughly swayed by Lowes's demonstration and because he regards the issue of priority as perhaps not "susceptible of absolute demonstration." The parallel texts *Riverside* inherits appropriately express, not the certainty that Gg is a later text, but a doubt about where authority lies.[19]

Robinson provides parallel texts for reasons that, given his historical situation, seem to me sensible. But today his hesitation seems much less necessary. The closest Chaucerian parallel appears NPProl: there two authorial versions descend, and editors have printed what they believe the later one, Chaucer's final authorial intention. In the case of LGWProl, since temporal anteriority can be determined (Gg is later), a standard

---

[18] George B. Pace and Alfred David adopt this procedure in *A Variorum Edition, Vol. V, Part 1*: the authorial version appears, with all variants displayed, at 59–64, but the volume also includes an edited version of the scribal recension at 55–56.

[19] Here and in subsequent paragraphs, I cite F. N. Robinson, *The Works of Geoffrey Chaucer* (Boston: Houghton, 1957), 839; the discussion continues on 840.

critical edition in single column should logically accept a heavily
emended Gg as its sole basis,[20] and print F, if at all, somewhere else.
Donaldson in fact adopts such a rule of final intentions and gives only an
emended Gg version. But *Riverside*'s parallel text format, given the
editors' prior rejection of Robinson's logic for two texts, implicitly
identifies a different situation as the relevant analogue. The F prologue,
authorial as competing versions of Truth probably are not, circulated far
more extensively than Gg, and was printed as Chaucer's text for
centuries. Thus, with somewhat better warrant than the scribal recension
of Truth, it has every right to be considered a *textus receptus* important
to the tradition and to be reprinted.

But Robinson does not simply print F because of doubts about the
authority of Gg. In his notes, he adds a statement indicative of a logic
different from that of final intentions: "The chief objection to regarding
[Gg] as the revision is probably the fact that some excellent poetry in F
has been sacrificed in the rearrangement." And he acknowledges that his
parallel texts allow readers access to this poetically-superior version. This
invocation of poetic quality, while it ignores the author altogether, has
attracted strong modern support. "Excellent poetry" (or excellent poetry
of the kind Robinson likes) apparently did not appeal to Chaucer when
he revised LGWProl: this "excellence" has been identified on thoroughly
modern, not authorial, grounds. But such a judgement has appealed to at
least two editors, Baugh and Fisher, who print F as a single-column text
and suppress Gg altogether.

Here the closest analogy isn't Chaucerian at all, but *Piers Plowman*.
The "poetic powers" of Langland's B text, as perceived by modern
readers, have kept that version of the poem in constant circulation. (In
contrast, the "less poetic" C text was only printed separately in 1978.)
Editors, on the basis of modern taste, violate Langland and Chaucer's
plain intent in revising their poems one last time. In both cases,
Langland's C and Chaucer's Gg, revision was a mistake from which the
poet should be exculpated and the reader spared. But, of course, the traditional presentation of *Piers Plowman* suggests a rationale for printing F
and Gg in parallel—as one indication of the author's continuing poetic
concerns. This example reveals, I think, confusions about the degree to
which editors of Chaucer feel they should seek an author's authority. The
two texts appear as an unargued act of conflation; or the revision does
not appear because the poet can't or shouldn't have meant it.

---

[20] Robinson points out, 913, the large numbers of Gg scribalisms, a view recently
seconded by George Kane, "The Text of *The Legend of Good Women* in CUL MS
Gg.4.27," in Douglas Gray and E. G. Stanley, eds., *Middle English Studies Presented
to Norman Davis* (Oxford: Clarendon, 1983), 39–58.

Multiple-text conflation elsewhere among "the minor poems" reflects similar lapses of attention. In these cases, editors have been too willing to see transmissional problems as merely a property of the variants considered in isolation and have rarely scrutinized the evidence as something historically generated, a property of each individual witness to the text in its own right, a property which emerged at some distinct point in the transmission history of that text. Here the possibility of more powerful analyses through such tools as codicology—what the physical forms of manuscripts tell about the production of this copy—remains very open. Such analyses, as Edwards's of "Anelida," may lead to new editions which seek to provide open access to a properly irreducible multiplicity.

As a way of drawing together these arguments, consider what amounts to a single reading in PF—those lines now always printed as 680-92, the roundel sung by the birds. Vincent Di Marco and Larry D. Benson, the most recent editors of the poem, deserve congratulations for the editorial forthrightness with which they present this passage: they identify some lines as the editorial supply, extant in no witness, which they are. Although in line 675 Chaucer calls this inserted lyric a "roundel," this term misdenominates what the scribes present. The printed text has been reconstructed hypothetically, on good historical principle, from French models; Skeat prints it in this form and has the grace to put lines he supplies in italics; something like Skeat's form has been followed by every subsequent editor.[21]

But the issue of silent reconstruction, impeccable given its assumptions, troubles me less than does the manuscript evidence here. From that perspective, I remain unconvinced that anything exists here to be reconstructed. The twelve witnesses at this point (four copies lack this portion of the poem)[22] offer seven different options, whose diversity a standard collection only denatures:

1. silent omission, i.e., the text runs from 679 to 693 across the blank line separating stanzas (so FfLtT).
2. an indicated omission, in two forms:
   (a) in the blank between 679 and 693 appears the line "Que (Qui

---

[21] For the text, see Walter W. Skeat, *The Complete Works of Geoffrey Chaucer*, 6 vols. (Oxford: Clarendon, 1894), 1:359; and for the basis of the reconstruction, 1:524-25 (675n).

[22] The information in *The Riverside Chaucer*, 1147, also suggests twelve witnesses. But Di Marco there (in addition to several errors in the manuscript foliations he provides), implies that P ends at line 687, rather than the correct 667. And at least for this lection, Th, William Thynne's print, has manuscript authority independent of its normal sources Cx and/or Pynson.

Th^1) bien ayme a (om. CxRTh^1) tarde oublie" (so BCxFRTh^1).
(b) a blank space left for a rime royale stanza (so Gg^{1}H).
3. a text of some description written continuously after 679; this text
   has a single origin but descends through at least two (and perhaps
   three) different exemplars:
   (a) the form of Gg^2 = 680-84, 687-89 (added in the blank 2.b., Gg^1,
       above).
   (b) the form of J = 683-84, 687-89.
   (c) the form of DTh^2 = 680-81, 683, 682, 687-89 (687 absent in D;
       lines I call Th^2 follow immediately on 2.a., Th^1, above).

Moreover, although the question is immensely difficult in this poem, the
distribution of these variants does not correspond to patterns of
attestation usual elsewhere in PF: the manuscripts do not display their
normal genetic affiliations.[23]

Editors have always discussed this spate of readings as if all of them
existed simultaneously, in a sort of Platonic vacuum. Typically the lection
has been taken detached from any of that descriptive bibliographical
study Bowers and Tanselle would see as basic in any edition of a printed
book. Thus, everyone states that Gg^2, the material added in the blank
(Gg^1), is written by "a later scribe:"[24] the unwary reader is permitted
to suppose something like a contemporary corrector. Alas, no. The eight
lines are written into the blank space left by the original scribe in a
bastard secretary, apparently from its ligatures, copied by a scribe more
used to writing textura; simply on a palaeographic basis, s/he added
these materials no earlier than circa 1460-1470 and likely later still
(although before circa 1500), in any case minimally half a century after
the main scribe. By blandly designating this a "later hand," editors have
allowed readers (and, I suspect, themselves) to assume that the roundel

---

[23] As is thoroughly typical with the "minor poems," there is no published full
collation. A reader without access to the witnesses must rely on Chaucer Society
transcripts; useful notes in *Riverside*, 1002 (677n) and 1150 (680-92n); and John
Koch, ed., *Geoffrey Chaucers Kleinere Dichtungen* (Heidelberg: Winter, 1928), 97.
Derek Brewer's usually helpful edition, *The Parlement of Foulys*, 2d ed. (Manchester:
Manchester University Press, 1972), does not offer an actual collation here (see 98).
[24] Even, quite surprisingly, M. B. Parkes and Richard Beadle, *The Poetical Works
of Geoffrey Chaucer: A Facsimile of Cambridge University Library MS Gg.4.27*, 3
vols. (Norman: Pilgrim, 1979-80), 3:4. No edition, excepting Manly-Rickert for *The
Tales* and Root's separate volume for *Troilus*, provides even the most rudimentary
palaeographical descriptions, and even article-length coverage remains at best spotty,
e.g., Eleanor Prescott Hammond, "MS. Longleat 258–A Chaucerian Codex," *Modern
Language Notes* 20 (1905): 77-79. Vast amounts of codicological work remain to be
done, even on well-known manuscripts of *The Tales* and *Troilus*. For the minor poems,
Julia Boffey provides a fine start in *Manuscripts of English Courtly Love Lyrics in the
Later Middle Ages* (Woodbridge: Brewer, 1985).

in fact is not a bit of conflation but integral to Gg's text. Thus, they can assume that while it represents something copied in by someone else, it still derives from Gg's usual exemplar, always perceived as of higher quality than that available to the other scribes. Such can not be the case.[25]

Moreover, only one of the witnesses with a text between 679 and 693 can be appreciably older than Gg[2]. Although J contains a chronicle of London with other materials ending at 1432/33, the manuscript was produced somewhat later, near mid-century.[26] D was copied by a named scribe, John Brode, also responsible for John Rylands Library, Eng. 113, a *Canterbury Tales*; he can be placed in the 1480s.[27] And Th, William Thynne's *Works*, went to press in 1532. Moreover, Thynne's sources are pellucid and traceable: he used either Cx or Pynson's derivative edition as copy-text (drawing Th[1] from it) but also, as he often did elsewhere, consulted one or more manuscript versions for alternative readings (here the exemplar of D, which provided Th[2]). In short, there is absolutely no evidence for the existence of the text some manuscripts provide between 679 and 693 before something like the 1440s. This I, at least, find deeply troubling.

But my malaise intensifies when I come to consider, as an editor is supposed to do, the lines some manuscripts provide in the context of the remaining variation. At this point, it is appropriate to join the PF scribes to see what they had just copied when they came to the point where modern editions print the roundel. Chaucer describes the birds singing, as they customarily do, and continues:

> The note, I trowe, imaked was in Fraunce;
> The wordes were swiche as ye may heer fynde,
> The nexte vers, as I now have in mynde.
>
> (677-79)[28]

---

[25] Note that Ff, generally considered to be drawn from the same tradition of exemplars as Gg[1], has variant 1 above.

[26] Charles Lethbridge Kingsford, *English Historical Literature in the Fifteenth Century* (Oxford: Clarendon, 1913), 86-87, dates the whole soon after the lists of London officers which end 1433; Robert E. Lewis and Angus McIntosh, *A Descriptive Guide to the Manuscripts of the* Prick of Conscience (Oxford: Medium AEvum Monographs, 1982), 117-18, are considerably more circumspect about date (s. xv), although they acknowledge the lists as a *terminus a quo*. I am grateful to Jeremy J. Griffiths, currently preparing a catalogue of St. John's College manuscripts, for his opinion—"s. xv[2/4], near the end, in the decade 1440-50."

[27] Daniel W. Mosser presented preliminary results from his continuing study of Brode at the Kalamazoo International Congress, 8 May 1987; see also M. B. Parkes, *English Cursive Book Hands 1250-1500* (Oxford: Clarendon, 1969), plate 3 (ii) and p. 3.

[28] I take this opportunity to indicate that minor readings scattered through this text

A scribe at all attentive to his text must have been aware that something had gone badly wrong here. For having copied these lines, which promise "the wordes" of a song, on the evidence most manuscripts give, the scribe would find in his exemplar "the nexte vers" announcing, not the song, but its cessation: "whan the song was do." I find no compelling reason for believing that this was not the experience of virtually every scribe when initially confronted with PF 679/693: excepting J and perhaps D, they all found what they did not expect, a frankly discontinuous text, and they were left to their own inclinations and devices to cope with the problem.[29] From this lacuna and the resulting effort to fill it through multiple manuscript consultation, the profuse (and non-genetic) variation I have outlined emerges.

In defending a reading, an editor must account for all the scribal behaviors s/he observes in light of the hypothesized text. Here one can most easily explain the behavior of those scribes at the extremes— thorough honesty and thorough dishonesty (or pure somnolence). The first group produced the variant labelled 2b: Gg and H recognized textual discontinuity, knew they had no way to deal with it, and indicated its presence in their copies. They, just as every scribe but one who copied the poem, appear to have had no earthly idea what a "roundel" is: they simply assumed the minimal loss of a stanza.[30] The other crowd, those scribes responsible for the variant I call 1, either paid no attention to what they copied or took evasive action: although they can not be

---

are quite susceptible to various presentations. In lines 677 and 678, Gg reads in isolation from all other copies; *Riverside*, which I quote, accepts one such unique reading and rejects the other. I think this is correct, but would accept and reject in a different distribution. In 677, read "maked" or "made," as all copies but Gg; "trowe" has sounded -e, which the Gg scribe may have contaminated with the following "maked" of his archetype—he writes "trow." But in 678, read with Gg against all other copies and delete "heer." This reading looks to me like a combination of objection to the metre and scribal overkill, overspecification; given what scribes appear to have found in their exemplars after line 679, the reading was offered in consummate bad faith.

[29] D's exemplar appears also to have been used by Lt and was certainly derived from T: on this basis, one would expect that it did not include the roundel, procured by Brode from another source. (There are signs of sporadic consultation of a copy not like LtT scattered throughout D.)

[30] It is more than an accident that one scribe, responsible for the exemplar available to DTh², did his best to reproduce something *not* like a roundel but like the other seven-line stanzas of the poem. S/he transposed lines 682 and 683 so that the block of poetry started *abab*, as if a piece of rime royale. The transposition creates an anacoluthon, apparently unnoticed by the archetypal scribe, for the two derivatives introduce different smoothings to accommodate it (682 And] Hast D, Whiche Th²). And John Brode went a step further: in D he suppressed line 687 altogether so that he copied only seven lines and produced a textual block homogeneous with the other stanzas on the page (even if it does not rhyme as they do).

accused of having positively misrepresented their exemplars, if they noticed discontinuity, they plainly did not feel compelled to announce it to their readers. These scribes surely felt that, whatever the state of the text, they weren't responsible either for it or for attempting to improve it.

The scribes who produced option 2a at least saw a problem, although they coped with it a tad deviously. Chaucer promises that subsequent verses will give "the wordes" the bird sang; and although he insists that they sang a French note, he makes no parallel promise to reproduce it. These scribes responded to the instructions in the text as best they could—an activity requiring a double misreading. "Vers" in line 689 is probably Chaucer's plural; the scribes contented themselves with supplying "a next verse." But incapable of giving what Chaucer promised, "the wordes," they could only offer a French note. Unlike the two "solutions" I have already discussed, either of which might occur independently to any scribe of appropriate moral character, this particular insert happened, I should think, only once. Its appearance in five copies not all usually affiliated represents a combination of licit archetypal descent and multiple exemplar consultation. On that basis, especially given B and Cx's routine access to this copy or its progeny for other texts, this "solution" likely is an innovation in F.[31]

The scribes whom every editor since the nineteenth century has followed give a text, variant 3 in its different manifestations. The preponderance of the evidence suggests that the entire text, whatever its handling in surviving PF manuscripts, was imported, originally from outside the PF tradition. In Gg^2 and Th^2, the lines have been added to the usual exemplar behind the copy. In D and J, given their textual continuity, the lines may already have been intruded into the scribe's source-text. Such behavior is datable and occurred in an already advanced stage of the textual tradition.

Beyond the disposition of the variants, which implies that no early scribe saw anything other than what FfLtT record, an interstanzaic blank line at 679/693, some details in the *textus acceptus* are troublesome. In line 684, "smale foules" might well be a licit form by which the singing birds could refer to themselves. But 687 "they," 688 "hem," and 689

---

[31] Skeat is certainly right to suspect the "the note" as non-Chaucerian; see 1:525 (677n). But Philip Brett, to whom I'm grateful for the information, tells me that Skeat's reason for suspicion is misplaced. Although Brett describes F's apparent direction to adopt a setting made for an octosyllabic text to the longer lines of the surviving roundel (unknown, I think, to F) as "a slightly indelicate choice," he believes that a skilled medieval musician could have dealt with the resulting problems during performance. In such a context, the performer could have split notes or taken full advantage of opportunities afforded by melisma.

"they" seem less plausible examples of self-reference: one would expect the birds to have sung "we," "us," "we." The inset lyric we receive does not look as if it were ever intended for feathered singers.

The lyric attracted the scribe who first inserted it into PF (where it spread to at least two and perhaps three lost copies) for two reasons. It was a roundel, and it clearly referred to events like those PF describes, birds singing to celebrate the spring. But its form in the earliest manuscript to reproduce it seems to me telling. Either J, whose text, so far as it goes, is the most acceptable of the four,[32] or the scribe of his exemplar edited the poem. Apparently conscious of the need to achieve a good fit between Chaucer's text and extraneous materials, he over-adapted the poem to context by suppressing its generally spring-y first triplet, and he copied only those lines which refer to bird-song. The roundel may be Chaucer's—I do not seek to determine authorship, and I like the poem enough to hope it's his. But I don't think the preponderance of the evidence allows me to believe that it's what Chaucer wrote following PF 679. If he wrote anything, and in the state of the evidence, that is not certain, it has not been transmitted to us. And the generations of editors who have printed something like a PF 680–92 have simply replicated intelligent fifteenth-century conflational behavior: in the guise of seeking an author, they have perpetuated what the handbooks they are following have told them to avoid, those vicissitudes normal in fifteenth-century poetic transmission.

If this argument—that PF 680–92 is a mid-fifteenth-century intrusion, Chaucerian perhaps but not part of PF—is acceptable, what does an editor do? Two possible honest forms of presentation seem appropriate. First, one can follow a modest tradition established by past editors and print ellipses: rows of dots have appeared in other contexts where material is plainly wanting, after "Complaint to his Lady" 22 or "Former Age" 55, for example. Perhaps more germane, because involving a similar query about an extant *textus receptus*, is Pratt's handling of *Canterbury Tales* A 164 and E 1305–6: he leaves blank lines, two of them partial, and provides textual notes.[33] Alternatively, one could print the poem from Gg as emended but completely enclosed in brackets. (The Gg text will at least indicate the basic substance of what does not survive, a poem of more ornate stanza-form than the remainder of PF, while the brackets will alert even the most heedless reader and direct him or her to the notes for

---

[32] Gg^2, the only full version with correct line order, nonetheless requires at least three emendations: 680 thy] om. Gg; 682 longe] la^{r}ge Gg; 684 smale] smal Gg. In addition, various editors have corrected other readings, e.g., 681 this] thes Gg; 683 on lofte] o lofte or olofte Gg; 689 synge] ben Gg.

[33] See Robert A. Pratt, *The Tales of Canterbury* (Boston: Houghton, 1974), 6 and 345.

further information.) In addition to texts sundered and in parallel, editions will need to indicate texts thoroughly discontinuous.

My third example is deceptively simpler, a case of minor variation in "General Prologue" 217. Of the Friar Chaucer says:

> Ful wel biloved and famulier was he
> With frankeleyns over al in his contree,
> And *eek* with worthy wommen of the toun.
>
> (215-17)

Or so read the important manuscripts Ad³ Ch Ha⁴ Hg, while the similarly important Cp El En¹ Gg Cx¹ omit "eek." Both lines are eminently acceptable—the Hg version with "eek" a "normal" hendecasyllabic line, the El version without the word that variation usually called a "headless line." Readings of this sort occur with extraordinary frequency in the tradition of *Tales*, for example at KnT 1095:

> This prison caused me nat *for* to crye,

where I cite the text of Ad³ El En¹ Gg Ha⁴; Ch Cp Hg Ne omit the italicized word and have simple "to." Here El's "for" produces a hendecasyllable; the Hg version begins as if "headless," but at mid-line has juxtaposed stresses, a "Lydgatian," "broken-back," or "fifteenth-century heroic" verse.

An editor here encounters difficulty because, whipsawed between two conflicting imperatives, s/he must and must not make a choice: editors do get paid to print A Text. Yet no compelling logic for a choice between one variant or the other exists in these lines. Given, as is quite typical of these instances, the expletive words whose inclusion creates hendecasyllables, one hesitates between ascribing the words certainly to poet or to scribes. Both sets of lines, in either variant form, are probably metrical, and either version could be the poet's. After all, he wrote lines, nearly universally attested, with expletive readings, like *"Ful* many a deyntee hors hadde he in stable" (A 168), in situations where he could have offered a "headless" line.³⁴ Moreover, studies of attestation like Manly and Rickert's, even ignoring the circular reasoning by which they were created, will not resolve such variants: expletive readings of this sort are created and suppressed by scribes independent of archetypal affiliation and produce the impression of convergent genetic groups in traditional stemmata.

In the present state of knowledge, Greg's rule of copy-text provides

---

³⁴ One must qualify even this pellucid case. One of the nine scribes I cite, while s/he did not change the metrical form, nonetheless rejected expletive *Ful* for a more purposive anticlericism; En¹ writes *For* instead.

the only expedient for dealing with such lections. Following Greg, in legitimately doubtful instances (not all such examples are "legitimately" so), the editor allows the form of the manuscript chosen as copy-text for the edition to determine what s/he prints. This action is a kind of resignation: the copy-text is printed, not as correct, but as an acceptable reading in a context where correctness may not be determined. (Again, one may point to the usefulness of explicit textual notes which indicate this fact to users of the edition.) But if one now recalls my earlier discussion of tale-order, one can see that following Greg's principle in such cases of doubt potentially creates a multiple *Canterbury Tales*. For the two variants above, Blake's text prints Hg's eek/–; *Riverside* prints El's –/for; were there editions which followed the actual readings of Cp and Ha⁴ (and not just, as I suggested, their tale-order) they would complete the full array of possibilities by offering –/– and eek/for, respectively.

The alternative to Greg's rule and to a thoroughly multiple text is choice. But the editor of *Tales* will get to make roughly the same choice among variants at a very large number of points, and thus s/he will eventually do more than just create a presumption about Chaucer's metrical usage (and, given Chaucer's centrality, about the whole history of English meter and poetry 1300–1550). Especially if the editor's choice rests on universal principle—extreme versions of this act would invariably choose hendecasyllables, with occasional "headless" lines tossed in, or invariably choose the verse most metrically difficult—s/he will conclude by pre-writing the history of English meter for those who use the text to find. Someone researching English metrical history might well be better served by less emphatic pursuit of behavior deemed authorial and by concomitant access to the forms of individual manuscripts near the head of the tradition.

That preferable return to the manuscripts suggests one possible move toward a resolution of some metrical variants—although not a "ready expedient" like Greg's rule. All *Tales* manuscripts, or some appropriate selection like the nine I cite, can be entered into a data bank and surveyed, not for possible rectitude but for simple scribal habit in specific verbal-metrical contexts. If one cannot openly determine the anteriority of one reading over another, one can determine how individual scribes react to certain possible lections. One could then answer such questions as how often Hg includes the word *eek* when attested elsewhere in the sample, how often it has the phrase *and eek*, how often it reproduces "headless" lines. Such a data bank may reveal a variety of distinctive scribal profiles—Ne's *eek* or *whan that* or *forto* behavior as distinct from Gg's, for example—and may thus control one's sense of what attestation means at any single point in the text.

However onerous, such a study promises some minor surprises, at least on the basis of one cursory, if not erratic, sampling I have made. I did not read Manly-Rickert's full variant corpus but restricted myself to surveying two metrically important expletives, *ful* and *eek*, as they appear in an edited text, *Riverside*'s A 1–750. First, both words, in this sampling based upon editorial acceptance and not the manuscripts themselves, almost certainly are Chaucerian and necessary to an authorial meter in most places they occur. I find thirteen examples of *eek*, thirty-four of *ful* (and may have missed others): six *eek*'s and fourteen or fifteen *ful*'s[35] are unanimously attested in the nine manuscripts I survey, and in most other instances variation is limited to one or two copies. Two meter-bending suppressions of *eek* and fifteen of *ful* occur in but a single manuscript of the nine and, from their isolation, probably emerged in transmission.

Second, this variation is not random, and at least two distinctive scribal profiles emerge. The copyists of the *a* and *b* archetypes (En[1]; and Cx[1] to 567, Ne thereafter) show an animus against expletive *eek* and *ful*: between them, the two families account for two meter-affecting suppressions of *eek* nowhere else attested and thirteen similar suppressions of *ful*.[36] An editor should probably consider the evidence of these manuscripts in other situations tainted: their omission of an expletive may simply represent scribal predeliction and may indicate nothing about a retained Chaucerian reading from their archetypes. In contrast, some manuscripts, obviously those on which the *Riverside* editors based their text, preserve these metrically useful expletives in the overwhelming number of instances: El replaces *ful* with a conjunction once (A 215) and has every other example of both words except the problematic A 217; Ch has two substitutions of equally expletive words (*wol/wel* at A 22 and 615) and includes A 217 *eek*, along with the remainder;[37] Hg has the expletive substitution at A 615, includes A 217 *eek*, and has but a single

---

[35] I take 615 *ful* as such an agreement, since although no less than six copies (Ad[3] Ch En[1] Ha[4] Hg Ne) in fact read *wol/wel*, all readings show the same metrical form and attest an expletive word here. Ordinarily, *wel/ful* would resist resolution, but here *wel good* in the preceding line has attracted the subsequent lection.

[36] *b* (Cx[1] + Ne) rejects *eek* three times, *ful* thirteen times (one example of *ful*, A 539, gives a more emphatic reading); En[1] rejects *eek* four times, *ful* five times (including two examples of emphatic substitution, A 168 and 221). *b* eight times rejects *ful* with no support from other manuscripts; En[1], three times; they together reject another example of *ful* and two of *eek* in lections where they agree only with each other. Thus, they are solely responsible for fourteen of the twenty-six lections with variation.

[37] Ch deserves considerably more attention than it has ever received. The text was compiled from a variety of different archetypes and its apparent conservatism here probably reflects, as Manly and Rickert suggest, its access at this point to something like the copy available to Hg.

other omission (A 132 *ful*, partly supported by Ha⁴); Cp lacks only two
eek's, neither a unique omission.[38]

All but a handful of the variants, whatever their metrical effect, appear
purely transmissional, the results of either *ab* animus or of quite isolated
behavior—both within the particular lection and in the scribe's overall
activity. Three more widely attested readings may be resolved openly, on
the basis of context and disposition of variants, and were likely produced
in transmission.[39] Problematic remain A 217, with which I began this
discussion (and about which I remain agnostic); A 132 *ful muchel*] *al*
Ha⁴, *muchel* Hg (where I would follow Hg only if copy-text); and A 489
eek] *om*. Ad³ Cp Cx¹ Gg, the one fruit of this truncated study of two
isolated features with metrical effect.

Every editor I have found since Skeat prints A 489 *eek*—wrongly, I
would suggest. Including the word creates accentual patterns not easily
paralleled elsewhere (e.g., second-syllable stress on *offryng* within the
line); omitting the word would produce a much preferable "headless"
line. Presumably the five manuscripts which preserve the word have it
as an almost automatic hiccough after *and*. Printing A 489 without *eek*
would contribute to a more various *Canterbury Tales* than readers have
seen heretofore, not simply in its metrical patterning (A 489 with *eek* is
a hendecasyllable, if an awkward one) but also in its manuscript
sources.[40]

These examples indicate what I perceive as a double bind which
effects author-centered textual criticism when applied to Chaucer's
works. On the one hand, the author is single, and given his canonical
status, must look singularly so in the same way, say, Spenser or (perhaps
the nearest analogue) Pope does. But as virtually always in textual
criticism, this authorial Chaucer can be discovered from multiple sources,
here a sort particularly resistant to modern notions of book-production.
These require some radical reduction to meet the needs of authorial

---

[38] The other manuscripts show no discernible tendencies: Gg varies 5x (3x unique,
2x by substitution), Ha⁴ 5x (3x, 2x), Ad³ 4x (0x, 0x, an absence suggestive either of
thoroughgoing conflation or of a careful reliance on inherited readings).

[39] A 634 *eek*] *om*. Ad³ En¹ is the product of inadvertent (and perhaps independent)
haplography before *lekes*; A 196 *ful*] *om*. Ad³ Cx¹ Ha⁴ removes a hypermetric syllable,
very likely authorial, to create a "normal" line, and A 212 *ful*] *om*. by the same three
manuscripts is similar (although the scribes failed to heed Chaucer's usual elision of
many a, and the line is not hypermetric).

[40] Within the very limited confines of my survey, the use of two words in lections
already editorially approved (and with no search for added *ful* or *eek* elsewhere), the
witness with the greatest number of acceptable readings, although narrowly, is neither
Hg nor El, but Cp. The only one of its readings among these forty-seven lections I
might reject would be A 217—and I would print that, were El my copy-text. (Contrast
Hg at A 132, 217, 615; El at A 215, agreeing with Cp in A 217.)

singularity. Thus editors are compelled toward a measured unity of presentation.

Such a unity is "measured" because it is only a modern scholarly convention foreign to the materials by which one finds Chaucer. *The Works* have a venerable editorial history which sanctions some presentations and not others. These conventions governing the forms under which Chaucer gets consumed often remain unexamined. They silently shape approaches to the manuscript multiplicity which editors must discipline to unity and can restrain, as much as enable, editorial thought. *The Canterbury Tales* should appear a continuous canonical text, as it does in El; PF should include a roundel, as it does in some manuscripts; everyone should print A 489 *eek*, since El and Hg have it. And serious deviation from norms established by past texts undermines the entire enterprise: it destroys that assurance of being in touch with the author that the reader of an edited canonical text should have. At some point and in some instances, convention of its own inertia overrides investigation of the varying manuscripts from which the text is formed. Editors must account for that multiplicity, reproduce it somewhere, but not investigate it too strenuously.

Fortunately, the evidence remains in all its robust plurality. A great deal of it, given the constraints of convention, has not been examined to the extent that it deserves. In many places, ranging from large readings (like tale order) to small (like a single *eek*), the sources convey a Chaucer unread. Thoughtful consideration of such manuscript alternatives may produce a rather different, a more fractured and various Chaucer the author.

Chaucer's Meter:
The Evidence of the Manuscripts

DEREK PEARSALL

T alking about meter is a hazardous business. For one thing meter is
very important. Though it might easily slip one's mind, given that nine-
tenths of the critical writing on Chaucer never mentions the fact,
Chaucer's poetry is written in verse, and the way we read that verse and
respond to its musicality, whether in our heads or when reading aloud,
is presumably an important part of our interpretation of and response to
its meaning. Another hazard, given that the matter is an important one,
is that rational debate is even more difficult than usual, since interpretation must in the end be based on an intuitive "feel" for the music of
Chaucer's verse, and none of us is going to be very ready to allow that
someone else's intuitive feel is better than our own, or to be easily
persuaded out of our very good opinion on the matter. There *is* the
evidence of the manuscripts, which will be the subject of this paper, but
instinct, ingrained habit, prejudice, and the determination to prove one's
opinion right are more potent shaping forces, and are the reason that
discussions of meter always end in tight-lipped fury and the painful
recognition that one's colleagues are not as likeable or intelligent as one
had thought. A third hazard is the role of meter in the determination by
editors of unoriginal readings. An editor does not have to have a theory
of meter in order to edit a verse text, but, in an area where theories are
increasingly hard to come by, it is possible to have a theory of meter, and
editors usually avail themselves of the opportunity. The editor's theory
of meter thus becomes entrenched in the text, acquires something of the
sacramental quality of the text, and comes to be even more strenuously
defended as a recovered rather than a perceived reality. The subject
seems to be one that invites intransigence. The following discussion,
which will confine itself to the pentameter couplet of the *Canterbury
Tales*, will attempt a greater flexibility.

For a long time there has been a theory of meter behind the practice
of Chaucerian editors, one which has therefore exerted considerable
influence upon the way in which Chaucer is read. The best and clearest
statement of this theory, as always, is by Skeat, in his general introduction to the six-volume Oxford Chaucer.[1] Skeat was not immune to the

---

[1] *The Complete Works of Geoffrey Chaucer*, ed. W. W. Skeat, 6 vols. (London:

influence of fanciful theories, and he flirts for a while with a notion of speech-waves and a law of monopressures derived from an anonymous tract published in Edinburgh of which he was surely wrong to say that it "deserves to be better known" (lxxxiv). But he does not allow this to interfere much with his analysis, which has the kind of Skeat-like pragmatism that makes it seem not a theory at all. He finds, from his reading of the Old French ten-syllabled line, that there were sixteen possible varieties of the line, allowing for the addition of an extra unstressed syllable at the caesura or line-end, the omission of the unstressed syllable at the line-beginning or caesura, and the permissible permutations of these four kinds of license. He considers that Chaucer "freely accepted" the principle of adding a syllable at the caesura or line-end (the so-called feminine ending), that he "allowed himself to accept" the principle of dropping the unstressed syllable at the line-beginning (the "headless" line), but that he "disliked" all four types of line in which the unstressed syllable at the caesura was omitted (the "Lydgate" or "broken-backed" line).

Skeat's language is delightfully disingenuous: what Chaucer "allowed himself to accept" is clearly something that Chaucer accepted against his better judgement, or, more properly, against Skeat's better judgement, and the way is clear for the editor to remove as many of these unfortunate evidences of indulgence as he decently can. With the Lydgate line, Skeat's distaste is as marked as the "dislike" that he attributes to Chaucer. Such lines, he says, "introduce a most disagreeable jerk into the middle of the line, such as he very rarely allows" (lxxxviii), adding that Lydgate, nevertheless, "did not shrink from these unmelodious forms." Lydgate's failure to shrink from it may have been, to Skeat, a sufficient condemnation of the practice, though the line he quotes, presumably one of the worst he could find, does not seem to me unspeakable:

> Up he roos maugre all his foon.[2]

It is clearly difficult to talk about single lines out of context.

Later in his introduction, Skeat returns to a discussion of the Lydgate line, as if bracing himself for a disagreeable task. It is a license, he repeats, "of which Lydgate availed himself to a painful extent" (xcii). Of Chaucer he says:

> It is clear that his ear disliked it; yet there seem to be just a few cases that cannot fairly be explained away, the MSS being sadly

---

Oxford University Press, 1894), introduction on "Versification," lxxxii–xcvii.

[2] The line is from Lydgate's *Siege of Thebes*, and appears as line 2195 in the edition of A. Erdmann, EETS, 108 (London: Oxford University Press, 1911). Skeat quotes from an earlier edition.

unanimous. It is better to learn the truth than to suppress what we should ourselves dislike. (xcii)

The line he quotes as an example of the sad truth of Chaucer's betrayal of his good ear is *Merchant's Tale*, E (IV) 1682:

> My tale is doon:—for my wit is thinne.[3]

He admits that this cannot be mended (without conjectural emendation based on meter, that is): the *done* offered by the two worst manuscripts is, as he says, "impossible." With another problem line, *Melibee*, B 2141 (VII.951), Skeat allows the truth to be ever so slightly obscured, if not suppressed:

> I meane of Marke, Mathew, Luk, and John.

"Four MSS," he comments, "have a tag after the *k* in *Mark*; hence I have printed *Mark-e*. But I fear it can hardly be justified" (xcii). One could not reasonably ask for more honesty, except that Skeat might have mentioned that one of the manuscripts with a tag is the Ellesmere (San Marino, California, Henry E. Huntington Library, MS. 26.C.9), which had such a profound influence generally on Skeat's view of Chaucer's text and meter in the *Canterbury Tales*. Nor could one ask for a better demonstration of the way in which an editorial assumption becomes enshrined in his text, even though he acknowledges that his assumption is insecurely based. And there is, to be sure, absolutely nothing wrong with the line: the meter is perfectly apt to the rhetorically emphatic syntax of the list of evangelists.

Skeat quotes two other Lydgate lines as "unsatisfactory." One is *Monk's Tale*, B 3384 (VII.2194), which he does not cite, but which appears in his text thus:

> "Goth, bringeth forth the vessels," [tho] quod he.

He emends as indicated, citing in his note lines B 3391, 3416, 3418, where the plural *vessels* is similarly spelt. I'm sorry to say that F. N. Robinson, in his edition, shows no such scrupulousness, and simply emends *vesseles* without comment or textual note. The line is not one that we are going to like, I must admit, but we might be prepared to admit a certain metrical licence at the junction of direct speech and speech prefix (much as in alliterative verse speech-prefixes are often

---

[3] Quotation, here and in the following examples, is from Skeat's text and not from his introduction. Alternative fragment numberings refer to the edition of F. N. Robinson, *The Complete Works of Geoffrey Chaucer*, 2d ed. (Cambridge, MA: Houghton-Mifflin, 1957), which is used for all other quotations from Chaucer, unless otherwise indicated.

extra-metrical), where the pause in the continuity of sense might accommodate a metrical pause.

The second line that Skeat quotes as unsatisfactory is *Monk's Tale*, B 3535 (VII.2346)—he is using Fragment B for nearly all his examples:

> And Hermanno, and Thymalaö.

It is impossible to imagine what this line could have deteriorated from, or why a scribe might have made a mistake with it. It is evidently what Chaucer wrote, and he accepted the Lydgate line and the metrical stress on *and* in the context of a list of these strange-sounding foreign names, and as part of the desire to encode the correct pronunciation of Thymalaö, and the correct rhyme, in the metrical structure of the line. No one has emended this line.

Another interesting feature of Skeat's discussion of meter is his emphasis upon the medial pause, for which he found manuscript support in the care and regularity with which the virgule is inserted in the Ellesmere MS to indicate the caesura.[4] It was for this reason that he welcomed Chaucer's practice of introducing an extra unstressed syllable at the caesura, particularly when this syllable was a light one such as an inflexional final -e. Not only that, but he considered that normal elision, as of -en, or -er, or final -e with following initial vowel or h-, was inhibited at the caesura, so that an extra unstressed syllable was often created in this way. In this Skeat departed from the strict rules of elision and scansion established by Ten Brink[5] and read lines such as the following with greater freedom:

> Which that my fader in his prosperitee.
>
> > (B 3385, VII.2195)
>
> That god of heven hath dominacioun.
>
> > (B 3409, VII.2219)

---

[4] I have myself found no impelling reason to share Skeat's respect for the positioning of the virgule in the Ellesmere manuscript (nor for that matter in Hengwrt): it is sometimes unusually apt, often not so, and is clearly scribal in origin. G. B. Killough, in a valuable essay on "Punctuation and Caesura in Chaucer," *Studies in the Age of Chaucer* 4 (1982): 87–107, concludes likewise that the virgule is scribal, but considers that the placement is highly regular, and in accordance with well-established tradition.

[5] B. Ten Brink, *Chaucer Sprache und Verskunst* (Leipzig, 1884), translated by M. B. Smith as *The Language and Metre of Chaucer* (London: Macmillan, 1901). For an account of the history of the study of Chaucer's meter, with full bibliography, see T. F. Mustanoja, "Chaucer's Prosody," in Beryl Rowland, ed., *Companion to Chaucer Studies*, 2d ed. (New York and Oxford: Oxford University Press, 1979), 65–94. See also the very useful essay by A. T. Gaylord, "Scanning the Prosodists: An Essay in Metacriticism," *Chaucer Review* 11 (1976): 22–77.

Skeat even added final -e's to his copy-text (the Ellesmere) so as to create the kind of line that he liked, the most famous example being the second of the opening two lines of the *General Prologue*:

> Whan that Aprille with his shoures sote
> The droght of Marche hath perced to the rote.

Neither Hengwrt (Aberystwyth, National Library of Wales, MS. Peniarth 392D) nor Ellesmere has this final -e for *March*, and it is completely unetymological. Note also how Skeat has added an -e to *Aprill* in the first line, though in that case the purpose is to convert a headless line, which we remember is the kind of line Chaucer occasionally allowed himself to accept but would evidently not allow in the very first line of his great poem, into a line with reversal of the first foot and in no danger of turning into the dreaded Lydgate line, whatever the pronunciation of *Aprille* (Hengwrt has *Aueryll*, Ellesmere *Aprill*).

Skeat's fondness for the medial pause has to do with his general opinion that Chaucer's verse should be read slowly and with deliberation, with careful attention to feminine endings both at caesura and at line-end. (An analogy that he does not mention might be with the pronunciation of the alexandrine of French classical drama.) He explains his opinion thus:

> We may believe that, in old times, when poetry was recited by minstrels to large assemblies, the enunciation of it was slow and deliberate, and the pauses were longer than when we now read it to a friend or to ourselves. . . . The minstrel's first business was to be understood. Many speakers speak too fast, and make too short pauses, till experience teaches them better (xc).

The generalization about minstrel delivery seems to me to be mistaken: I cannot imagine a slow and deliberate enunciation of a tail-rhyme romance like *Sir Launfal*, where speed is essential to the bright, bitty, and trivial nature of the narrative performance. There is nothing to sustain deliberation. Chaucer knew this style exactly and catches it with unerring precision in *Sir Thopas*: the reader of these jog-trot tail-rhyme stanzas invariably finds himself going faster and faster, as if the accelerator were stuck. But I think Skeat is right about the Chaucerian pentameter, and it is quite possible to believe that one of Chaucer's purposes, especially after his early work in the short couplet, was to slow down English verse, and to make it capable of bearing a richer cargo of meaning. His introduction of the pentameter, the type of verse which most of all resists the compulsive onward drive of traditional English meters such as the four-stress alliterative line and popular ballad meter, may be seen as an important element in this strategy.

Skeat's emphasis on the medial pause seems therefore to be well-judged, and it seems a little inconsistent of him to be so severe on the Lydgate line, or at least the good Lydgate line, especially when he accepts that the caesura may on quite numerous occasions necessarily preserve final -e from elision (xci), as in this line from the *Nun's Priest's Prologue* (B 3989, VII.2799):

> Than had your tale al be told in vayn.

The effect of hiatus is not unlike that of the Lydgate line, which is perhaps one reason why the stricter metrists of the fifteenth and twentieth century have taken advantage of the liberal sprinkling of final -e's in early manuscripts to emend the line and read as follows:

> Thanne haddë yourë tale be toold in veyn

or

> Thanne haddë your tale al be toold in veyn.

The first is presumably the reading of the line intended by revisers in the group of heavily editorialized manuscripts represented by Corpus Christi College, Oxford, MS. 198, British Library MS. Lansdowne 851 and the Petworth MS, the latter is the reading explicitly preferred by Sisam:[6] both have a metronome-like regularity and neither it seems to me can bear comparison with the naturalness and syntactic adequacy of the line as first quoted.

One has to accept, perhaps, that there are various kinds of medial pause, including both genuine hiatus and also the sense of deferred continuity or demurral which is what I think Skeat really prefers, that delicious drawing out of a half-sounded final -e or of a complex consonant cluster that recognizes artifice and self-conscious pleasure in musicality at the same time that it defers to the insistence of the line and the continuity of sense. The opening lines of the *General Prologue* will illustrate the variety of Chaucer's techniques:

> Whan that Aprill with his shoures soote
> The droghte of March hath perced to the roote
> And bathed every veyne in swich licour
> Of which vertu engendred is the flour. . . .

---

[6] The edition by K. Sisam referred to is that of *Chaucer: The Nun's Priest's Tale* (Oxford: Clarendon Press, 1927). All references, here and subsequently, to variant readings in MSS and printed editions of lines from the *Nun's Priest's Tale* are detailed and discussed more fully in my edition of *The Nun's Priest's Tale* for the *Variorum Edition of the Works of Geoffrey Chaucer*, general editors P. G. Ruggiers and D. C. Baker, vol. II, part 9 (Norman, OK: University of Oklahoma Press, 1984).

At the same time there should be no persistent loitering, and the practice of many readers, of always giving full syllabic value to feminine endings and even of supplying them when they are not there, becomes in the end a kind of strait jacket. I have heard readers go on with the next lines,

> Whan Zephirus eek with his sweete breeth(-e)
> Inspired hath in every holt and heeth(-e)
> The tendre croppes. . . .

The effect is to deny rather than to defer continuity, and to overemphasize line-end at the expense of Chaucer's daring enjambement.

One should also recognize, even whilst acknowledging the potential importance of the medial pause, that flexibility and variety are even more important considerations for Chaucer. At times his verse can move with frenetic speed, and the passage that everyone would go to as an example, the breathtaking finale in the bedroom of the *Reeve's Tale*, is notable for the infrequency of feminine endings, the complete absence of headless or Lydgate lines, and the almost complete swallowing of the medial pause in the headlong onrush of the verse.

The system of versification that Skeat outlined for Chaucer, though in his own practice it was modified by his own admirable pragmatism, became subsequently more rigid, and was reinforced in the paragraphs on versification in a hundred introductions to texts of Chaucer, and in an editorial practice that tended to follow Skeat closely. It was the increasing rigidity of the system that I think goaded James G. Southworth and Ian Robinson into asserting that Chaucer did not write pentameter, that his verse was not indeed metrical at all, but rhythmical, and came from essentially the same mold as traditional alliterative verse.[7] Their view depended on their belief that final -e was never sounded in Chaucer's versification, a belief that has been conclusively shown to be false on several occasions,[8] and also on an eccentric interpretation of the prosody of Chaucer's followers. The usual view is that the secret of his versification was lost with the loss of sounded final -e, already an archaic practice in his own day, and that English poets tended to revert to the older traditional semi-alliterative type of measure, described by C. S. Lewis as "a long line divided by a sharp medial break into two half-lines,

---

[7] J. G. Southworth, *Verses of Cadence: An Introduction to the Prosody of Chaucer and His Followers* (Oxford: Basil Blackwell, 1954); J. G. Southworth, *The Prosody of Chaucer and His Followers: Supplementary Chapters to Verses of Cadence* (Oxford: Basil Blackwell, 1962); I. Robinson, *Chaucer's Prosody: A Study of the Middle English Verse Tradition* (Cambridge: Cambridge University Press, 1971).

[8] E.g., by E. Donaldson, "Chaucer's Final -e," *PMLA* 63 (1948): 1101-24; M. L. Samuels, "Chaucerian Final -e," *Notes and Queries* 217 (1972): 445-48; D. Burnley, "Inflexion in Chaucer's Adjectives," *Neuphilologische Mitteilungen* 83 (1982): 169-77.

each half-line containing not less than two or more than three stresses."[9]
Here is an example from the fortunately little known poet George Ashby,
who purports to be writing rhyme royal:

> At the ende of Somer, when wynter began
> And trees, herbes and flowres dyd fade,
> Blosteryng and blowyng the gret wyndes than
> Threw doune the frutes with whyche they were lade.[10]

Southworth and Robinson argue, on the contrary, that Chaucer's
followers really understood Chaucer's versification and it is nineteenth-
century scholars who have got it wrong. Southworth scans Chaucer using
musical notation, producing for instance the reading of the opening lines
of the *General Prologue*, as they appear in Ellesmere (figure 1).[11] I
hope (in my reading aloud) that I am not doing an injustice to Southworth's reading of these lines, though I do, I admit, find it difficult to
conceive of an injustice being done to a reading so bad. His claim, in
opposing a system of versification that he sees as being over-rigid and
mechanical, is that Chaucer must be read more naturally, in accord with
the rhythms of prose and colloquial speech ("it is the movement of a
highly developed English speech").[12] This of course is the interpretation
generally offered of the scansion of alliterative verse—that it is a highly
wrought version of speech, with the syntactical and rhythmical patterns
of speech to some extent formalized and systematized, and that it is, to
that extent, strictly speaking non-metrical.

I have to make it clear at this point that I know exactly what "metrical" means in relation to English verse. A metrical system posits the
existence of a regular line, or regularly repeated pattern of lines, with an
arbitrarily fixed number of stresses regularly disposed, the regularity of
disposition being temporal, and based on the isochronous interval. Such
a metrical system may be *accentual* (what Coleridge propounded in his
preface to "Christabel" as his "new" principle) or *syllabic*: to be more
exact, and simpler, there may be less or more regularity in the distribution of unstressed syllables. This, of course, does not affect in any way
the almost unlimited local variations that may be worked in individual

---

[9] C. S. Lewis, "The Fifteenth–Century Heroic Line," *Essays and Studies* 24 (1938):
28–41. For further discussion of fifteenth–century prosody, see D. A. Pearsall, ed., *The
Floure and the Leafe* (London and Edinburgh: Nelson, 1962), introduction, 59–62; D.
Pearsall, *John Lydgate* (London: Routledge and Kegan Paul, 1970), 60–63.

[10] Opening lines of "A Prisoner's Reflections," in George Ashby's *Poems*, ed. Mary
Bateson, EETS, 76 (London: Oxford University Press, 1899).

[11] Southworth, *Verses of Cadence*, 66–67. Figure reproduced by kind permission
of the publishers.

[12] Southworth, *Verses of Cadence*, 91.

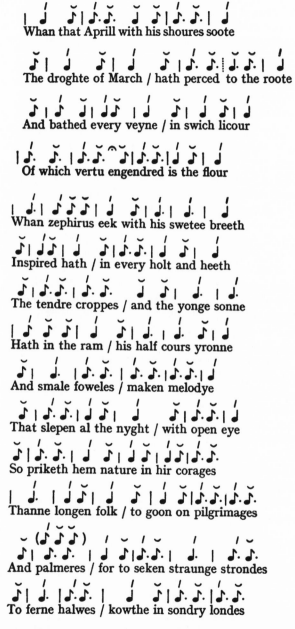

Figure 1. Reproduced, by permission, from J. G. Southworth, *Verses of Cadence: An Introduction to the Prosody of Chaucer and His Followers* (Oxford: Basil Blackwell, 1954), 66-67.

lines, in the interests of rhythm, by rhetorical and syntactic patterning, often in tension with and counterpointed against the metrical pattern. Alliterative verse is non-metrical because the rhythmical interest is found, as Bliss points out, "not in the more or less exact accommodation of the speech-material to the metrical pattern," but in the variation in the patterns of individual half-lines, which are themselves "selected from among the rhythms which occur most commonly in natural speech."[13] Whether this remains entirely true of later Middle English alliterative verse, and whether there is not there some accommodation to the increasingly dominant metrical forms of verse, would be another question, and the answer would certainly take in the process already alluded to by which the "metrified" four-stress alliterative or semi-alliterative line infiltrates the Chaucerian pentameter.

It would be possible to acknowledge that there is already influence of this kind being exerted upon Chaucer. I did, after all, in a moment of high excitement on the very first page of my book on *Old English and Middle English Poetry*, call the alliterative four-stress line "the secret power and anvil of the pentameter."[14] The audacity and freedom of Chaucer's handling of the pentameter may have something to do with tunes that were ringing in his head from older forms of English verse. If it were this inheritance that Southworth was genuinely trying to draw attention to, there would be much to be said for his iconoclasm. But reading according to his system of musical notation suggests that what he is doing, without realizing it, is simply to reduce Chaucer to the compound four-stress meter which, with its close affinities with dancing, marching, and popular music, lies at the root of all English popular verse. It is the meter of folk song and nursery rhyme, and is characterized by regularity of primary and secondary stresses, frequent absence of intermediate unstressed syllables, and a primacy of metrical stress over speech rhythms which allows, for instance, for things like pause-stresses in secondary positions. Here is an example where the intermediate unstressed syllables are mostly present:

> Up the airy mountains, down the rushy glen,
> We daren't go a-hunting for fear of little men.

And here is an example where they are mostly absent:

> Deedle deedle dumpling, my son John,

---

[13] A. J. Bliss, "The Appreciation of Old English Metre," in *English and Medieval Studies Presented to J. R. R. Tolkien*, ed. N. Davis and C. L. Wrenn (London: Allen & Unwin, 1962), 27–40; see 29.

[14] Derek Pearsall, *Old English and Middle English Poetry*, Routledge History of English Poetry, vol. 1 (London: Routledge and Kegan Paul, 1977), 1.

Went to bed with his trousers on. . . .

Once this jingly meter is in your head it is very difficult to get it out, and even the most orthodox pentameter will collapse into its jog-trot rhythms:

Clóse by those méads, for éver crowned with flówers,
Whére Thames with príde survéys his rising tówers,
Thére stands a strúcture óf majestic fráme,
Whích from the néighbouring Hámpton takes its náme.

I mangle thus these lines from Pope (*The Rape of the Lock* 3.1–4) as a terrible warning against any attempt to argue a "rhythmical" reading, in Southworth's sense of the term, of Chaucer's verse.

It remains true, though, that the over-rigid interpretation of Chaucer's pentameter that Southworth was reacting against was itself a distortion of Chaucer's versification. As Manly and Rickert pointed out in 1940:

Current theories of Chaucer's versification are based, not upon the text as found in the MSS, or as established by critical processes, but upon the artificial text made regular by all the devices at the disposal of the scholar.[15]

It has always been possible for editors to produce regular decasyllabic lines by selection among the variants offered by the manuscripts, whose scribes, indeed, were often prompted by the same concern for regularity. But study of the text as it is presented in the Hengwrt manuscript, which has a special claim to textual authority that is now generally recognized, and to an only slightly lesser extent in the Ellesmere manuscript, which has been rather unfairly impugned by the editors of the Variorum Chaucer, including me, compels one to recognize a difference in metrical practice between what must be Chaucer's and what must be his editors'. The freedom and generosity in the conception of the rhythmical possibilities of the pentameter, the audacity of variation and experimentation, and the subtle sense of the relation between rhetorical and syntactical impetus and rhythmical variation, are surely positive characteristics of the creative poet at work, while the mending and smoothing of lines to produce a mechanically regular syllable count or alternation of stressed and unstressed syllables, at the expense of natural speech rhythms, are surely likely to be characteristic of the improving scribe or editor.

A statement like this needs to be backed up with specific examples,

---

[15] J. M. Manly and E. Rickert, eds., *The Text of the Canterbury Tales: Studied on the Basis of All Known Manuscripts*, 8 vols. (Chicago: University of Chicago Press, 1940), 2:40.

and the examples I shall give will all be from the *Nun's Priest's Prologue*
and *Tale*,[16] where a small but significant number of emendations
continue to be made by editors for the sake of meter, and more
particularly for the sake of restoring a more regular decasyllabic line. I
begin with two lines I allowed myself, in the Variorum edition, to emend
(to adopt Skeat's phrase), but which I now think need no emendation:

> "I crye on the mynystres," quod he
>
> (B 4233, VII.3043)

Ellesmere and most other manuscripts add *out* after *crye*, and are
followed by all modern editors. This certainly makes for smoother meter,
but the Hengwrt reading, with the abrupt break in the line created by the
inhibition of elision, could be seen as conveying more emphatically the
outrage of the speaker. Both phrases, *crye on* and *crye out on*, seem to
be equally idiomatic. The second line appears thus in Hengwrt:

> As man that was affrayd in his herte
>
> (B 4468, VII.3278)

Ellesmere and most other manuscripts have *affrayed*, for obvious
metrical reasons, and are followed by all modern editors. Chaucer uses
both forms, *affrayd* and *affrayed*, but a case for *affrayd* could be made
here on the grounds that the sustaining of the stressed syllable that is
necessary to carry the voice over the following hiatus adds emphasis to
the key word in the line.

The examples that follow might be regarded as clearer examples of the
mending of meter in Ellesmere. Ellesmere is followed by all editors in
"improving" the following headless line,

> For a preestes sone yaf hym a knok
>
> (B 4504, VII.3314)

by adding *that* after *For*. Ellesmere alone has this reading; the two
usages, *for* and *for that*, are equally idiomatic. The following Lydgate
line, or at least the Lydgate line effect created by inhibition of elision at
the caesura,

> Who so wol seke Actes of sondry Remes
>
> (B 4326, VII.3136)

---

[16] All quotation, of text and variant readings, is from the edition cited in note 6
above. Supplementary quotation from Ellesmere is from the collation of Ellesmere
given in P. G. Ruggiers, ed., *Geoffrey Chaucer, The Canterbury Tales: A Facsimile and
Transcription of the Hengwrt Manuscript, with Variants from the Ellesmere
Manuscript* (Norman, OK: University of Oklahoma Press, 1979).

is restored to syllabic regularity by Ellesmere, which adopts the reading *seken*, with full infinitival ending, for *seke*, as do most modern editions. Yet the line is perfectly readable in Hengwrt. Simple syllable counting seems to be the reason for the change that Ellesmere makes in this line,

> Than is a Clokke or any Abbey Orlogge
>
> (B 4044, VII.2854)

by substituting *an* for *any*. Most modern editors follow Skeat's lead in adopting the Ellesmere reading, even though elision of the final *y* of *any* with the initial vowel of *abbey* (which is pronounced with the accent on the second syllable, of course), will produce a perfectly regular line for those who want it. Ellesmere also removes the extra syllable in the following rather striking line,

> A dong Carte wente as it were to donge lond
>
> (B 4226, VII.3036)

by omitting *wente*. Skeat followed suit, but other modern editors have been happy to accept the line as it appears in Hengwrt and other early manuscripts.

Sometimes the editor of Ellesmere makes problems for himself, as for instance in this line, where he shows his usual pedantic concern for removing the contracted form of the third person singular:

> Comth of the grete superfluitee.
>
> (B 4117, VII.2927)

The line, now thought to have too many syllables with the substitution of *cometh* for *comth*, is further emended by the omission of *the* and the substitution of the ungrammatical strong form of the adjective. The line now reads,

> Cometh of greet superfluytee

which is sufficient in itself to deny the Ellesmere editor much of an ear. What modern editors do, characteristically, is to adopt the uncontracted form from Ellesmere (or more likely from Skeat, who has exerted a powerful influence on subsequent editors), but to ignore the other Ellesmere emendations in the line. They possibly assume that *cometh* is contracted in pronunciation if not in spelling.

Ellesmere, however, for all the comments I have made, here and elsewhere,[17] on its editorializing propensities, is on the whole very

---

[17] E.g., in the Variorum edition of the *Nun's Priest's Tale*, 97-99, and in *The Canterbury Tales* (London: Allen & Unwin, 1985), 10-14. I think the Variorum editors have felt themselves under pressure to denigrate Ellesmere as part of their determina-

close to Hengwrt. Indeed, there are one or two occasions when the *eek*'s
which were fairly liberally thrown around by fifteenth-century editors in
their attempts to regularize meter appear in Hengwrt but not Ellesmere:

> Ran Cow and calf and eek the verray hogges.
>
> (B 4575, VII.3385)

> The hope and pryde eek of hire enemy.
>
> (B 4594, VII.3404)

To be consistent, I suppose I should be suspicious of these *eek*'s, but
then, there are good Lydgate lines and bad Lydgate lines, and these
would be bad ones. A nice illustration of the positive value of Ellesmere
for understanding Chaucer's meter is provided in a line that appears in
a portion of the *Nun's Priest's Prologue* not present in Hengwrt:

> Ye quod oure hoost by Seint Poules belle
>
> (B 3970, VII.2780)

Modern editors have had a good deal of trouble with this line, which they
have mended by reading *hooste* for *hoost*, a form which appears
elsewhere in Chaucer with syllabic final -e, but not in this line in any
important manuscript, or by reading *seinte* for *seint*, a form which is
found in the heavily editorialized British Library MS. Harley 7334, but
which itself needs a great amount of special pleading. Editors are clearly
desperate to avoid the Lydgate line, but it seems to me here not only
acceptable but superior, with appropriate emphasis given to the first
word of the Host's oath by its position after the mid-line break.

The testimony of Hengwrt and Ellesmere combined is thus formidable,
and the most striking examples of editorial emendation based on an over-
rigid theory of the regularity of Chaucer's versification come where the
joint testimony of the two manuscripts is rejected. The following
headless line,

> And of many a maze ther with al
>
> (B 4283, VII.3093)

is emended by nearly all editors by the addition of *eke* after *And*, a
reading picked up from Cambridge University Library MS. Dd.4.24, which
alone of all reputable manuscripts has it. The same manuscript provides
the reading (*Ipassed*) that Skeat adopts in order to eliminate another
headless line,

> Was complet and passed were also
>
> (B 4379, VII.3189)

---

tion to defend Hengwrt. It is not necessary: the differences between the two are clear
enough, and Ellesmere remains an exceptionally good witness.

though later editors have been content to accept the line (*complet* may be accented on either syllable in Chaucer). A harder case is this Lydgate line in Hengwrt:

> And when the fox say that he was gon.
> (B 4608, VII.3418)

The hiatus comes between *fox* and *say* (as often, the virgule in Hengwrt and Ellesmere, inserted here between *say* and *that*, is completely arbitrary and misleading), and the line is by no means difficult, given the possibility of drawing out the final double consonant of *fox*. But some modern editors, including F. N. Robinson, prefer to pick up the reading *the cok* for *he* from Dd.4.24, which gives good meter, with stress reversal after the caesura, and possibly better sense.[18] This emendation is certainly preferable to that of Skeat, who adopted *igoon* for *gon* from Harley 7334, a manuscript that still had some shreds of respectability hanging about it in his day, even though Chaucer's normal form would be *agon*.

Resistance to the quasi-Lydgate line created by inhibition of elision at the caesura has induced many modern editors into accepting the various remedies offered by fifteenth-century editors. Nearly all accept the insertion of *wolde* before *han* in the second line here:

> Was lyk an hound and wolde han maad arest
> Up on my body and han had me ded
> (B 4090–91, VII.2900–901)

even though the artificial raising of *and* in the original Hengwrt-Ellesmere line produces an appropriately petulant stridency into Chauntecler's account of his dream. Nearly all editors accept *answered* from editorializing manuscripts such as Corpus 198 and Harley 7334 in their desire to avoid mid-line hiatus in the following line:

> The hostiler answerde hym anon.
> (B 4219, VII.3029)

The virgule after *hostiler* in Hengwrt and Ellesmere, though I have said that the positioning of the virgule in these manuscripts has no general authority, might suggest that *answerde* was to be pronounced, unusually, with the accent on the first syllable, to produce a rather nice Lydgate line. Elsewhere, two successive lines present similar problems to metrical purists:

---

[18] It is worth recalling here that Dd.4.24, as the best representative of the alpha tradition, has often been thought to preserve, on occasions, original but rejected Chaucerian readings ("first shots"). See *Nun's Priest's Tale*, Variorum ed., 99–100.

> And preyde hym his viage to lette
> As for that day he preyde hym to byde.
>
> (B 4274-75, VII.3084-85)

In the first line few modern editors have adopted the early expedient of picking up *preyed* from manuscripts such as Corpus 198 and Dd.4.24 in order to avoid the hiatus of *preyde hym*, but most adopt *for to lette* for *to lette*. It may be that they are accepting the hiatus in the early part of the line and are simply doubtful about the pronunciation of the final -e of *viage*, but the suspicion remains that they are introducing the extra syllable in order to avoid the hiatus. In the second line, nearly all editors—though not Robinson in this case—accept the reading *abyde* for *byde* offered by large numbers of manuscripts and so avoid hiatus.

Finally, two lines with extra syllables might be mentioned as examples of the embarrassment afforded to editors by the apparently irregular versification sanctioned by Hengwrt and Ellesmere. The first,

> And in this Cart heere he lyth gapyng upright
>
> (B 4232, VII.3042)

is metrically unusual, but Sisam, in his excellent edition of the *Nun's Priest's Tale*, has suggested that it may be effective in conveying the impression of "hurried and excited speech."[19] Other modern editors have little time for such niceties, and most follow manuscripts such as Corpus, Lansdowne, and Petworth in omitting *heere*, even though, from the textual point of view, there is no plausible explanation of the generation of the reading of Hengwrt and Ellesmere from the variant. Similarly, in this line,

> But herkneth to that o man fil a gret mervaille
>
> (B 4266, VII.3076)

nearly all editors avoid metrical irregularity by omitting *herkneth*, the authority again being Dd.4.24. Other manuscripts, such as Corpus 198, Lansdowne, and Petworth, tinker with the line in different ways, in their attempt to produce a regular decasyllable. The omission of *herkneth* is difficult to justify from a textual point of view, since there seems no good reason why the word should have been introduced by a scribe. Its presence can be defended in terms of the "dramatic effect in reading" that it creates, as Manly and Rickert suggest; and Sisam thinks it may be one of the "extra-metrical asides" that Chaucer sometimes allows when narrative and dramatic discourse converge.[20]

---

[19] Sisam, *Nun's Priest's Tale* (see note 6 above), 41.

[20] Manly and Rickert, *Canterbury Tales*, 4:515; Sisam, *Nun's Priest's Tale*, 42.

Inevitably, the many examples that have been given above of editorial management of Chaucer's meter will seem mechanically isolated out of context, and it is true that surrounding lines would have to be quoted and talked about to demonstrate fully the value of the scansion offered. Ideally, the whole poem would have to be read aloud. But even in this abbreviated manner of presentation it is possible to see how Chaucer's versification, or what can reasonably be inferred to be Chaucer's versification, has been misrepresented by generations of editors and metrists. Whether it is the editors who mislead the metrists, or vice versa, it would be hard to say, but both seem to have an interest in devising systems that obscure the freedom, variety, and flexibility of Chaucer's meter.

Authorial Vs. Scribal Writing
in Piers Plowman

CHARLOTTE BREWER

The editions of the A and B texts of *Piers Plowman* published by George Kane and E. T. Donaldson[1] have been variously received by the critics over the last few years. When Kane's A-Text came out in 1960, it was greeted with acclaim and praise.[2] Kane's joint edition of B with Donaldson, which appeared fifteen years later in 1975, excited similar respect and admiration, but also roused a few dissenting voices.[3] In this article, I wish to examine some of the critical responses to the edition of B, and suggest that further study of the rich store of material presented in both this edition and Kane's earlier one brings to light evidence which conflicts with the premises underlying the two editorial enterprises.[4] My material falls into five sections. In section 1, I try to show that the most useful way to assess the two editions is to examine the relationship between editorial premises and the individual decisions in which the premises result. In section 2, I outline the two major theoretical positions open to *Piers Plowman* editors: either that Langland wrote a series of rolling revisions of the poem, or that he wrote three discrete versions

---

[1] George Kane, *Piers Plowman: The A Version* (London: The Athlone Press, University of London, 1960); George Kane and E. T. Donaldson, *Piers Plowman: The B Version* (London: The Athlone Press, University of London, 1975). Both have recently (1988) been reissued in second editions, though with minimal alteration and supplement.

[2] See, for example, the reviews by Morton Bloomfield, *Speculum* 36 (1961): 133-37; J. A. W. Bennett, *RES* 14 (1963): 68-71; Gervase Mathew, *Medium Ævum* 30 (1961): 126-28; David C. Fowler, *Modern Philology* 58 (1960-61): 212-14; P. M. Kean, *Library* 16 (1962): 218-24.

[3] See the reviews by Traugott Lawlor, *Modern Philology* 77 (1979-80): 66-71; John A. Alford, *Speculum* 52 (1977): 1002-5; J. A. W. Bennett, *RES* 28 (1977): 323-26; Thorlac Turville-Petre, *Studia Neophilologica* 49 (1977): 153-55, Derek Pearsall, *Medium Ævum* 46 (1977): 278-85; David C. Fowler, *YES* 7 (1977): 23-42; E. G. Stanley, *Notes and Queries* 23 (1976): 435-37; Manfred Görlach, *Archiv* 213 (1976): 396-99.

[4] The following analysis of Kane and Donaldson's work is only made possible by the immense scholarship evident on every page of the A and B editions. I shall argue that their hypotheses and methods are, in some respects, misconceived, but I am overwhelmingly aware of the debt of gratitude owed the two editors by every reader of the poem. I am also grateful to Malcolm Godden for reading and advising on an early draft of this article.

that are, theoretically at any rate, reconstructable from extant manuscript evidence. Kane and Donaldson adopt the second of these positions, and section 3 returns to the theme of section 1 by looking at the textual decisions which result from their editorial premises, in particular their distinction between scribal and authorial readings. Section 4 describes the discrepancy between the editorial methodology of the A and the B editions, and section 5 looks in detail at one of the problems arising from this discrepancy, a problem that illustrates the close relationship between editorial theory and judgements on individual readings.

I

The Athlone A and B texts of *Piers Plowman* represent the fruit of many years of exhaustive labor on the poem. It is difficult for any outsider, that is, anyone who has not spent the long period of toil and devotion demanded of the two editors, to comprehend fully the immensity of editing the A and B versions of *Piers Plowman*; we can only guess at it, and admire their courage and tenacity. A certain deep respect and accompanying humility is detectable in all the reviews, even the more critical ones, and several point out that Kane and Donaldson's work represents the near-fruition of a project first undertaken (by Chambers and Grattan) before 1909.[5] Kane and Donaldson lay implicit claim to such a response when they warn their readers against ill-conceived criticism, by which they seem to mean the criticism of anyone who has not, like them, struggled up the A- and B-Text Parnassus. The last two sentences of their magisterial introduction throw down a gauntlet to reviewers. The textual evidence, and their interpretation of it, has, they say, "been laid wholly open to scrutiny in the preceding pages of this introduction. Whether we have carried out our task efficiently," they add, "must be assessed by reenacting it" (220).

The average critic and reader, even the *Piers Plowman* enthusiast, is unlikely to devote a lifetime to the task of "reenacting" Kane and Donaldson's textual decisions in order to satisfy the criteria they lay down for anyone aspiring to judge the enterprise as a whole. On the other hand, while it is perhaps unfair of Kane and Donaldson to disenfranchise their potential critics in this way, it is surely right that one

---

[5] See R. W. Chambers and J. H. G. Grattan, "The Text of 'Piers Plowman,'" *Modern Language Review* 4 (1909): 359–89. Chambers and Grattan describe how Skeat allotted them the task of a new edition of A for the Early English Text Society in "The Text of 'Piers Plowman': Critical Methods," *Modern Language Review* 11 (1916): 257–75 (see 265).

should attempt a critique of their edition on their own terms: by scrutinizing their text in relation to the principles by which it is constructed, and vice versa. But this is no easy task, as reviewers have complained, despite the editors' own acknowledgement that an edition such as this "must above all be open to its users" (211–12). The layout and organization of *The B Version* make judgement of both textual principle and practice, both methodology and its implementation in hundreds of separate instances, very difficult indeed. The introduction is remarkable for its opacity: not because the editors write in an obscure or obfuscatory style, but because they present their material without any of the normal aids to comprehension that a reader might wish for.

Kane and Donaldson's editorial thesis is outlined in the 209 closely written pages comprising chapters 2–5 (chapter 1 contains their description of the B manuscripts). There are no headings or subheadings within these four chapters, despite the architectural shape and intricate windings of the argument. The reader must first work through the whole, and then return to reread several times over, marking his or her own copy with paragraph headings, numbering the various points that make up sub-arguments, and independently mapping out the shape and substance of the introduction. Many of the stages in Kane and Donaldson's argument are punctuated by long lists of agreements which function as illustrations or substantiations of some assertion or conclusion; to pause to look each of these up in the text, checking it against the critical apparatus, appreciating how it functions in context, and then reckoning up its significance as a constituent within the list where it appears, and hence its contribution towards the immediate and ultimate argument, is a lengthy and cumbersome task.

Reading the text itself is equally difficult. Each word, each line in the text must be checked against the critical apparatus. The apparatus (quite conventionally, of course) records only those manuscripts deviating from the edited text. But not all the manuscripts of A and B bear witness to all the canonical text of the versions; to make sense of the apparatus one must first construct for oneself a table showing where each of the manuscripts has defective text, so that one does not inadvertently assume that a reading is attested by a manuscript which in fact omits this particular line.[6] Since many of Kane and Donaldson's chosen readings are very poorly attested, this chore is particularly important. Some of their chosen readings are attested by no B manuscript at all: in instances where Kane and Donaldson judge the archetypal reading of the B manuscripts to be corrupt, they frequently emend it to the equivalent text of A and/or C. So

---

[6] The table can be put together from information on the individual manuscripts in chapter 1.

the reader needs to keep handy a copy both of Kane's text and of the C-Text, and be ready to turn to equivalent passages to trace whether Kane and Donaldson's reading originates from one of those two sources, or whether, instead, it is the product of the editors' conjectural emendation.

Most important of all is regular comparison of Kane and Donaldson's edited text with their explanation for their editorial decision. But these explanations are almost irretrievably buried in the introduction; there is no key, no index, and as I have said, no division or subdivision of the introduction other than into long chapters. Again, the reader has to do the work independently: reading through the introduction, one must continually turn forward to the text and mark page references in the margin that refer back to individual discussions or listings of readings in the introduction.[7] As there are several thousand of these, the labor involved is Herculean; but to do it the other way round, to look up the explanation in the introduction as and when one comes upon a reading in the text whose credentials one wishes to explore, is so time-consuming as to be practically impossible.

Some of this work is inevitable, for example the checking between text and apparatus. But the editors could easily have supplied a table of manuscript defections, cross-indexing between text and introduction, and headings and sub-headings within the introduction; for it is inconceivable that they did not compile and use such aids themselves. It is not clear why they did not pass on such virtually indispensable material to the reader.

The absence of sufficient editorial aid, together with the sheer difficulty of the introduction, has considerably hamstrung criticism of Kane and Donaldson's edition. In his impressive review, the most thoroughgoing and ambitious yet published, Lee Patterson has stated that, so far, "virtually all criticism [has been] directed at the fitness of individual readings." And he explains that such criticism is inadmissable: "criticism at the level of counterexample, no matter how often made, is inconsequential as a criticism of the edition as a whole. Moreover, if these criticisms derive from editorial principles sharply different from those that govern the readings in question, and especially from the perspective of an editorial tradition that overvalues attestation as evidence of originality, then the criticisms are irrelevant." [8]

---

[7] Kane provides a separate section discussing some individual textual decisions at the end of his edition (433–57); the explanation for many others, however, must be sought out in the body of his introduction, which like that of his later edition of B is without index or headings within the chapters.

[8] Lee Patterson, "The Logic of Textual Criticism," in Jerome J. McGann, ed., *Textual Criticism and Literary Interpretation* (Chicago: University of Chicago Press,

This seems to me overstated. Not all criticisms have been as local as Patterson suggests—that is, functioning on the level of "counterexample." Most critics have recognized the theoretical significance of Kane and Donaldson's work, and have discussed the edition in specifically theoretical terms; although they illustrate the consequences of the two editors' principles by citing individual examples.

Kane and Donaldson's major editorial innovations can be briefly summarized under the following three heads. Firstly, like Kane earlier, they reject recension as a practicable means of editing the poem, and instead rely on a process of discrimination between manuscript variants: analyzing them so as to determine which (if any) was the original, and the one most likely to have given rise to the others by some process of conscious or unconscious scribal error. The principles for this were set down and fully described by Kane in his edition of A (Kane, 115–72). Secondly, Kane and Donaldson now believe that Langland wrote according to a strict, though eccentric, alliterative pattern, and they emend and reconstruct readings accordingly (131–40). Thirdly, they agree with the previously established view that the supposed archetype of the extant B manuscripts was seriously corrupt, and they take advantage where they can of equivalent A and/or C text to emend this corruption, using the two other texts as a control on the accuracy of B (128 ff.).

Critics have taken issue with all three of these principles. On Kane and Donaldson's criteria for detecting the direction of scribal error, John Alford has pointed out that "the great danger of [Kane and Donaldson's] method . . . is the possibility that scribal tendencies of the fourteenth and fifteenth centuries may be used to answer uniquely twentieth-century questions. By means of an infinite variety of scribal 'errors,' we can make the text say almost anything our ignorance requires."[9] The only way of illustrating the force of this statement, which is a comment on an editorial principle, is to give an example of its workings in action, which Alford does (he argues that Kane and Donaldson are wrong to emend the reference to Haukyn's *wife* at B.14.28 to Haukyn's *will*.) Thorlac Turville-Petre sheds further doubt on their principles for identifying scribal error. Derek Pearsall (and others) object to Kane and Donaldson's views on Langland's metrical practice. Turville-Petre and David Fowler particularly object to the use of A and C as controls on B. As I have said, all these reviewers substantiate their objections to Kane and Donaldson's editorial principles with one or more examples (infelicitous, or unjustifiable, in their view) of the effect Kane and Donaldson's principles

---

1985), 55–91 (68–69).
    [9] Alford, 1003.

produce on their text. To write off these criticisms as merely irrelevant listing of "counterexamples" seems a little unfair.

Patterson goes on to say "the only way such criticisms could be effective would be if they were part of a sustained effort to provide a contrary hypothesis by which to explain the phenomena—to provide, in other words, another edition." Again, this seems to me a questionable comment. One can examine and criticize the various stages of Kane and Donaldson's argument, so as to test it for any weaknesses or lapses, without being obliged to provide an alternative hypothesis (let alone an alternative edition) to validate one's views. Patterson claims that "the methodology of the natural sciences teaches us that a theory can be disproven only by a better theory," and hence that "until one appears, then, the Kane-Donaldson edition must and should stand as, not only the best *Piers Plowman*, but the true one."[10] Leaving on one side the question of truth, it is possible to question whether the methodology of the natural sciences (or that of any other intellectual discipline) does in fact teach us this. To take one of several possible examples: no one would now claim that, because no economist has been able to come up with a similarly universal theory commanding wide acceptance, Keynesian economics "must and should stand as, not only the best economic theory, but the true one." Keynesian economic theory has been shown to be untenable on its own terms, and this has been satisfactorily demonstrated in the absence (so far) of any universally accepted alternative theory.

One of Patterson's main points is that criticisms of the Athlone edition should be in the first place directed at its methodology, and that criticisms of the way in which that methodology has been implemented must be secondary, and will operate at a different level. This seems superficially attractive, and right, but has implications and consequences he himself does not explore. In fact, textual principle and practice mesh far more intimately and pervasively than Patterson acknowledges. Every stage of Kane and Donaldson's argument is backed up with lists of scores of individual readings, and each of these stages can be assessed only in relation to the cumulative persuasiveness of the interpretations the editors make of those individual readings. This is clearly recognized by Kane and Donaldson themselves: "Our text must be assessed not generally but in its detail, by the quality of the arguments with which we support that detail and the appropriateness of its readings" (140).[11] But

---

[10] Patterson, 69.

[11] Cf. their caveat on the reliability of their method of classifying the B manuscripts: "Because the method requires exercise of judgement at every stage, in the determinations of originality which afford its data, in the tracing of complex variation, and in the

Patterson's discussion is largely theoretical; he never subjects individual readings and emendations to scrutiny, but instead takes on trust Kane and Donaldson's various judgements on these, and examines only the way in which the results of individual textual decisions are cumulatively deployed to build up the two editors' overarching view of the textual transmission of the poem.[12]

But it is possible (although, for reasons I have described, laborious) to analyze Kane and Donaldson's edition in a way that takes into account both their methodology and its manifold implementation: extensive study of their text can bring to light information not provided by the two editors, but reflecting back significantly both on Kane and Donaldson's textual principles and on the manner in which they implement them.

An excellent example is presented by David Fowler in his devastating review of their edition, a review based on an analysis of their text which, he says, took him over two months to make. Fowler seems to have been prompted by his objections to many individual emendations in the B-Text to make a proportional analysis of Kane and Donaldson's emendation rate. He shows that they emend the reading of the archetypal B-Text with considerable unevenness: over stretches of the poem where A and B read equivalent text (2,200 lines), they emend one reading every sixty-two lines to restore alliteration; over stretches of text new in B (1100 lines), they emend one reading every eight lines to restore alliteration.[13] In other words, Kane and Donaldson detect far more (alliterative) error in the B archetype where A is not available as a control than they do where this control is present. So striking a variation in the perceived rate of originality of B is remarkable, to say the least, and at first sight highly disturbing. The obvious conclusion is that it is attributable to Kane and Donaldson's varying editorial policy rather than to genuine fluctuations in the B archetype's accuracy.[14] It may be that there is a plausible explanation for the variation which also saves Kane and Donaldson's text, although I cannot think of one. But whether or not such an explanation exists, it is regrettable that the editors do not themselves provide the

---

discrimination of variational and genetic groups, it implies successive possibilities of error" (19).

[12] In keeping with this, he takes the view that if one of Kane and Donaldson's readings is correct, then they all must be—unless their editorial principles have been *misapplied* in any instance (Patterson, 68-69). This is to misunderstand the painstakingly atomic nature of their editing procedure. Cf. Kane: "each crux is unique," so that "the authority of a text of this kind must vary from line to line" (165). Would Patterson agree that if one of Kane and Donaldson's readings is wrong, they all must be?

[13] Fowler, 25.

[14] Fowler supposes the variation is attributable to the different authorship of A and B.

figures on their emendation rates, and consequently do not offer any explanation for them.[15]

Studying the *effects* of Kane and Donaldson's editorial principles, then, can provide us with additional, and essential, information about those principles. It is not enough to assess them in an artificial vacuum.[16] Before attempting to examine some comparable detail myself (in section 5 below), I shall try to outline some major characteristics of Kane and Donaldson's theoretical position on the poem.

II

Both editions, as everyone knows, inherit (ultimately, from Skeat) the hypothetical model of three original texts: it is supposed that Langland wrote first A, and then two revisions, B and C. (It is illuminating to trace back through Skeat's prefaces to his various editions the process by which he lighted on the three text hypothesis; it is a much more problematic process than is sometimes supposed, and one which deserves separate treatment.)[17] Most of the fifty-odd manuscripts of the

---

[15] No acknowledgement of the problem is provided in the revised edition of B (1988), which is an exact reprint of the first edition without any alterations or additions.

[16] This point is also illustrated by the fact that A. V. C. Schmidt adopts many of Kane and Donaldson's editorial principles to come up with a substantially different text. See *The Vision of Piers Plowman*, 2d edition (London: J. M. Dent & Sons, 1987). Paradoxically enough, Patterson goes some way towards an implicit acknowledgement of the crucial relationship between theory and practice in a footnote to his article, where he records findings "at least at first sight, disquieting," produced by an analysis of Kane and Donaldson's implied assumptions on the relative rates of originality of the three texts (Patterson, 217). Where A, B, and C read equivalent text (Patterson estimates this as some 1900 lines), once every fourteen lines (on average), B and C wrongly reproduce a reading which was correctly preserved in A. Where A and B alone read equivalent text (400 lines), once every 1.3 lines (on average), B wrongly reproduces a reading correctly preserved in A. In other words, scribes tended to miscopy B especially in those places where Langland completely rewrote C. Kane and Donaldson could of course claim that Langland was motivated to rewrite C precisely because of this inaccuracy in B; on the face of it though, it looks as if the two editors were more inclined to emend B to A's reading when C was absent than when it was present. (The apparent disparity between Fowler's and Patterson's figures is, I think, due to the fact that Patterson, unlike Fowler, differentiates between the presence and absence of C, and does not restrict himself to counting only those emendations made *causa metri*.)

[17] See W. W. Skeat, ed., *Parallel Extracts from 29 MSS. of Piers Plowman, with comments, and a proposal for the Society's Three-text edition of the poem*, EETS, o.s. 17 (London, 1866); *Langland's Vision of Piers Plowman. The Vernon Text; or Text A*, EETS, o.s. 28 (London, 1867); *Langland's Vision of Piers Plowman. (Text B)*, EETS, o.s. 38 (London, 1869); *The Vision of William concerning Piers Plowman . . . Text C,*

poem that survive fall roughly into three distinct narrative shapes, those of A, B, and C. As a rule, the A manuscripts go up to Passus 11 or 12, the B manuscripts contain this material in an occasionally very different form, together with the addition of an extra nine passus, and the C manuscripts have a reworked version of the B material. It would be difficult to deny that these three shapes do exist, and do explain satisfactorily the manuscript situation—up to a point, that is.

But the model of three, and three only, original texts has two major limitations. First, there are a number of maverick manuscripts, among them Bodley 851 (Z), the former Ilchester MS, and Huntington 114, which cannot at first sight be easily assimilated into the ABC model.[18] Second, if one compares the manuscripts by lines and readings rather than by broad narrative shape, the multiplicity and diversity of variational readings begin to strain credulity: can this chaos really be related back to just three original versions?

To explain the chaos of divergent and convergent readings, editors can in the first instance turn to one of two obvious hypotheses. One hypothesis takes on board the possibility that Langland may have written more than just three versions of the poem, so that the textual complexity of the surviving manuscripts may bear witness to authorial as well as to scribal variation; the other hypothesis resolutely retains the three-text premise, and explains the manuscript chaos by suggesting that scribes interfered with and corrupted the poem in what must be a uniquely complicated example of textual transmission.

As one might expect, the two alternative hypotheses have substantial and mutually irreconcilable implications. The first hypothesis, as I have indicated, responds to the manuscript complexity by assuming that the three-text theory may be wrong, or at least, inadequate. According to this view, Langland may have written more than three versions of the poem, and the manuscripts may therefore bear witness to intermediate versions

---

EETS, o.s. 54 (London, 1873); *The Vision of William concerning Piers Plowman in three parallel texts* ... (Oxford: Oxford University Press, 1886).

[18] On Bodley 851, see *Piers Plowman: The Z Version*, ed. A. G. Rigg and Charlotte Brewer (Toronto: Pontifical Institute of Medieval Studies, 1983), and George Kane, "The 'Z Version' of *Piers Plowman*," *Speculum* 60 (1985): 910-30; on the Ilchester manuscript, see Derek Pearsall, "The Ilchester Manuscript of *Piers Plowman*," *Neuphilologische Mitteilungen* 82 (1981): 181-93; on Huntington 114, see Venetia Nathan and George Russell, "A *Piers Plowman* Manuscript in the Huntington Library," *Huntington Library Quarterly* 26 (1963): 119-30 and Wendy Scase, "Two *Piers Plowman* C-Text Interpolations: Evidence for a Second Textual Tradition," *Notes and Queries*, n.s., 34 (1987): 456-63. Despite the efforts of Kane-Donaldson and Schmidt to assimilate them into the B-text, it is possible that B manuscripts R and F may also indicate evidence of authorial versions other than the canonical A, B, and C; see further below.

between A, B, and C (or versions coming before or after them.) This would explain why it is difficult to fit the manuscripts into a neat three-text mold: there never were three original, separate texts. Langland may have revised, rewritten, re-rewritten, and/or used partially revised copies of his poem to re-write, in a way that makes it impossible to reconstruct any three putative originals. (Indeed, since it is often supposed that Langland spent his life rewriting the poem, it is perhaps odd that we should think to restrict his rewritings to two only, B and C.) Any pre-printing text will by definition survive only in versions more-or-less tainted with scribal error; the first hypothesis takes this premise further, and allows for the possibility that the processes of composition and of transmission may have got inextricably tangled. As Bennett suggests in his review of Kane and Donaldson, just as Joyce gleefully incorporated printer's errors into *Finnegans Wake*, so may Langland have done something similar with scribal errors when writing and revising *Piers Plowman*.[19]

In great contrast, the second hypothesis preserves the notion of the author turning out three, and three only, quite discrete versions of the poem. On this view, the distinctiveness of Langland's writing is such that these three versions can, at least theoretically, be in some way distinguished from the writing practices of the scribes who copied them. Since this hypothesis preserves the three-text premise, it has to suppose that the complexity of variational readings is due solely to the fact that scribes interfered radically, consistently, and (most important of all) identifiably with the poem.

Clearly, Kane and Donaldson have edited their two editions on the second hypothesis. They do raise the question of the validity, integrity and authenticity of A, B, and C in both their editions, but only briefly, and in highly theoretical terms. Perhaps unsurprisingly, they conclude that there were only three original versions, and that everything pointing away from this is scribal (Kane 19-20; Kane-Donaldson, 70-72.) Closely linked to this conclusion are a number of significant and pervasive assumptions about Langland as author, sometimes clearly set down in black and white and sometimes not. For example (and they do make this perfectly clear), they assume that Langland's writing was of a totally consistent and invariably high quality, and of a completely different order

---

[19] The recent debate on Hans Walter Gabler's edition of *Ulysses* (New York and London: Garland Publishing Inc., 1986) has raised questions of editorial methodology which shed interesting light on editing Langland. At the time of writing the most useful summary articles are those of Edward Mendelson, "Diary," *London Review of Books*, vol. 10, no. 19, 27 October 1988, 29, and Charles Rossmann, "The New 'Ulysses': The Hidden Controversy," *New York Review of Books*, vol 35, no. 19, 8 December 1988, 53-58.

from anything a scribe was capable of, so that, once editors have worked out his (supposed) *usus scribendi* from the corrupt manuscript evidence, they can turn round and apply this standard back to the manuscripts, and usually distinguish infallibly between what Langland would have written and what is the result of scribal tinkering or misprision.[20] This applies down to the smallest textual detail. (There is a troubling element of circularity here, although it is true that all editing involves some degree of comparable circularity; see Kane-Donaldson, 212.) The notorious example of this is Kane and Donaldson's metrical theory: they assume that Langland wrote according to one and one only alliterative pattern, so that lines not conforming to this pattern are, *prima facie*, scribal.[21] This has been pounced on by their critics. More generally, the assumption that Langland wrote to a consistently high standard is in some ways a peculiar one given the evidence we have about the poet. Langland's obsessive rewriting of the poem, involving deletion of lines and readings as well as additions, suggests that, in his own opinion at least, the quality of his output could vary.

Another example of Kane and Donaldson's beliefs about Langland (and one which, in my view, they never convincingly or even explicitly argue for) is their assumption that he revised his poem from A to B to C in a logical and consecutive way, never, for instance, going back to an A reading for his C version, having written something different for B. Agreement between A and C against B is thus regarded as *prima facie* evidence that the B archetype is corrupt, and in almost all cases where this occurs Kane and Donaldson emend B to read as AC.[22] Kane and

---

[20] Examples of this belief abound throughout their introduction; one occurs at 82 ff., where the two editors repeatedly consider, and reject, the possibility that readings in B which they judge defective in comparison with equivalent ones in AC could be attributable to a failure of judgement in the poet: "in this situation it seems to us right to reject the possibility of the erratic poet for the established certainty of the inaccurate copyist." Kane and Donaldson never, so far as I can see, consider the possibility that their identification of the respective quality of some of these readings might be fallible.

[21] Their method of argument is revealing here. They judge that "almost a third of the B version's two-stave lines are scribal from considerations other than of versification" (136), and take this as an overwhelmingly strong indication that *all* two-stave lines are scribal. But the propositions (1) that scribes frequently corrupt by dropping a stave, and (2) that Langland sometimes wrote two-stave lines and considered them acceptable, are not mutually exclusive. As Donaldson pointed out over thirty-five years ago, there is no good reason for "the assumption that a poetic revision will never produce the same mechanical pattern as a scribal error." See E. T. Donaldson, "The Texts of 'Piers Plowman': Scribes and Poets," *Modern Philology* 50 (1952-53): 269-73 (271).

[22] See, e.g., 149 ff. The principle that AC vs. B agreement is to be interpreted as due to scribal error in B, rather than authorial revision, seems to have been first expressed in print by Elsie Blackman, a pupil of Chambers and Grattan, in the article

Donaldson also assume that each time Langland rewrote, he rewrote for the better, so that a reading in B which is (by their lights) inferior to the equivalent one in A, is necessarily a scribal reading. (*The Prelude* has often been held up as a counterexample to this theory of progressively improved authorial revision.)

It is clear why Kane and Donaldson should have made these assumptions. Believing in three texts as they did, and having to get these out in a reasonable form to the printer, they were under what Derek Pearsall has called "the pressure of the search for editorial certainty."[23] To acknowledge the possibility of more than three original versions, of inconsistent revision, of authorial and scribal interdependence, all these things that the first hypothesis is capable of tolerating, is to do away altogether with the possibility of constructing a three-text critical edition of the poem; for such possibilities fatally undermine the grounds on which such an edition can be produced. (This is the reason, presumably, why the first of the two editorial hypotheses I outline above has never been seriously contemplated by an editor working to produce a critical edition of the poem.)[24]

But the three-text model, and the assumption of the second hypothesis that editors can meditate on the tangle of manuscripts to construct, or reconstruct, something satisfactorily close to three original texts, has never been finally established. Some editors of selections from the poem at the turn of the century seem to regard the question as not finally settled,[25] while Kane and Donaldson themselves make it clear that they believe that the C-reviser, at any rate, produced his version with some substantial inattention to detail.[26] If this is true, then it significantly undercuts the notion that editors can painstakingly restore scribal copy to original pristine masterpiece simply on the grounds of superior poetic quality. In 1955 E. Talbot Donaldson suggested that B manuscripts R and

---

summarizing her 1914 University of London thesis: "Notes on the B-Text MSS. of *Piers Plowman*," *Journal of English and Germanic Philology* 17 (1918): 489-531 (518). But Chambers had adumbrated the principle in "The Authorship of 'Piers Plowman,'" *Modern Language Review* 5 (1910): 26 ff.

[23] "The Ilchester Manuscript of *Piers Plowman*," 192.

[24] Skeat's three texts were not critical editions so much as occasionally emended texts of Vernon, Laud, and Huntington 137, as Chambers and Grattan point out in "The Text of 'Piers Plowman,' " *Modern Language Review* 4 (1909): 359-89. They themselves, in their aim to produce a critical text of A, reject the possibility that the "the author issue[d] from time to time additions to his work, so as to give rise to a series of transitional texts" (377).

[25] See, e.g., J. F. Davis, ed., *Langland: Piers Plowman Prologue and Passus I-VII. Text B* (W. B. Clive, London: University Correspondence Press, 1897), vii-viii.

[26] See, e.g., 125. The editors provide no comparable discussion of the characteristics of AB revision, except very briefly at 75.

F might represent a B version written by Langland before producing the B version proper.[27] Needless to say, he later repudiated both this theory and the remarkable speculation which accompanied it:

> I wonder whether, in the present instance, the peculiarities of the B-MSS are not more easily attributable to the revisions of a poet than the machinations of a contaminator. Everything we know of the B- and C-poet suggests a constant and loving reviser of his poem. Indeed, I sometimes wonder whether the C-text, the B-text, and even the A-text are not merely historical accidents, haphazard milestones in the history of a poem that was begun but never finished, photographs that caught a static image of a living organism at a given but not necessarily significant moment of time.[28]

In 1981 Pearsall discussed the possibility that the Ilchester MS might represent a fourth, a D-text of the poem—written by Langland himself— but turned away from re-opening the question of "the exclusive integrity of the three texts" as "almost too complicated to bear thinking about."[29] Four years earlier Anne Hudson had tackled the question more directly, when she said in a discussion of Kane and Donaldson's edition of B,

> one is tempted to wonder whether adequate consideration has been given to the likely way in which the revisions were made—almost certainly haphazard, spread over a period of time, often re-revising or restoring the first reading, quite probably using more than one copy.[30]

This takes us firmly back to the position of the first editorial hypothesis: the view that the chaotic state of the manuscripts may be as much a reflection of the way in which the author composed the poem, as it is of the way in which the poem was transmitted.

Underlying these two editorial positions are two fundamentally divergent theories of textual criticism. The first position is close to the work of Jerome J. McGann, who has been prominent in a movement of

---

[27] Skeat's hypothesis was that MS R was "a copy of the B-text *with later improvements and after-thoughts*"; see *Langland's Vision of Piers Plowman. (Text B)*, EETS, o.s. 38 (London, 1869), xii.

[28] "MSS R and F in the B-Tradition of Piers Plowman," *Transactions of the Connecticut Academy of Arts and Sciences* 39 (1955): 179–212 (211). Donaldson's repudiation of these views seems to be implied in note 101, 64 of *The B Version*.

[29] "The Ilchester Manuscript of *Piers Plowman*," 193.

[30] Anne Hudson, "Middle English," in *Editing Medieval Texts*, ed. A. G. Rigg (New York and London: Garland Publishing Inc., 1977), 34–57 (44). John Norton-Smith makes some similar observations in chapter 1 of his *William Langland* (Leiden: E. J. Brill, 1983).

historical, almost sociological interest in textual criticism, fastening on
such topics as (to quote him) "the interpretive force of editorial
interventions," and "the social character of literary productions of all
kinds." It is this approach which underlies Patterson's analysis of Kane
and Donaldson's edition, for he undercuts his praise of their work (as
quoted above) with an attempted deconstruction of the editorial premises
they bring to it. Patterson detects two contradictory elements in these
premises: on the one hand a Romantic notion of the poet as genius,
whose work can be distinguished from the corruptions of careless
copyists by a process of (inevitably subjective) aesthetic scrutiny, and on
the other hand an insistence on the necessity for rigorously logical
analysis of the textual evidence. Both these elements, Patterson argues,
have more to do with Kane and Donaldson's cultural and intellectual
environment than with anything intrinsic to Langland. Recent textual
work concentrating on the activities of scribes rather than (or, at least,
as well as) authors falls in with this more self-conscious editorial stance.
It will be already apparent that I align myself with this sort of approach,
as illustrated for medieval editing in (for example) Hudson's essay already
quoted and some recent articles by Derek Pearsall, rather than with the
almost Platonic, or (in the philosophical sense) realist approach of Kane
and Donaldson.[31]

III

As my discussion so far will have made clear, the central problem
confronting the editor of *Piers Plowman* is the decision between the two
alternative textual camps outlined above: one explaining the textual
variation in the manuscripts as due to a more or less indeterminate
combination of authorial rewriting and corrupt scribal transmission, the
other attributing it to corrupt scribal transmission alone. Essentially, this
decision boils down to determining the degree to which one can
distinguish between authorial writing and scribal variation. The editor
must be prepared to account for the manifold differences between manu-

---

[31] A good deal of work has recently appeared (and continues to appear) on the
theory of editing. See, e.g., Jerome J. McGann, *A Critique of Modern Textual Criticism*
(Chicago and London: University of Chicago Press, 1983), Derek Pearsall, "Texts,
Textual Criticism, and Fifteenth-Century Manuscript Production," in Robert F. Yeager,
ed., *Fifteenth-Century Studies* (Connecticut: Archon Books, 1984) and "Editing
Medieval Texts," in Jerome J. McGann, ed., *Textual Criticism and Literary Interpretation* (Chicago and London: University of Chicago Press, 1985), 92–106. Kane's remarks
in " 'Good' and 'Bad' MSS," *Studies in the Age of Chaucer*, Proceedings 2, 1986
(Knoxville, 1987), 137–45, seem intended as a response to Pearsall and Patterson. See
also note 19 above.

scripts and versions of the poem—differences that must be referable either to the poet or to the scribes—in terms of a number of assumptions: about Langland's methods of and motives in revising, about his judgement of his own work, about the relations between authorial and scribal *usus scribendi*. Interestingly enough, few of these assumptions are explicitly dealt with (and acknowledged as assumptions) in the introductions to the two Athlone editions.

Kane and Donaldson's three-text premise requires that they distinguish absolutely between the texts of A, B, and C. This is not as easy or straightforward as it sounds, since over substantial stretches of the poem either all three, or two, of the versions read essentially equivalent text. Considerable manuscript variation characterizes these passages as much as it does the rest of the poem: the question then arises, is the variation due to authorial revision or to scribal corruption? The variation comprises two different categories: first, where the manuscripts of any one version disagree among themselves over any particular reading, and second, where similar disagreement is found in the equivalent reading of the other version(s) too. I shall now turn to look in detail at the way in which first Kane and then Kane and Donaldson treat these two categories.

In my view, Kane never recognizes the theoretical importance of the question whether variation within a version is to be attributed to scribal or to authorial variation. Without any prior discussion, he treats as premise his assumption that Langland would have been responsible for only one (at most) of the variants in any textual crux, and he uses this premise to analyze variation in the A tradition, in particular to distinguish between authorial and scribal *usus scribendi*. He assumes that, of any two main variants, that supported by the majority of manuscripts will be authorial and that supported by the minority scribal, and thus, through characterizing the minority readings, he is able to identify a wide range of scribal tendencies to error.[32] If Kane had allowed for the possibility that more than one of the variants in any textual crux might have been authorial, he would not have been able to establish his categories of scribal error in this way, categories taken over and adopted without

---

[32] He summarizes his procedure as follows: "The frequent recurrence of *presumably unoriginal variants* with similar effects on the substance of the poem, and therefore presumably made from similar motives, allows the editor to deduce the existence of several general tendencies of scribal substitution. . . . Such circumstances both account for the large number of material variants and afford a means of interpreting these in crucial passages" (143–44; italics mine). This method corresponds precisely to that described in the major work of textual criticism in the tradition which Kane inherited from Chambers and Grattan: see B. F. Westcott and F. J. Hort, *The New Testament* (Cambridge and London: Macmillan and Co., 1882), 2:23–24.

further question by Kane and Donaldson for their edition of B (129). This is a very clear example of how prior textual premise determines an editor's analysis of textual variants, whether fully acknowledged by the editor or not. (I discuss Kane's criteria for detecting scribal error more fully elsewhere.)[33]

Kane and Donaldson consider the possibility of authorial revision within the B tradition towards the end of their discussion of B manuscript textual relationships. They write as follows:

> The text of RF contains about 175 lines not found in WHmCrGY-OC²CBmBoCotLMS [*viz.*, the remaining B-MSS, other than H]; and these latter manuscripts (with H where it is a B text) contain about 170 lines not found in RF. These differences have suggested some form of authorial differentiation: specifically, that RF might preserve an authorial form of the poem intermediate between B and C; or conversely that the text of WHmCrGYOC²CBmBoCotLMS might incorporate changes made by the poet (63-64).

They explain that both these explanations rest on inaccurate assumptions: first, that the B manuscript tradition was otherwise relatively uncomplicated (sc. in comparison with that of A), and second, that RF were genetically linked with LM, which "made it difficult to account for differences between these pairs of manuscripts, or agreements of LM with WHmCrGYOC²CBmBoCot against RF, except by assuming some form of authorial intervention, or contamination" (64). "But it is now clear," they say, "that the difficulty was unreal": "Full collation of the B manuscripts has done away with any impression of their uniformity of attestation; they are frequently and strikingly corrupt"; and full collation has also brought to light the extensive cross-cutting agreements between all the manuscripts, which places the apparently inconsistent relationships of LM in a context of a far more general inconsistency. (Kane and Donaldson attribute this inconsistency to convergent scribal variation.) The problem of attestation of different lines remains, however, and Kane and Donaldson explain this as the result of mechanical error on the part of the two scribes responsible for the two respective common ancestors (see 64-69). They conclude that the apparent distinctiveness of the two manuscript families in B is referable to scribal omission of lines, not to authorial addition of them; and they thus preserve intact their theory that textual complexity in *Piers Plowman* is due to corrupt scribal transmission, not to authorial rewriting.

I think there are two objections to Kane and Donaldson's analysis here.

---

[33] "The Textual Principles of Kane's A-Text," *Yearbook of Langland Studies* 3 (1989): 67–90.

First, they make no comment on the distinct oddness of their theory: why is it that the two scribes concerned omitted copy in this way? As far as I can make out from their lists of manuscript defections and peculiarities in the introductions and critical apparatuses of the two editions, no other *Piers Plowman* scribes (of either A or B, that is) omitted comparable quantities of lines. One hundred and seventy-odd lines is a very large number to account for; and it is also peculiar that the (supposedly accidental) omissions of the longer passages do not result in narrative disruption.[34]

My second objection is that Kane and Donaldson discuss the matter principally in terms of *lines*, not of readings. Yet later in their introduction they argue that MS F contains more than 100 original readings not found in the other manuscripts (165 ff).[35] It seems to me that this peculiarity might also be referable to the question of different authorial rewritings of B; but Kane and Donaldson never re-open it. Their prior conclusion that Langland wrote only one version of B, a conclusion they based on an analysis of F's lines, not its readings, does not seem to have allowed them to respond to the evidence presented by the readings in an unbiased way. There is a striking contrast between the apparent rigor with which they discuss various explanations for F's authentic readings, and their failure to investigate the most obvious one, that F may represent a separate, authorial strand of the B tradition.

Even if they are right in their belief that the differences between RF and the remaining B manuscripts (except H) do not in any way reflect the original existence of different authorial *versions* of B, that is still no reason for discounting the possibility that they may reflect original authorial *rewritings*. Langland may have revised or retouched his poem sporadically, word by word rather than line by line (or passage by passage). We have no reason to think this *prima facie* unlikely, especially since something similar has been suggested in the case of other authors. The textual peculiarities of the manuscripts of *Troilus and Criseyde* have led their most recent editor, Barry Windeatt, to say of Chaucer's process of composition:

> The existence of traditions of scribal copying of the poem need not drive the temporal and material wedges of separate "versions" or editions of the text between the superimposed layers of composition. . . . The very notion of editions and versions draws a definite-

---

[34] A point made by Derek Pearsall in his review of *The B Version* (cited n. 3 above). See also David Fowler, 34 ff. The two sets of omitted lines are listed in Kane and Donaldson, 66–69.

[35] In thirty of these instances, R is defective, so that "F's reading is explicable as probably or possibly that of the main genetic group (RF)."

ness of identity and integrity from the world of print which is inapplicable to the age of manuscript, when the complete and material difference between a modern author's working drafts and his published appearance in print could be less distinct.[36]

The second category of *Piers Plowman* textual variation, that between one tradition and the next, is considered somewhat more explicitly in both A and B editions. Kane states: "In practice the intrinsic likelihood that the authorial revision responsible for the major differences between versions will also have introduced smaller differences, makes it impossible to say of many lines whether their various forms in the three versions originated with scribe or author" (147 n. 1). This contrasts significantly with the self-confidence of Kane and Donaldson's pronouncement, where they state as axiomatic the principle that "not all [variations between the three versions over text common to all] can be authorial; some must necessarily have been created by scribal variation in one or more of the archetypal traditions" (75). While this may seem reasonable, Kane's earlier diffidence on the possibility of being certain which of the variations can be confidently determined as scribal, which authorial, is conspicuous by its absence. Later, Kane and Donaldson describe how they determined "whether differences between the archetypal readings in the B tradition and those of AC or A or C were created by authorial revision or scribal variation," and comment

> This minute delimitation of versions, which, we appreciate, is the most crucial operation in the whole editing of *Piers Plowman*, we have endeavoured to conduct with restraint, permitting ourselves to reach conclusions only in cases which seemed beyond serious doubt (149–50).

Various critics have argued that several of their textual decisions can scarcely be admitted under this description; meanwhile, the very language Kane and Donaldson use in their development of this statement reveals their underlying resistance to the possibility that authorial variants rather than scribal corruption are responsible for differences between the archetypal versions of the three texts:

---

[36] Barry Windeatt, "The Text of the Troilus," in *Essays on Troilus and Criseyde*, ed. Mary Salu (Cambridge: Boydell and Brewer, 1979), 1–22 (21–22). Malcolm Godden posits similar sporadic authorial revision as an explanation for textual relationships in the manuscripts of Ælfric's Catholic Homilies: "One suspects that much of the revision of detail originated when Ælfric was checking newly copied manuscripts for errors, rather than as a deliberate process of revision, and that revisions were often copied sporadically from one pattern-manuscript to another within Ælfric's scriptorium," *Ælfric's Catholic Homilies*, EETS, s.s. 5 (Oxford, 1979), lxxxvi.

> we *accepted* as authorial not only all large differences of structure or meaning, but also every small difference which did not seem explicable in terms of scribal imperception or evident stupidity, and every stylistic difference which might conceivably reflect an author's taste rather than a scribal tendency of variation. Where we could see so much as a possibility that the difference between B and another version might reflect some authorial intention we *allowed* this full force. Further we *allowed* the greater likelihood of finical and relatively insignificant revision in certain positions ... [e.g., where Langland was unarguably responsible for substantive differences between A and B or B and C; italics mine] (150).

This suggests that their expectation is of scribal error, and that they are prepared to admit the possibility of scribal accuracy only under certain specified conditions.[37] The last sentence also suggests that the same phenomena were interpreted as symptomatic of scribal corruption or of authorial revision depending on their position in the text rather than on any inherent characteristics, a criterion which does not seem to square with the scrupulousness of those listed immediately above.

Kane and Donaldson's introduction furnishes many further instances of the editors' certainty about their discrimination of scribal from authorial readings, even though the criteria they bring to bear on their decisions are never fully discussed or justified. They say of instances where they do detect authorial revision between versions that

> the determination of the likelihood is inevitably subjective; *a posteriori* because a purpose imputable to the author, as the whole poem reveals him, seems discernible behind the change; or aesthetic because the change seems of a kind which a poet rather than a scribe would make. In other words such differences suggest enlargements of imaginative conception, insights into new modes of development, altered senses of the poetic or doctrinal value of topics, or intensified homiletic purpose (75).

These remarks make it clear that Kane and Donaldson do not consider the possibility of whimsical, inconsistent revision, or revision from a good to a less good reading, whose purpose may not now be recoverable by an editor. Kane and Donaldson also in practice reject the possibility that Langland may have decided against an A reading for his B text, but

---

[37] Kane and Donaldson together appear to have a significantly higher expectation of scribal error than Kane alone did earlier. Compare, for example, Kane's remark that "the majority of scribes did, after all, copy a very large number of words in a great many lines faithfully, often to the extent of keeping spelling and dialect forms of the exemplar" (Kane, 126).

subsequently have reinstated it in C (75 ff.). It is clear why these
possibilities should have been unpalatable: they remove the rationale by
which one may distinguish with confidence between authorial and some
scribal readings.

An examination of the textual apparatus to even a short specimen
passage of their text reveals that Kane and Donaldson emend the
archetype of B to read as A very considerably indeed. Comparison of their
text with that of Kane shows that many of the differences between the
readings of Kane's text and of the B manuscripts are construed by Kane
and Donaldson as indicating corruption in the B archetype rather than
authorial revision between A and B. Such differences vary from the very
minor (e.g., singular as opposed to plural nouns where the meaning of
the context is unaffected, or omission or inclusion of *And* at the
beginning of a line) to major lexical changes between the versions. The
B archetype or majority B manuscript reading is emended to read as
Kane's A-Text even when the C manuscripts are in agreement with the
B manuscripts. Kane and Donaldson justify such emendation by their
hypothesis that in his revision of B to C Langland used a scribal copy of
his original B-Text (although one less flawed than the archetype of all
existing B manuscripts), so that many agreements between B manuscripts
and C manuscripts are due to the same post-archetypal corruption.[38]
This means that in practice their text of B very closely resembles that of
Kane's A (much more so than does Schmidt's B-Text, although Schmidt
adopts many of Kane and Donaldson's editorial principles.)

Such consistent emendation of B to read as (Kane's) A argues distinct
views on Langland's methods and motives in revising A. Unfortunately,
Kane and Donaldson nowhere provide us with a detailed account of what
they believed these were. The reader is not left completely helpless; one
can infer, for example, that Kane and Donaldson assume Langland did
not revise his poem to make B readings more explicit and more emphatic
than the corresponding ones in A, since B readings with these characteristics are invariably struck out as scribal. But the editors do not justify or
defend their implicit assumptions on Langland's mode of revision, and it
seems perhaps unfair that the reader should be reduced to such
inferences. It would have been very useful if Kane and Donaldson had
spelt out clearly the ways in which, in their view, B differs from A, so as
to justify their decisions on textual cruces where, despite the overwhelm-

---

[38] See chapter 4, "The C-Reviser's B Manuscript," 98–127. Such emendation raises
a difficult problem for the editor of C: if Langland incorporated a B reading identified
by Kane and Donaldson as scribal into his C-revision, does that not amount to authorial
sanction? Or is the editor of C to revise his text to read as (Kane's) A? Further: if
Langland found the reading acceptable, might that not indicate that Kane and
Donaldson's identification of error is fallible?

ing or unanimous testimonial of B manuscripts, they make B read the same as A. It would also have been useful if they had explored more explicitly the implications of their pervasive use of Kane's A-Text during the early part of the poem, for this raises some substantial methodological problems for their two editions. In the remainder of this article, sections 4 and 5 below, I shall look at one of the major consequences of this.

IV

In some respects, Kane and Donaldson's heavy reliance on Kane's A-Text appears unremarkable. In establishing the text of any one version of the poem, it might seem obvious to take into consideration the readings of the other two versions. This was recognized by Chambers and Grattan in 1916: "So inter-related are the texts, that before you can have a final A-text, you must have an adequate B- and C-text."[39] But Kane took a different view on the matter, pronouncing strongly in his edition of A (albeit in a footnote) as follows:

> The limitation to A variants [in establishing the text of A] is unavoidable, since this is an edition of the A version. In theory all variations of corresponding lines in the three versions might afford indications of a common, presumably unrevised original form of such lines. In practice the intrinsic likelihood that the authorial revision responsible for the major differences between versions will also have introduced smaller differences, makes it impossible to say of many lines whether their various forms in the three versions originated with scribe or author. The editor of any version is thus restricted to the evidence of the variants in manuscripts inferentially descended from the archetypal copy of that version. He will employ the evidence of variants from other versions only in special circumstances. . . . This restriction is to be regretted, since it cannot fail to have some effect on the quality of the text of each version. But it is inherent in the nature of the editorial problem (147 n. 1).

One type of "special circumstance" is "when most or all of the A variants for a passage are unsatisfactory in a way which casts doubt on their originality, and when, at the same time, the reading of another version could easily and naturally have given rise to the A variants if it had been

---

[39] "The Text of 'Piers Plowman': Critical Methods," *Modern Language Review* 11 (1916): 257–75 (271). Chambers and Grattan note that this principle had been acknowledged by Thomas A. Knott, in "Essay Toward the Critical Text of the A-Version of 'Piers the Plowman,'" *Modern Philology* 12 (1915): 129–61 (129).

the original of A as well" (157).

It was identification of such instances on a massive scale in the B manuscripts which led Kane and Donaldson to believe that the B archetype was seriously corrupt. Between editing A and editing B Kane changed his views radically on the acceptability of using the evidence from one tradition to determine originality in another, returning to the position held by Chambers and Grattan. In the Athlone *B Version*, he states that "the editor of A now considers that he allowed insufficient weight to readings from other versions in his editing, and that his earlier view of the situation (Vol I, 147n. 1 and 157) was mistaken." His present view is that "determination of originality in any version must include consideration in the first instance of all differences between the versions" (75).[40]

Kane and Donaldson set down logically and clearly the reasons for this:

> Given single authorship and a sequence of composition where B is the middle version [of the three versions of the poem] its editors are placed in an unusual logical position. For about a third of the poem, that is to the end of B X, there are many single words, as well as passages of various length, where the three versions recognizably correspond and can be minutely compared at the textual level with respect to local expression and to technical form, without distraction by larger considerations of meaning and structure. Because inaccurate copying axiomatically occurs at all stages in the transmission of manuscript texts all differences of reading revealed by such comparison are possible indications of unoriginality. Not all can be authorial; some must necessarily have been created by scribal variation in one or more of the archetypal traditions. Therefore determination of originality in any version must include consideration in the first instance of all differences between versions and in the second particularly of those differences not evidently or probably resulting from authorial revision. In the editing of B this principle has special force because the archetypal text of B can be compared over so much of its length not only with the text of A or the text of C but also, where all the versions correspond, with both, that is with two texts of itself preserved in distinct manuscript traditions. There are thus exceptional resources for assessing the quality of the B archetype (74-75).

In this crucial respect, therefore, Kane's text was constructed on a

---

[40] Cf. 164: "It is comparison with readings outside the tradition of the B manuscripts which enables accurate assessment of the quality of their archetype and its frequent correction."

radically different principle from that of Kane and Donaldson. They refer
to this difference between the two editions only in three footnotes to the
B-Text introduction (on 75, 159, and 205), despite the fact that the
textual principles involved are, in my judgement at least, of sufficient
importance to merit full treatment in the main body of the introduction.[41] For the shift in editorial methodology between A and B produces
a substantial problem for the Athlone project. When, time after time,
Kane and Donaldson dismiss the reading of archetypal B and revert to
that of Kane's A, they do so without rethinking the editing of A. But Kane
arrived at his A reading by a process of textual analysis that Kane and
Donaldson reject as inadequate; that is, Kane took into account the
readings *only of the A manuscripts* in establishing his text, and not those
of B and of C manuscripts. Thus Kane and Donaldson's final text is based
on mutually inconsistent premises: in implementing their B-text methodology, they treat as relevant evidence textual decisions arrived at by an
irreconcilably different methodology, that of Kane's A.[42]

V

Couched in such theoretical terms, this inconsistency may seem troubling
but not necessarily significant. But when one looks at the two edited
texts and at the relevant variational readings, its serious consequences
become immediately apparent. Unfortunately, it is impossible to elicit the
necessary information easily, for one must compare the text and critical
apparatus of Kane's edition of A with those of Kane and Donaldson's of
B over a stretch of the poem long enough to constitute a significant
sample. Kane and Kane and Donaldson evidently did this themselves over
the entire B-Text, in order to carry out their B-text methodological maxim
that B should be compared with A and C over the entirety of the text to
which the two other versions bear respective witness. But they do not
offer the full results of this comparison to the reader.

I have compared the text and critical apparatus of Kane's A with those
of Kane and Donaldson's B for the prologue up to the end of B passus 7.
This has yielded the interesting discovery that among many of the A
manuscript variants rejected by Kane are readings that, whether adopted
by Kane and Donaldson or not, are also the readings of the B-Text

---

[41] It is conceivable that Kane-Donaldson recognized the shift as posing significant
problems for their editorial enterprise only at a late stage in their composition of the
B-Text introduction, and hence were unable to take full notice of these in the body of
their text.

[42] I make this point in "The Textual Principles of Kane's edition of the A-Text."

archetype. All the A manuscripts have some B readings; some A manuscripts, in particular the apparently genetic group EAMH^3, have a large
number of B readings. The figures are as follows.

B readings in A manuscripts

T	10
R	37
U	38
D	22
Ch	15
H^2	23
V	61
H	79
J	52
L	57
E	94
A	65
K	55
W	84
N	63
M	127
H^3	41
Z	173

I discuss the full implications of these figures elsewhere;[43] meanwhile,
I wish simply to summarize various reasons why, in my view, they
challenge the theory and practice of the Athlone editions of A and B.

First, Kane nowhere indicates to his readers the existence of such
agreements between B and the A variants that he rejects for his text; for
as we have seen, he did not believe it necessary to take into account the
readings of other versions when establishing his text of A. The reader

---

[43] See my unpublished D. Phil. thesis, "Some Implications of Z for the Textual
Tradition of *Piers Plowman*" (University of Oxford, 1986). These figures are the result
of a handmade collation of the readings of Z, and of the A and B manuscripts as given
in Kane's and Kane-Donaldson's texts and critical apparatuses. It is likely they would
be supplemented by a computer collation. Perhaps the most remarkable feature of the
B element in A manuscripts is that, diverse as they are, the overwhelming majority of
B readings are also found in Z. Each A manuscript shares on average 60–70% of its B
readings with Z, while Z has in addition a substantial number of independent B
readings. I believe this feature can be shown to demonstrate both the extreme
likelihood that Z represents an authentic, authorial version of *Piers Plowman*, written
by Langland before he wrote A, B, and C, and that Kane's and Kane-Donaldson's
choice of original readings in the A and B texts are frequently in error.

may well wonder whether, if Kane had taken into account these agreements, he would have judged the A variants concerned differently, especially since their reading is often found not only in B but also in C. An agreement between an A manuscript reading, B and C might well be taken to be the original reading of all three texts. But in many instances, as I have said, Kane chose the other A variant for his A-Text—and Kane and Donaldson emend the B-Text reading to that of Kane's A. This produces the following line-up of agreements:

Ka (some A-MSS) and KD (few/no B-MSS)] other A-MSS, B and (often) C.

It could be that there is acceptable justification for Kane's and Kane and Donaldson's choice in these instances. Kane offers no justification, since he does not acknowledge that such a pattern of agreement exists.

My second point concerns Kane and Donaldson's treatment of these agreements. Evidently, since they did consult the readings of the other *Piers Plowman* versions, they knew of the existence of agreements between the B-Text and A variants rejected by Kane. They signal their presence, however, only where B *and* C are in agreement with the A reading rejected by Kane, and where they themselves reject the B reading—in other words, only in what one might take to be the most damaging of these instances. Surprisingly, they do not regard these agreements as in any way challenging or undermining Kane's (and their own) textual decisions. Instead, they take agreements between rejected A variants, B and C against their two texts as confirmation of their decisions, in the following way:

the observable generation in one textual tradition of certain specific kinds of readings by the identifiable operation of known scribal tendencies establishes something like a certainty that the same or similar readings in another tradition will have a similar origin. We therefore reject the possibility of authorial revision (102).

The logic seems to be that the more often a variant occurs, the less likely it is to be original.[44] This passage makes it very clear that Kane and

---

[44] This assumption is in direct opposition to Kane's original views on the significance of majority manuscript support for a variant, on which he based his criteria for detecting the direction of scribal variation: "In practice unanimity of support must be accepted as establishing the strongest presumption of originality, unless the reading attested by all the manuscripts is patently unsatisfactory" (148). Cf. Kane-Donaldson, 129n.1, and "The Textual Principles of Kane's A-Text," where I attempt to show that Kane's identification of the "known scribal tendencies" referred to here is in fact predicated on the assumption that variation in A manuscripts is never due to authorial revision.

Donaldson are determined to attribute much textual variation within and (especially) between versions to scribal miscopying, and reluctant to admit the possibility of authorial rewriting.

The sceptic might well wonder whether Kane and Donaldson were not driven into this position by the prior decisions of Kane's A-Text. The discovery that many A variants agreed with B, a fact presumably unknown to Kane,[45] must have forced Kane and Donaldson to choose between various alternatives. They could have considered the possibility that Kane might have made wrong decisions in editing A; this in turn would mean either that his criteria for detecting scribal error had been at fault, or that he had applied them wrongly. Or, secondly, they could assume that Langland wrote more than one version of A, so that Kane's A represents one of these versions, and the variants agreeing with B another. But this would undermine one of the fundamental bases of their editorial position, that allying them to the second, not the first, of the two textual camps I outline in section 2 above, that Langland wrote only three, quite distinct, versions of the poem. Thirdly, they could try to explain the agreements between A variants and B as the result of scribal contamination, scribes of A introducing (corrupt) archetypal B readings into their exemplars; this explanation, however, brings with it further problems, and was sensibly rejected.[46] Fourthly, they could stick to the reading of Kane's text, and argue, as above, that the B and C readings are the result of scribal error of *precisely the same kind* that generated the A variant rejected by Kane in the first place. Whether this argument is correct or not, it seems unfortunate that the two editors did not inform the reader that these agreements exist, and consequently did not discuss, or even notice, the substantial methodological issues they imply.

All four of the possible explanations outlined here imply further corollaries, some of them extremely complex. It will be clear that it is impossible to assess the respective likelihood of any of them without turning to a detailed examination of the readings themselves: as I have argued throughout this article, textual premise and textual practice mesh intimately and pervasively. (The appendix below lists five representative agreements to give some idea of the issues involved.)[47] In my view, it is often difficult to support Kane and Donaldson's choice between variants, if one takes the readings of all the versions into account.

---

[45] There are several indications that Kane was unaware of agreements between A manuscripts and B: see item (i) in the Appendix below.

[46] I discuss the problems in full in "Some implications of Z."

[47] The impossibility of deciding between the various theoretical explanations without looking in detail at the readings concerned illustrates the weakness of some aspects of Patterson's assessment of Kane and Donaldson's edition; see section 1 above.

Sometimes the readings are hard to distinguish between on the grounds of poetic quality; in some of the other cases, where one variant is arguably superior to another, I do not see how we can invariably rule out the possibility that it was Langland who revised the worse reading to the better, or the better reading to the worse.

In each individual case, prior textual premise will play a significant part in determining the editor's decision. Editors belonging to the first of the textual camps I describe in section 2 will find it difficult to justify emending manuscript evidence, because they will not wish to posit unvarying authorial quality of writing, or invariable improvement on revision. Editors such as Kane and Donaldson, who belong to the second camp, will edit according to similarly prior, but different notions about Langland's poetic consistency, and his motives for revision. Evidently, it is impossible to edit without starting from views on manuscripts, author(s), and scribes which must in the first place be unsubstantiated premises. During the course of editing, these premises may be repeatedly modified, although this will mean returning to early textual decisions and re-thinking them. Kane and Donaldson's work in both A and B Versions stands as a monument to scholarship. I have tried to show, nevertheless, that in some respects, they did not explore as explicitly as they might the reasons for their initial premises, and that in others, they did not review and adjust earlier judgements so as to take account of the development of their later thought.

Appendix[48]

(i) Z.7.5 / A.7.5 / B.6.5 / C.8.3

ZBC and A-MSS EAMH[3]:   Haued Y hered that haluacur any
                                 ysowed hit aftur
Ka: Hadde y [erid] þat half akir

See Ka 446; RB 19. Kane rejects readings which complete the line after *haluacur* on the grounds that they do not explain omission from the other manuscripts. He regards the reading of EAMH[3] as a scribal filler of the same status as that of TChH[2] ("so me god helpe") and makes no reference to the fact that it is the reading of B and C. In view of the readings of the other versions, it seems likely that EAMH[3]'s reading was that of A also.

(ii) Z.2.94 / A.2.86a-7 / B.2.123 (not in C)

ZB and A-MS M: *Dignus est operarius* hys hure to haue
Ka: *Dignus est operarius mercede [sua]*
                          Worþi is þe werkman his mede to haue

See RB 55-56; for Kane's choice of *mede*, see Ka 436. There are several possible explanations for Z and M's reading: that it was original to A, and that Kane prints a scribal expansion; that Z and M were contaminated from B, or that both their reading and that of Kane were authorial variants in the A tradition.

(iii) Z.7.60 / A.7.60 / B.6.66 / C.8.67

ZB: Schal haue leue by oure lord to lese
                         here in heruest

---

[48] Line references throughout are to the following editions: for Z, *Piers Plowman: the Z Version*, ed. A. G. Rigg and Charlotte Brewer (Toronto: Pontifical Institute of Medieval Studies, 1983) [RB]; for A, *Piers Plowman: The A Version*, ed. George Kane (London: The Athlone Press, University of London, 1960) [Ka]; for B, *The Vision of Piers Plowman*, ed. A. V. C. Schmidt, 2d ed. (London: J. M. Dent & Sons, 1987) [Sch]; and for C *Piers Plowman*, ed. Derek Pearsall (London: Edward Arnold, 1978). *Piers Plowman: The B Version*, ed. George Kane and E. Talbot Donaldson (London: The Athlone Press, University of London, 1975) is referred to as "KD."

A-MSS MH³: Shal haue leue (be) oure lord to leuyn
here in heruist

Ka: Shal haue be oure lord þe more here in
heruist

(C: Shal haue leue by oure lord to go and
glene aftur me)

See RB 19 and 93, where we discuss the reading somewhat inadequately
with the comment that "the sequence of corruption in A-MSS . . . is not
easy to discern." In fact Kane (446–47) attempts to reconstruct this
sequence:

> The variants *haue leue* (MH³), *be allowed* (N), *byhynde* (W), may
> be accounted for as memorial reflections of manuscripts of the B
> version. But one circumstance is disturbing: the ease with which
> the adopted A form of the line might have derived from an original
> *haue leue . . . to lese here*, simply through early omission of *leue* .
> In a line so affected, reading *Shal haue be oure lord to lese here in
> heruist, to lese* would quickly become *þe lesse*, and this nonsense,
> on the suggestion of the context, would be corrected to *þe more*,
> as in the form adopted.

These remarks are strikingly perceptive in view of Kane's ignorance of
Z, whose evidence (if Z does indeed represent a pre-A version of the
poem written by Langland) corroborates his reconstruction of the original
A reading and suggests that the A archetype was corrupt here, and that
Kane should have emended it. (The other members of MH³'s variational
group, E and A, are both defective at this point.)

(iv) Z.5.88 / A.5.55 / B.5.72 (not in C)

ZB: To make mercy for ys mysdede by-
twene God ant ys soule

ys soule ZB and A-MSS LKEM; his pore soule A-MS V] hym Ka and
KD; cf. To gete mercy of god in helpe of his soule A-MS W; Tho
makyn mercy for his sowle betwyn god and hym of mysdede A-MS
A

Kane lists V's reading here among those substitutions where scribes
"consciously or unconsciously, if sometimes without intelligence or taste,
strained to participate in the experience that [the poem] recorded, as
well as to contribute to its purpose" (138–39).[49] Clearly this is a pos-

---

[49] 138–39; I can find no discussion of the reading in KD.

sible interpretation of the evidence, assuming that *hym* was original. But *soule* is not manifestly inferior on any inherent grounds to *hym*; indeed, one could argue that as it is more precise, so it is more poignant and moving in Lechery's prayer of despair, since it stresses that the only important part of Lechery is his soul: he *is* his soul. One could therefore argue for the contrary direction of corruption, from *hys soule* to *hym*, and assume that scribes could change their exemplars in a way that blunted the effect of the original rather than exaggerated it. And in fact, four pages before his discussion of *hys soule/hym*, Kane identifies as typically scribal any variations in readings where "the change is in the direction of flat statement, simplifying not only language but connotation, and sometimes losing or altering denotation. It favours the obvious and the colourless, and rejects language pregnant, or mannered, or fanciful" (134). The *hys soule/hym* variation is thus an example where two different criteria, both generally acceptable (and accepted), for detecting scribal variants can be applied to the evidence to produce opposite results. How are we to tell whether the more straightforward or the more fanciful reading is the original? Kane notes that "change ... in the direction of flat statement" is to be distinguished from "the effect of some substitutions to increase emphasis of statement," which is "a separate matter" (134 n.1). But he offers no criteria by which one is to make this distinction. I would argue that the variation *hys soule/hym* better fits the category of scribal flattening, with *hys soule* as the original, than the category and direction of scribal corruption to which Kane assigns it. The textual evidence of the other two versions in which the line is found vindicates this judgement: Z and all the B manuscripts read *hys soule*.[50]

(v) A.5.116 / B.5.198 / C.6.208; not in Z

Ka: And was his prentis ypliȝt his profit to
                                          loke
                                          loke Ka and KD] wayte BC and A-MSS
                                          AMH[3]

KD class *wayte*, the BC reading, as a "lexically easier" scribal substitution for original *loke*, and emend accordingly. I can find no specific treatment of the variation in Kane; he may either also have judged *wayte* to be lexically easier, or have adopted it as the majority reading of the A

---

[50] With the exception of B-MS F, which has a different form for the b-half of the line.

manuscripts.[51] *OED* and *MED* evidence does not show that the required sense of either reading is harder or easier than the other,[52] so it is difficult to make sense of KD's rejection of *wayte*. Nor is it obvious why either reading should have been replaced by the other as a result of visual error. C's agreement with B in *wayte* endorses Schmidt's decision to retain the archetypal B reading, especially since it is unanimously attested by the B manuscripts. Possible explanations for the readings are (1) that there were two A versions, one of which read *loke*, the other *wayte; or* (2), that *loke* is a scribal error in the A tradition, reproduced for their B-Text by KD despite the fact that it is found in none of the B manuscripts.

---

[51] *loke* is found in all A manuscripts other than AMH[3] containing this line.
[52] See *OED* s.v. "wait" v.3c; *MED* s.v. "look" v. 6(e.).

Middle English Romance: The Limits of Editing, the Limits of Criticism

A. S. G. EDWARDS

Probably more than textual and literary critics of other periods and genres the student of Middle English romance responds to recent developments in literary theory with a sense that *plus ça change*. Current concerns with the disappearance of the author and the consequent impossibility of determining intentionality are, for the romance editor, nothing new. What I wish to briefly explore are some of the responses to these problems and their implications, both theoretical and practical, for the actual interpretation of the text.

Romance (I will be talking here only about verse romances) is the most textually slippery of all Middle English genres. There are several reasons why this is so. The first and most fundamental is the nature of the surviving materials with which the editor has to work. These often seem to thwart the most modest efforts to recover originality. At one extreme are a significant number of romances which survive in only single, usually late, often incomplete copies, either in manuscript[1] or printed form.[2] The most obvious example is the famous seventeenth-century Percy Folio manuscript which contains unique copies of ten romances.[3] And its owner, Bishop Thomas Percy, was in the eighteenth century among the first to perceive the problems of textual restoration in the light of the paucity of available evidence. Percy's efforts to deal with this problem earned him the disapproval of his contemporaries. In the last edition of his *Reliques* published during his lifetime he was compelled to acknowledge the nature and extent of his editorial interventions:

---

[1] Of the ninety-four separate verse romances recorded in the revised *Manual of the Writings in Middle English*, ed. J. B. Severs, vol. 1 (New Haven, CT: Connecticut Academy of Arts and Sciences, 1967), nearly fifty survive in only a single manuscript.

[2] Six of the verse romances listed in the *Manual* survive only in a printed edition: *Golagros and Gawain, The Jeaste of Syr Gawayne, Rauf Coilyear, Scottish Alexander Buik, Roswall and Lillian,* and *The Knight of Curtesy.*

[3] These are: *Guy and Colbrond, The Legend of King Arthur, Sir Lancelot du Lake, King Arthur's Death, The Green Knight, The Turke and Gowin, The Carle of Carlile, The Marriage of Sir Gawaine, King Arthur and King Cornwall,* and *Sir Lambewell.* In addition, the Percy Folio provides the only manuscript authority for two other romances: *Eger and Grime* and *The Squyer of Lowe Degree.*

The Second poem in this Volume [he writes] titled the Marriage of Sir Gawaine having been offered to the Reader with large conjectural Supplements and Corrections, the old Fragment itself is here literally and exactly printed from the Editor's folio MS. with all its defects, inaccuracies and errata; that such austere Antiquaries, as complain that the ancient copies have not been always rightly adhered to, may see how unfit for publication many of the pieces would have been, if all the blunders, corruptions and nonsense of illiterate Reciters and Transcribers had been superficially retained, without some attempt to correct and emend them.[4]

Even this acknowledgement hardly adequately indicates the extent of Percy's editorial interventions with respect to this poem and to others in his collection.[5]

It is easy to disparage Percy's activities, to sneer as Ritson and other later editors have done at the "ingeniousness" of his editorial procedures. Yet his analysis of the factors that led him to his position remains sound and quite typical of the problems confronting an editor of Middle English romances. Such analysis does not lead necessarily to the position that Percy takes, but one can perhaps understand how such a position derived from his understanding of the editorial role and the way it was essentially thwarted by the available evidence. This frustration led naturally, if not defensibly, to an attempt to fulfill his sense of the editorial role—the recovery of what the author wrote—even at the cost of inventing such authorial intention when confronted with incomplete or textually intractable materials.

Percy's excesses have perhaps been a factor in the much more limited sense of their role reflected in the work of later editors. They have often tended to adopt much more cautious strategies. Many editions of Middle English romances are really transcripts rather than edited texts, with little attempt at the recovery of original readings. In its most extreme form such caution makes the editor the preserver of the aberrations of transmission.[6]

But such an editorial stance is not generally the outcome of supine passivity. More often it derives from a growing understanding of the complexities of romance transmission, complexities which usually

---

[4] *Reliques of Ancient English Poetry*, 4th ed. (1794), 3:350.

[5] For a valuable survey of Percy's treatment of his manuscript see W. J. Bate, "Percy's Use of the Folio-Manuscript," *Journal of English and Germanic Philology* 43 (1944): 337–48.

[6] For a recent example (in an otherwise excellent edition) see Frances McSparran's treatment of the de Worde fragments in her edition of *Octavian* (EETS 289 [London: Oxford University Press, 1986]); cf. my review in *Speculum* 63 (1988): 436–37.

manifest themselves when the editor has more than one witness to deal with. If a text surviving in a single witness invites extensive conjecture (at least for Percy), a text surviving in more than one is likely to demonstrate the futility of such conjecture. The reconstruction of "what the author wrote" necessarily entails a reconstruction of the processes by which error could have been engendered. In theory (and with other kinds of texts, in practice) a multiplicity of witnesses is of assistance in determining originality. For the editor of romance texts problems often prove more intractable. He, or she, often confronts the problem of extracting a discernibly superior and original reading from among a number of existing ones that do not lead directionally to the identification of one that is conspicuously better. Indeed, the recovery of a single original text is often crucially, irretrievably obscured. This seems due in large measure to the role of the minstrel as the prime agent of romance transmission.[7] The assumption of some form of oral, minstrel circulation is the most reasonable way to explain the variations between the surviving manuscripts of many romance texts. After composition the text would be recited by the minstrel, who would modify it according to audience, special circumstances, his sense of his capacity to improve the original, or uncertainties of memory. At various stages, reconstituted versions of the text would be transcribed; then the same processes would doubtless be repeated. The researches of A. C. Baugh have demonstrated the ways in which witnesses, often clearly descended from a common single original, like the manuscripts of *Bevis of Hampton*, reveal processes of improvisation and substitution presumably occasioned by the factors I have just noted. He reaches the rueful conclusion:

> the variations between the manuscripts containing these longer narratives are often quite striking, so great that it is generally impossible to establish a single critical text with the variants adequately reported in footnotes. Indeed, the attempt to do so has at times obscured the extent to which the different manuscripts differ from one another except where these differences are so extensive as to force the editor to print long passages independently in the notes. If it were not for certain bookish productions one might venture the observation that the number of what are really separate versions of a story is in direct proportion to the length of the story.[8]

---

[7] See A. C. Baugh, "The Middle English Romance: Some Questions of Creation, Presentation and Preservation," *Speculum* 42 (1967): 1-31, and his "Improvisation in the Middle English Romance," *Proceedings of the American Philosophical Society* 103 (1959): 418-54.

[8] Baugh, "Improvisation in the Middle English Romance," 435.

This would be discouraging enough to any editor in quest of original readings. But, more recently, William Holland has raised arguments that are even more fundamental in their implications for the rediscovery of originality. His conclusions are based on an examination of the transmission of *Arthur and Merlin* and comparative analysis of a large body of other romance material. They are profoundly dispiriting to the aspiring editor and critic:

> the extent to which the diction of the verse romances is conventional has not been completely appreciated. . . . [Formulas], far from being a "mere convenience" form . . . the very heart of the narrative; they are the means by which the story is told. The verse romances, those in couplets as well as more complex stanazs, are by their very nature conventional. They do not fail of originality, but ignore it. And it is for this reason that oral variation could so easily occur.[9]

For many romances it would seem that triteness is all. To attempt to apply the principle of *difficilior lectio*, as a number of editors have done, may therefore be inherently futile since the quest for originality may well properly lie in seeking the most banal rather than the most difficult reading. This sharp delimiting of the possibility of editorial intervention inevitably also limits the role of the literary critic who also has to confront the untranscendable banality of such texts.

Such limitations are, if anything, only confirmed by the intermittent possibilities of identifying distinctive authorial method and practice. We can append authors' names to or suggest common authorship for only a few groups of Middle English romances. The results of such identifications afford little encouragement to either editor or critic. The largest group of works identified with a single author is that associated with Thomas Chestre, the putative author of *Sir Launfal*, *Libeaus Desconus*, and the southern *Octavian*.[10] The argument for common authorship depends to a significant degree on the assumption that there could not be two versifiers who could write so distinctively badly. As Maldwyn Mills points out, one crucial aspect of style shared by these works is the way in which words, phrasal patterns, and narrative devices all

> may be used with a singular disregard for their aptness to context; indeed, their significance to the problem of authorship lies not only

---

[9] William E. Holland, "Formulaic Diction and the Descent of a Middle English Romance," *Speculum* 48 (1973): 89–109; the quotation is from 105.

[10] The fullest account is Maldwyn Mills', "The Composition and Style of the Southern *Octavian*, *Sir Launfal* and *Libeaus Desconus*," *Medium Aevum* 31 (1962): 88–109.

in the fondness for certain words, phrases, or formulae, to which they bear witness, but in the fact that this common material is used in a manner that betrays a consistent desire to meet the needs of rhyme, at whatever cost to stylishness and sense.[11]

If this is a valid principle of canon formation, it is one that serves once again to curtail editorial and interpretive activity. Other possible attributions, such as *The Wedding of Sir Gawain and Dame Ragnell* to Malory,[12] or of *Generides* to the author of *The Flower and the Leaf*[13] are cross-generic ones that consequently provide no real assistance to the editor, whatever grist they may afford for the speculative mill of the critic.[14]

More generally, our assumptions about audience and milieu remain relatively insecure. To some degree this problem interlocks with questions of authorship. The apparent clerical provenance of a number of romance manuscripts and the evident Latinity of certain romance authors suggest a clerical origin for at least some romances.[15] This hypothesis receives its most striking endorsement from Ashmole 33, where what appears to be an early draft of parts of *Sir Ferumbras* is written on the back of documents connected with Exeter Cathedral.[16] It seems probable that clerics, probably in the service of secular or ecclesiastical nobility, had a role in the composition and dissemination of a number of romances, particularly in provincial contexts. The alliterative *William of Palerne*, surviving uniquely in King's College, Cambridge, MS. 13,

---

[11] *Lybeaus Desconus*, ed. M. Mills, EETS 261 (London: Oxford University Press, 1969), 65.

[12] See P. J. C. Field, "Malory and *The Wedding of Sir Gawain and Dame Ragnell*," *Archiv* 219 (1982): 374–81.

[13] See D. Pearsall, "*The Assembly of the Ladies* and *Generydes*" *Review of English Studies*, n.s., 12 (1961): 229–37.

[14] Mention should be made, however, of the judicious analysis by O. D. Macrae-Gibson of the possible common authorship of *Arthur and Merlin*, *Kyng Alysaunder*, and (perhaps) the *Seven Sages of Rome*. The criteria for common authorship established there could well have significant editorial implications; see his edition of *Of Arthour and of Merlin*, EETS 279 (London: Oxford University Press, 1979), 65–75.

[15] For discussion of authorship and audience see A. C. Baugh, "The Authorship of the Middle English Romances," *Modern Humanities Research Association Annual Bulletin* 22 (1950): 13–28; Karl Brunner, "Middle English Metrical Romances and their Audience," in *Studies in Medieval Literature in Honor of Albert Croll Baugh*, ed. M. Leach (Philadelphia: University of Pennsylvania Press, 1961), 219–26; and Derek Pearsall, "Middle English Romance and its Audiences," in *Historical & Editorial Studies in Medieval & Early Modern English for Johann Gerritsen*, ed. Mary-Jo Arn and Hanneke Wirtjes (Groningen: Walters-Noordhoff, 1985), 37–47.

[16] On this manuscript see Baugh, "The Authorship of the Middle English Romances," 25–26.

apparently produced for Humphrey Bohun, earl of Hereford, is one such possibility; *The Wars of Alexander*, discussed below, is another. And Harley 2253, containing *King Horn* was copied by a scribe with connections to the bishop of Hereford.[17]

But such probabilities must be balanced against the evidence of the Auchinleck manuscript, which implies an elaborate apparatus of commercial, metropolitan book production in place by the fourth decade of the fourteenth century, an apparatus possibly including an entourage of hack translators rendering Anglo-Norman romances into Middle English.[18] It seems best to insist with Derek Pearsall on "the range of possible audiences that need to be adduced for medieval English romance."[19] But the lack of either very secure general assumptions or ones of specific validity makes it difficult to postulate contexts of creation and/or audience that are likely to be of assistance to the editor.

It is only in atypical circumstances, like the *Wars of Alexander*, that the possibility of recovering such contexts offers the editor much assistance. Recently, in an important article, Thorlac Turville Petre has demonstrated how editors with great acuteness, much patience, and extended access to a computer might restore the text of this romance with a considerable degree of confidence.[20] One crucial factor in establishing such confidence is the identification of a specific Latin source which it can be shown was translated accurately. To be able to demonstrate such a precise relationship between source and text is itself very unusual among romances. Another factor is the establishing of a body of computer-based data that establishes criteria for characteristic collocations both within the poem and in related poems in the alliterative tradition. But the opportunities for such contextual reconstructions are rare and would not be of much help outside some portions of the alliterative tradition, where there are discernible constraints of verse form and, through verse form, on style.

The cumulative effect of all these circumstances, of transmission, style, authorship, and context, is to create for the editor a general sense of

---

[17] On King's College, Cambridge 13 and Harley 2253 see most recently A. I. Doyle, "English Books in and out of Court from Edward III to Henry VII," in *English Court Culture in the Later Middle Ages*, ed. V. J. Scattergood and J. W. Sherborne (London: Duckworth, 1983), 165–66 and the references cited there.

[18] See the introduction by D. Pearsall to *The Auchinleck Manuscript: National Library of Scotland Advocates' MS. 19.2.1* (London: Scolar Press, 1977), vii–xi.

[19] Pearsall, "Middle English Romance and its Audiences," 43.

[20] See his article, "Editing *The Wars of Alexander*," in *Manuscripts and Texts: Editorial Problems in Later Middle English Literature*, ed. Derek Pearsall (Cambridge: D. S. Brewer, 1987), 143-60.

indeterminacy: he must usually function in contexts where the usual pre-occupations with the recovery of originality cannot serve much purpose. This sense is likely to increase in proportion to the number of surviving manuscripts. The fewer the witnesses the greater the possibility of confident interpretation. One contrasts this situation with recent editorial and critical treatment of Chaucer's "romance" *Sir Thopas*, notably by John Burrow, where careful analysis of manuscripts and diction has led to a fuller appreciation of the structure and texture of the poem.[21]

But in the case of most romances the general problems I have noted are compounded by localized ones that impede the most elementary analysis. Several examples can be adduced from one of the most important sources for the Middle English romance, the Auchinleck manuscript. Here, even such a basic matter as our sense of closure can be at issue. The most recent editor of *Arthur and Merlin* points out that the poem "comes to an end, with no formula of conclusion" so that "a good deal of the plot is left in the air." He plausibly suggests a range of possible reasons why this is so, none of which is mutually exclusive, including scribal fatigue or the physical constraints of manuscript production: "Perhaps the 'general editor' of the [Auchinleck] manuscript decided that [the poem] as he knew it was too long for his anthology, and so directed the scribe to stop at what seemed a convenient point."[22]

Beginnings can also be a problem in Auchinleck. One thinks here most obviously of the prologue to *Sir Orfeo* as it appears in two of the three manuscripts. In the third, Auchinleck, the beginning of the text has been physically excised. The *Orfeo* prologue does appear elsewhere in the manuscript as the prologue to a different poem, *Lay le Freine*.[23] Elsewhere passages in *Sir Degarre* can be paralleled in both *Lay le Freine* and *Bevis of Hampton*.[24] Such carrying over of narrative "chunks" from one text to another within the manuscript seem to confirm the activities of a London scriptorium that combined transcription with redaction, pragmatically shunting passages according to whatever constraints obtained, whether of space or appositeness.[25]

---

[21] See various of his essays on *Sir Thopas* collected in *Essays on Medieval Literature* (Oxford: Oxford University Press, 1984).

[22] *Of Arthour and of Merlin*, ed. O. D. Macrae-Gibson, 2:161.

[23] The argument that these poems are by different authors is made by J. B. Beston, "The Case Against Common Authorship of *Lay le Freine* and *Sir Orfeo*," *Medium Aevum* 45 (1976): 153-63.

[24] See the discussion by Nicholas Jacobs, "*Sir Degarre, Lay le Freine, Beves of Hamtoun* and the 'Auchinleck Bookshop,'" *Notes & Queries*, n.s., 29 (1982): 294-301.

[25] A further instance of this tendency is the borrowing in the Ashmole 61 text of

This uncertainty as to the purposive location of passages of the text lessens the possibility of making confident assertions about some kinds of conscious verbal artistry in many romances. Or, at least, if a critic wishes to do so , it is a lot easier if the work in question survives only in a single manuscript. Thus, a critic of the romance *Athelstan* (which survives only in Gonville & Caius MS. 175) is on relatively safe ground in pointing to the purposive nature of the verbal repetitions in the testing scenes involving Sir Egeland and Sir Wymond.[26] The verbal parallels serve to juxtapose the fidelity of the former against the climactic punishment of the latter for his infidelity. One can contrast this relative certainty with a minor illustration from *Sir Degarre*. In the Rawlinson manuscript of this romance, the concluding episode, a battle between combatants who do not realize they are father and son, is introduced by a line ("To hym com prekand a joly knyghtt" [901]) that echoes one that opened the poem's initial episode, the rape of the maiden that engendered the child who is now fighting his father: "To hur com prikand a joly knyght" (82).[27] It would be tempting for the critic to argue that such parallelism is conscious, a crude but deliberate attempt to stress the causal relationship between these incidents. But such temptation should probably be resisted. The line is not repeated in the earliest text of *Sir Degarre*, the Auchinleck; and the Rawlinson manuscript has been characterized as "a very inferior one, much corrupted and padded out."[28] Such appreciation of the vagaries of textual transmission makes it difficult to repose much confidence in the originality and significance of specific passages in particular texts of a romance, even (or possibly especially) when they seem to have a particular allusive force. For example, in one of the two manuscripts of *Sir Gowther*, the eponymous hero, after his death "lyeth in a shryne of gold / And doth maracles, as it is told / And hatt Seynt Gotlake" (BL Royal 17.B.43). But in the other manuscript (NLS Advocates 19.3.1) we are told merely that Gowther is "a varre corsent parfett."[29] In the world of romance transmission it

---

Sir Orfeo of six lines from *Of Arthour and of Merlin*; see *Sir Orfeo*, ed. A. J. Bliss, 2d ed. (Oxford: Clarendon Press, 1966), xvi n. 1.

[26] As has been argued by Kevin S. Kiernan, "*Athelston* and the Rhyme of the English Romances," *Modern Language Quarterly* 36 (1975): 339-53.

[27] Line references to the version in Rawlinson MS. F. 34 are to the edition of this version in *The Breton Lays in Middle English*, ed. T. C. Rumble (Detroit: Wayne State University Press, 1965), 45-78.

[28] See *Medieval English Romances*, ed A. V. C. Schmidt and Nicholas Jacobs (New York: Holmes & Meier, 1980), 2:240.

[29] The Royal manuscript is cited from Rumble's edition of *The Breton Lays in Middle English* (see n. 27); the Advocates manuscript is cited from *Six Middle English Romances*, ed. M. Mills (London: Dent, 1973). I owe this observation to my former student Mrs. Joan Dwyer.

would seem rash to attach any interpretive weight to the greater specificity of the first passage. It could as well, if not more likely, be the result
of some attempt to introduce a snatch of local color by a scribe, minstrel,
or redactor, as be reflective of any original design.

Even when there is the possibility of establishing aspects of a text with
a relative degree of certainty, literary critics are not always willing to be
constrained by textual evidence. The attempt to apply aesthetic criteria
to discern authenticity carries particular risks. For example, Bruce
Mitchell has objected to a passage in the Auchinleck and Ashmole texts
of *Sir Orfeo* (the description of the dead and maimed in the King of the
Underworld's courtyard) as "an insensitive artistic blemish."[30] Certainly
the passage poses problems for those who, like Mitchell, approach the
poem with their critical presuppositions locked firmly into place. He feels
that "the faery world is a pleasant place,"[31] hence finds no place in his
critical scheme for such discordancies. Mitchell seeks textual validation
for his critical position from the absence of this passage in one manuscript of the poem, Harley 3810. But it does appear in the other two
manuscripts, Auchinleck and Ashmole 61. And it seems clear that Harley
and Ashmole "are dependent on a common ancestor, either descended
from or coeval with A[uchinleck]."[32] This suggests the greater likelihood not that Harley is original in its omission but that such omission
was probably caused by scribal error, occasioned by the lengthy passage
of anaphora at this point. I cite Mitchell's unconvincing argument because it shows the ways in which literary critics can be inclined to
impose interpretation on a text at precisely those points where the
textual evidence tends to a contrary conclusion.

But usually textual authority remains more indeterminate. This has not
stopped editors seeking to find it even when their own evidence suggests
that it does not exist. The quest for "authentic" readings can vitiate in
more fundamental ways even distinguished editorial undertakings. In
Maldwyn Mills's valuable edition of *Libeaus Desconus* an understanding
of the realities of romance transmission contends, at times, with a desire
to apply logical assumptions to the elucidation of materials that are
inherently whimsical. On the one hand, Mills believes there is a
distinguishable author for this romance, Thomas Chestre. But he posits
"a less than perfect archetype (or even original) and free revision by later

---

[30] "The Faery World of *Sir Orfeo*," *Neophilologus* 48 (1964): 157. The relevant
passages are lines 391–400 in Auchinbeck and 382–87 in Ashmole.

[31] "The Faery World," 156; most other critics have taken an altogether darker view
of the faery world and felt it to be structurally significant.

[32] A. J. Bliss, ed., *Sir Orfeo*, xv.

copyists."[33] Moreover, in such revision the "authors had differed from Chestre in degree rather than kind, and, like him, had relied to a large extent upon their memory in compiling their own versions of the story."[34] At the same time, he defines Chestre's style as one characterized by incoherence and contradiction.[35] It does not seem easy to proceed, as Mills does, from such perceptions about the nature of the text to discriminations that assess some passage as "authentic" or "more authentic" than others. Given the sort of authorial *usus scribendi* Mills has described, such discriminations seem open to question. And if there is no stable text, there can, of course, be no possibility of interpretation. The various versions of the text can perhaps only be usefully studied as discrete documents, of interest for what they reveal about the efforts of scribes and redactors to create their own texts out of Chestre's intermittent gibberish.

Nonetheless, other editors in somewhat different circumstances have felt it worthwhile to attempt the recovery of authentic readings. There have been several exponents in recent years of what has been termed "direct" editing. This involves attempts to apply systematic procedures of analysis at each point of variation to seek to recover the original reading. It is a method first extensively employed in Middle English editing by George Kane in his edition of the A-text of *Piers Plowman* and later to more controversial effect in his edition of Langland's B-text with E. Talbot Donaldson. It has also been thoughtfully applied to the editing of two romance texts, *The Awntyrs of Arthur* and *King Horn*.

Some sense of the problems of this method can be seen in the parallel performances of two gifted exponents, Robert J. Gates and Ralph Hanna III, who each produced separate editions of the *Awntyrs* within three years.[36] As Hanna, the later editor, notes, "[Gates's] views and my own frequently differ."[37] Indeed, divergence is at times so wide as to make

---

[33] *Lybeaus Desconus*, ed., M. Mills (see n. 11), 15.

[34] *Lybeaus Desconus*, 16.

[35] Cf. *Lybeaus Desconus*, 36:

Chestre again and again shows himself prepared to make almost any sacrifices ... to secure a rhyme. He will endow words with new ... or strained meanings, and introduce notions that are either quite at odds with the immediate context of the rhyme-word embodying them, or conflict with statements made a very short period of time earlier.

[36] *The Awntyrs of Arthure at the Terne Wathelyne: A Critical Edition*, ed. Robert J. Gates (Philadelphia: University of Pennsylvania Press, 1969); *The Awntyrs off Arthure at the Tern Wathelyn: An Edition Based on Bodleian Library MS. Douce 324*, ed. Ralph Hanna III (Manchester: Manchester University Press, 1974).

[37] Hanna, 55.

it hard to believe that both are actually working from the same body of evidence, as in line 444 which reads in Gates

[And dossours, and qweschyns, and bankowrs fulle bryghte]

but becomes in Hanna's edition

[With beddus brauderit o brode and bankers bry₃t].

[With beddus brauderit o brode and bankers bry$_3$t].

While variation between the two editions is not usually this extreme, it is extensive. And neither editor invariably provides full demonstration of the processes of scribal transmission that validate his restored readings. Nor does either editor address the question of the very limited body of evidence available to establish an authorial *usus scribendi*, in contrast to *Piers Plowman*. There are only four manuscripts of the *Awntyrs*, which, in its fullest form, comprises 715 lines. And Hanna argues that it is, in fact, two distinct poems (with a concluding stanza), of 338 and 363 lines respectively.[38] Given such small portions of text in so few manuscripts, given the formulaic nature of the poem's diction, and given Holland's general conclusions about the tendency to banality in such diction, it is possible to feel some methodological reservations about the scope of the editorial reconstructions on the text of this poem. As it is, we do not have a stable base upon which critical interpretations can be erected. Instead there exists a series of variant reconstructions, sustained by hypotheses, at times of different but often of equivalent force. The critic seems to feel free to accept or reject what he will from such conflicting reconstructions.[39] Rosamund Allen observes about the editing of the *Awntyrs*,

> In practice, different editors will have different opinions about the original form for any given set of variants and will offer different inspired conjectural guesses; the literary critics may present different interpretations according to which editor they follow, but this will also happen with single- or parallel-text editions, where the critic is simply selecting which fifteenth- instead of twentieth-century editor he favours.[40]

---

[38] The argument for authorship is developed most fully in his article "*The Awntyrs off Arthure*: An interpretation," *Modern Language Quarterly* 31 (1970): 275-97.

[39] Thus A. C. Spearing rejects on aesthetic grounds Hanna's apportioning of authorship because it violates his sense of the poem's "near symmetry"; see his *Medieval to Renaissance in English Poetry* (Cambridge: Cambridge University Press, 1985), 347 n. 23.

[40] "Some Sceptical Observations on the Editing of *The Awntyrs off Arthure*," in *Manuscripts and Texts*, ed. Pearsall (see n. 20), 24-25. Allen also notes (n. 78) Spearing's rejection of Hanna's editorial decision.

This is well put. It is not, however, clear to me where this situation leaves the literary critic. We live in a world of uncertainty principles. But the act of literary analysis, if it is not to be completely futile, requires a tolerable conviction that at least most of the words examined possess authority. The range of editorial divergence in the *Awntyrs* makes this an insecure assumption.

Rosamund Allen's own edition of *King Horn* helps to focus these problems of editorial intervention a little more clearly. She employs similar techniques of "deep" or "direct" editing, but the strategy of her edition is rather different from that of editors of the *Awntyrs*. Her detailing of the methodological implications of her method provides an elaborate discussion of specific readings and the general assumptions and procedures which she employs. Although convinced of the conscious artistry of the poem, she acknowledges the problems of her method:

> I am not unsympathetic to the critic who may decide that there is insufficient evidence to distinguish right readings from wrong, and hence to supply an indication of the author's *usus scribendi*, in a poem as short as *KH*. Such a critic will consider the conjectural emendations merely hypothetical; the large body of unclassifiable variants will confirm his impression that *KH* cannot be edited in this way. To this I can only reply that the method remains intrinsically sound, but may well be too fine a tool for the massive errors and displacements of a short, popular, and easy vernacular text, especially where there is thin documentary support from only three extant witnesses. The reader must judge.[41]

Once again, this is admirably put. It recognizes the necessary indeterminacy of the method, particularly as applied to such a text as *King Horn*. The basis of the method of "deep" editing is, of course, the identification of the harder reading often not present in any of the surviving witnesses. I have already discussed some of the general problems in applying such a method to romance texts. I would add that at some points I am struck by an apparent determination to make readings in *King Horn* either harder than they need to be or than the evidence allows. I hope one illustration, sufficiently pervasive to be representative, will indicate the nature of my concern here. It involves the treatment of the manuscript forms *god*, *christ*, and *iesu(s)*. These forms regularly appear in the manuscripts. But Allen regularly emends all these forms to *driȝte*, a single decision that involves her in some twenty

---

[41] *King Horn: An Edition Based on Cambridge University Library MS Gg.4.27 (2)*, ed. Rosamund Allen (New York: Garland Publishing, 1984), 35.

emendations unsupported by any of the witnesses.[42] In her discussion of this decision, which does indicate its extent, she argues that there is warrant for the emendation on the basis of a single occurrence of *driȝte* in her base manuscript.[43] Such singularity might, of itself, be sufficient reason to resist systematic, extensive emendation. And the weight given to this reading is further compromised by the fact that it appears only as a rhyme word. As with Gates and Hanna, one comes away from Allen's work with an overriding sense of a remarkably acute and courageous editorial intelligence. But, at the same time, it is not always easy to feel that the available evidence will bear the weight that is placed on it.

Where does this leave the critic? Often with a very limited role in elucidating romance. At times, a failure to perceive such limitations shows the critic to particular disadvantage, particularly when he requires the text to sustain a wholly inappropriate interpretive weight. One example of this is Kevin Kiernan's efforts to find comedy, even irony, in *The Squire of Low Degree*.[44] To try and demonstrate such qualities it is necessary to ignore the realities of transmission that have left us with variant versions of the poem that are late, corrupt, reflections of a design that was initially imperfect. As the poem's editor observes:

> If we had an entirely trustworthy text, unmutilated by copyists or reciters, we might fairly charge the author with remarkable density or remarkable carelessness in construction. But we are perhaps not warranted in holding the original author thus strictly to account.[45]

For Kiernan, poverty of invention and banality of diction become purposive elements in the poem's design, making it parodic and ironic. One need not strop one's Occam's razor for very long to doubt the usefulness of such an approach, sustained as it is at times by misreadings. Notions of burlesque and parody rest on a secure sense of the text and of the firm relationship between authorial design and audience. It is only by ignoring all the problematic aspects of the textual history of the romance that it is possible to perceive irony in the surviving forms of such a work.[46]

---

[42] These emendations appear in lines 46, 82, 86, 152, 162, 164, 171, 189, 419, 467, 561, 585, 675, 1075, 1156, 1215, 1306, 1334, 1353, 1560.

[43] The single occurrence is in line 1343; the form is briefly discussed on 76 without indicating the frequency of the emendation.

[44] Kevin S. Kiernan, "*Undo Your Door* and the Order of Chivalry," *Studies in Philology* 70 (1973): 345-66.

[45] *The Squyr of Lowe Degree*, ed. William Edward Mead (Boston: Ginn, 1904), lxxx.

[46] An inability to read the text is also an asset in such situations; he offers as an example of "another pun" lines 5-8: "He served the kyng her fader dere, / Fully the tyme of seuen yere; / For he was marshall of his hall, And set the lordes bothe grete

Indeed, if the preceding arguments possess any validity, there is little middle ground between textual and literary criticism in respect to the romances. The realities of composition and transmission serve, in many instances, to render at best indeterminate notions of purposive design and texture. And where texts cannot be established with even relative conviction, where, indeed, the concept of a text at all is difficult to sustain, critical activity becomes futile if it acknowledges the historical circumstances of the received text. That literary criticism of romances is possible at all is due to the fortunate survival of a number of relatively good, and usually unique, transcripts of a small number of texts, such as *Sir Gawain and the Green Knight*, the alliterative *Morte Arthur*, and *Havelok*.

---

and small." (I quote the de Worde text from Mead's edition.) Kiernan comments "when told of loyal, seven year service to a king, one thinks first in terms of knightly service. Here, though, it means the squire served the king *food*" (349). The passage goes on, however: "An hardy man he was, and wyght, / Bothe in batayll and in fyght" (9–10).

The York Cycle: Texts, Performances, and the Bases for Critical Enquiry

RICHARD BEADLE

Amongst the most hotly contested of recent debates in the interpretation of early English drama has been that concerning the staging of the York Corpus Christi cycle. The main issue is whether the fifty or so plays were presented processionally on pageant wagons at a series of stations along a route through the streets of the city, with each play being therefore given not once but twelve or more times in the course of a performance of the cycle, or whether the annual presentation was constituted by a single performance of the full text at one fixed location.[1] The bulk of the contested evidence has been drawn not from the text of the cycle itself, but rather from contemporary external documentary information held mostly in the civic archives at York. The manuscript containing the text of the cycle, now London, British Library MS. Additional 35290, has, as a codicological entity, seldom been invoked in the debate so far, since it has been traditional to place considerable reliance on the *editio princeps* published in 1885 by Lucy Toulmin Smith.[2] Miss Toulmin Smith's edition included amongst other things in the introduction a summary physical description of the volume, and along with the original text, recorded in footnotes the numerous marginal annotations added by later hands. Though doubtless adequate by the standards of the time, it has recently become clear that Miss Toulmin Smith's accounts of both the physical aspect of the manuscript and the later annotations were in various respects neither accurate nor complete, and that critical or interpretative notions based on them are often quite erroneous. The present study draws together some examples of these pitfalls, and one of its purposes is to establish a preliminary reorientation in that area where a distinction between textual study and critical enquiry, though traditional, is now better set aside.

A curious instance of a physical feature of the manuscript not alluded

---

[1] For a summary of the various positions taken in this debate see William Tydeman, *The Theatre in the Middle Ages* (Cambridge: Cambridge University Press, 1978), 114–20, and further references there.

[2] Lucy Toulmin Smith, *York Plays: The Plays Performed by the Crafts or Mysteries of York on the Day of Corpus Christi* . . . (Oxford: Clarendon Press, 1885).

to in Miss Toulmin Smith's edition is worth mentioning as it may have an unexpected bearing on the debate over the staging of the cycle. This is the quantity of black powder, seemingly soot, to be found in the gutters as the leaves of MS. Additional 35290 are turned. The presence of this substance was duly noted in the introduction to a recently published facsimile of the manuscript,[3] and it may indeed be readily observed in the facsimile itself. Chemical analysis would soon confirm whether or not the black powder is soot, but hazarding the guess that it is, why should such a feature—surely an issue on the furthest periphery of even codicological investigation—be of relevance to anyone concerned in the interpretation of the cycle in any of its numerous facets?

The answer to this question is complex and involves unravelling errors and misunderstandings of a kind that inevitably arise when the interpretative critic neglects the responsibility of understanding how codicological, documentary, or textual knowledge is arrived at and verified. On the basis of external evidence it is believed that MS. Additional 35290 was probably compiled at some time between 1463 and 1477. It was known locally as the "Register" of the York Corpus Christi cycle, and as such it evidently had the status of an official civic document.[4] Much new information about the Register has recently been gathered in a new edition of the cycle[5] and in the facsimile mentioned above. Almost the first thing that Miss Toulmin Smith said about the manuscript in 1885 embodied a significant misunderstanding of an important early documentary reference to it. She took a phrase in the city's Chamberlain's Accounts for 1554—"at the Trinitie yaites where the Clerke kepys the Regyster"—to mean that the manuscript "was at one time in the care of the priory of Holy Trinity in Micklegate, at the gates of which was the first station in the circle of performances through the city as early as 1399."[6] Miss Toulmin Smith's assertion has often been quoted to support arguments concerning the authorship and history of the manuscript,[7] but there is now wide agreement that the reference to the Common Clerk's "keeping" of the Register at the gates of Holy Trinity relates to one of the uses to which the manuscript was put. Keeping the

[3] Richard Beadle and Peter Meredith, eds., *The York Play. A Facsimile of British Library MS Additional 35290 together with a Facsimile of the* Ordo Paginarum *Section of the A/Y Memorandum Book* (Leeds: The University of Leeds School of English, 1983), xvii.
[4] Beadle and Meredith, *The York Play. A Facsimile*, ix.
[5] Richard Beadle, ed., *The York Plays* (London: Edward Arnold, 1982).
[6] Toulmin Smith, *York Plays*, xi–xii.
[7] See, for example, Hardin Craig, *English Religious Drama of the Middle Ages* (Oxford: Clarendon Press, 1955), 201; A. G. Petti, *English Literary Hands from Chaucer to Dryden* (London: Edward Arnold, 1977), 12.

Register at the first station was an activity of the Common Clerk (or his deputy) referred to in the surviving documents between 1527 and 1554, and his presence at the first station on Corpus Christi day, in all probability for the same purpose, can be traced as early as 1501. Current interpretation of this evidence is that keeping the Register involved the Common Clerk in sitting with extant manuscript open before him and checking what was spoken by the actors on the pageant wagons passing *seriatim* before him, against the text as set down in the book. Some of the marginal annotations added to the Register plainly derive from eyewitness observation of the plays in performance.[8] The first play is known to have been given at the first station annually at 4:30 A.M., in the early morning twilight, and the last of the fifty or so plays is unlikely to have moved off before early evening. To do his job properly the clerk must have needed artificial light and perhaps warmth, and the likelihood of burning torches or braziers nearby suggests one very obvious possible source for the quantities of soot which once evidently fell on the successively opened pages of the Register.

'Twere to consider too curiously to consider so? Perhaps. But the presence of what appears to be soot in the gutters of the York Register, though here but a speculative codicological observation, may yet have a place as another piece in the jigsaw of data concerning the processional staging of the cycle, which in turn bears directly upon the literary interpretation of the text. Why, for example, do many of the individual pageants begin with a greeting to the audience and end with a leave-taking? Alexandra Johnston has argued persuasively that the authors of the plays, conscious of the physical contingencies of processional presentation, made a virtue of the comings and goings of the wagons, invoking "the constant sense throughout each episode that the story of salvation history being unfolded before us consists of many journeys. . . . Salvation history is conceived as an unfolding procession. . . . This sense of travelling, of urgency, of leave-taking is built into the fabric of the play itself."[9] Several modern revivals have amongst other things sought to recreate something of this authentic sense of processional presentation, and literary and dramaturgic analysis of the plays must have constant reference to the fact that they "were as much custom-made for the method of presentation as vice-versa."[10] We are fortunate to have

---

[8] Beadle, *The York Plays*, 11-12, esp. 12 n. 9 for fuller treatments of the Common Clerk's "keeping of the Register."

[9] Alexandra F. Johnston, "The York Corpus Christi Play: A Dramatic Structure based on Performance Practice," in *The Theatre in the Middle Ages*, ed. H. Braet, J. Nowé, and G. Tournoy (Leuven: Leuven University Press, 1985), 362-73 (367).

[10] Richard Beadle and Pamela M. King, *York Mystery Plays: A Selection in Modern Spelling* (Oxford: Oxford University Press, 1984), xviii.

discovered evidence of how the town clerk watched them annually at the first station, pen in hand, the Register open before him, and quite possibly with the soot from burning torches falling on the open pages.

There are many specific instances where literary interpretation of the York plays, both severally or as a cycle, hinges upon information traditionally regarded as part of the domain of textual and related studies. Criticism of play XV, the Chandlers' pageant of the Shepherds, cannot be carried out satisfactorily on the basis of the 1885 edition, where Miss Toulmin Smith printed lines 51–57 (the moment of the appearance of the angel to the shepherds) as follows:

> iii Pas. Als lange as we haue herde-men bene,
>   And kepis þis catell in þis cloghe,
>   So selcouth a sight was neuere non sene.
> i Pas. We! no colle! nowe comes it newe i-nowe,
>   Þat mon we fynde.
>   Itt menes some meruayle vs emang,
>   Full hardely I you behete.[11]

Various emendations were proposed to "restore" an *ababcbc* rhyme scheme and bring this group of lines into conformity with the surrounding stanzas, and stage directions have been invented to give the apparently mute angel a part in the action. However, it was not noticed until recently that, in the Register, lines 51–55 appear at the foot of a verso and 56–57 at the head of a recto, and that an entire leaf is missing between them. Up to about sixty lines (or a third of the play as originally composed) have been lost, and comparison with complete shepherd plays extant in other cycles must serve to give some idea of what is missing.[12] The textual and interpretative problems raised by this lacuna are inseparable, and at present they remain very far from solution. The missing leaf was a singleton added to a regular quire, and both the reasons why it was required and the cause of its subsequent disappearance are obscure. There is internal and external evidence to suggest that the Chandlers' *Shepherds* was played "in tandem" at one station alongside its predecessor in the cycle, the Tilethatchers' *Nativity*, and moreover that both plays were revised during the lifetime of the cycle.[13] Extended consideration of the problem will involve a careful

---

[11] Toulmin Smith, *York Plays*, 120.

[12] Richard Beadle, "An Unnoticed Lacuna in the York Chandlers' Pageant," in *So Meny People, Longages and Tonges: Philological Essays in Scots and Medieval English Presented to Angus McIntosh*, ed. M. Benskin and M. L. Samuels (Edinburgh: privately published by the editors, 1981), 229-35.

[13] Beadle, *The York Plays*, 425-28. For the concept of performance of pageant plays "in tandem" (i.e., involving the use of two pageant wagons at one station), see

sifting and collating of codicological, textual, metrical, external documentary, and literary evidence, having regard to the analogues in English and French, and giving special attention to the early fifteenth-century Shrewsbury *Pastores* fragment, with its strong metrical and textual affinities with the York version.

Interpreting the nature of the York cycle text as a whole, and particularly its continuing development during the sixteenth century, demands equally close attention to matters of apparently peripheral, and in the following case, quite literally marginal detail. As Miss Toulmin Smith observed in 1885, the margins of the Register contain numerous annotations:

> Scattered through the volume are frequent small alterations or corrections, little nota and indications that *'hic caret'* or *'hic caret de novo facto,'* all of which are later than the text, most of them in a hand of the second half of the sixteenth century. In three places it is thus stated that the plays have been re-written, but no copy is registered,—'Doctor, this matter is newly mayde, wherof we haue no copy.'[14]

A number of significant interpretative points have come to hang on what Miss Toulmin Smith says here, and in what follows immediately in her introduction she goes on to assert that the "Doctor" apparently being addressed in three places by the annotator was Matthew Hutton, dean of York, who, from references in the civic archives in the late 1560s and 1570s, she believed was actively concerned in the revision of the plays to suit Protestant tastes. Recent research has revealed a rather different picture. "Doctor, this matter is newly mayde ..." is in fact a conflation of two separate later additions by the same hand on fol. 44r of the Register, against the beginning of the Spicers' pageant of the *Annunciation and Visitation*. Prior to the central episodes involving Gabriel, Mary, and Elizabeth this text has a prologue recounting the Old Testament prophecies of the Incarnation, for which the original compiler of the Register supplied no speaker's name, and Miss Toulmin Smith supplied the designation "Prologue" for the speaker of this part. The first addition by the later hand at the head of this speech consisted of the word "Doctour" [*sic* MS.] alone, and was clearly intended to rectify the original scribe's omission,[15] a fact confirmed by the summary description of the play in an early civic document, where the speaker of the prologue is

---

the note on the Masons' and Goldsmiths' text, 429–34.

[14] Toulmin Smith, *York Plays*, xv.

[15] Beadle, *The York Plays*, 110; Beadle and Meredith, *The York Play. A Facsimile*, xxxiv–xxxv.

identified as follows: "doctor declarans dicta prophetarum de nativitate Christi futura."[16] On another and subsequent occasion the same hand wrote partly next to and partly beneath the character-designation already supplied "this matter is | newly mayde wherof | we haue no coppy." Similar notes were later inserted against the Marshals' *Flight into Egypt* and the Barbers' *Baptism*, but contrary to the impression given in Miss Toulmin Smith's introductory remarks, neither is preceded by the appeal to the "Doctor" which she believed was intended at the beginning of the Spicers' pageant.[17] One unfortunate result of these misrepresentations of the manuscript evidence is the widespread notion, repeated in standard histories and studies of the early drama, that the later annotations in the Register relate to places in the text where doctrinal issues had attracted the attention of the reformers and alterations were made.[18] However, it is now known that the numerous notes of *hic caret*, *hic deficit*, and the like are largely the work of one hand, that of John Clerke, deputy to the Common Clerk of York in the mid-sixteenth century, and that many of the annotations must have been made whilst Clerke was engaged in "keeping the Register," as described above, that is, checking the manuscript against what was being spoken by the actors as each play came to the first station at Holy Trinity gates.[19]

It is becoming clear that the Register was often in Clerke's hands from at least the early 1540s to the late 1560s. He copied into it whole plays omitted by the original compiler, and his keeping of the Register during performance enabled him to annotate the volume in a variety of informative ways. He was able to note minor errors and omissions in the dialogue as originally set down when the text the actors were using was the same as what appeared in the Register, and when it was not he could note where plays had been revised wholly or in part. He also observed matters affecting the organization of the cycle, both externally and in performance, such as changes in the gild-ownership of plays, or episodes where plays originally recorded as separate had since been amalgamated, or were played "in tandem." He saw and recorded details of stage business and often specified cues for music, where the Register gave no

---

[16] Alexandra F. Johnston and Margaret Rogerson, eds., *Records of Early English Drama: York* (Toronto: University of Toronto Press, 1979), 1:18, in the *Ordo Paginarum* of 1415.

[17] Beadle, *The York Plays*, 161, 186; Beadle and Meredith, *The York Play. A Facsimile*, xxxvi.

[18] See, for example, Craig, *English Religious Drama*, 359; H. C. Gardiner, *Mysteries' End* (New Haven: Yale University Press, 1946), 74 n. 49; Petti, *English Literary Hands*, 12.

[19] P. Meredith, "John Clerke's Hand in the York Register," *Leeds Studies in English*, n.s., 12 (1981): 245–71.

indication. It is extraordinary that this eyewitness to the cycle during its last quarter-century of performance has taken so long to emerge from the shadows, and the assimilation of his evidence to the criticism of its literary and dramatic qualities is a matter of high importance.

Amongst the most significant things to emerge from an examination of Clerke's annotations, especially his "hic caret"-type notes and the places where he says that whole plays have been replaced, is the fact that the cycle was by his day very different in organization and content from what the compiler of the Register had set down some two generations previously. The evidence provided by Clerke's annotations suggests that the expression "the York cycle" is really no more than a convenient notional term to describe what was, in reality, a literary and dramatic entity capable of marked variation in form from year to year throughout its long performance history. Even the fairly full record of the text set down in the Register between 1463 and 1477 was in certain respects obsolete almost as soon as it was completed.[20]

It need hardly be said that this constitutes a situation impossibly resistant to the conventional objects of modern textual criticism, with its yearning towards definitive and unitary notions such as authorial intention, the authorized text of a work, and the act of publication. Here, even the primary document, the Register, bears witness to the existence of the text evolving over a lengthy time span, during which the processes of change were as unsystematic as they were continuous. A critical edition of the York plays, however, must needs be based on the Register, but as such is only capable of presenting a partial and fractional view of the reality of the cycle throughout its long history. The Register was in all probability compiled from copies of the individual pageants held by the various gilds, known locally as "originals," of which one late example has survived. In addition there would also have been separate parts written out for individual actors, known as "parcels," but no trace of such ephemera has survived at York.[21] Though doubtless very vulnerable to informal circumstances of transmission, if originals and parcels from York did exist they would naturally have at least equal status with

---

[20] For example, the compiler of the Register made no provision for a play on the subject of the Purification by leaving a gap in the appropriate place, between the Herod/Magi episode and the Flight into Egypt. It appears that the play was at that time defunct. Shortly afterwards, however, in 1477, it was decided to revive the Purification and to assign it to the Masons, whose registered play was a share in the Herod/Magi. A text for the Purification was not registered until 1567. See Beadle, *The York Plays*, 11, 434, and further references there.

[21] For an account of the various forms in which early play manuscripts are found, see P. Meredith, "Scribes, Texts and Performance," in *Aspects of Early English Drama*, ed. P. Neuss (Cambridge: D. S. Brewer, 1983), 13-29, esp. (for York) 15-17.

the Register in the establishment of a critical text. Supposing that as well as the Register one had every parcel and original used in relation to every performance of the York Corpus Christi cycle over anything up to two hundred years, and that all relevant archival material had also been preserved, then one could certainly begin to construct a historically truthful picture of "the York cycle." Such speculation may seem idle, but it at least brings home the gulf between what is possible on the basis of existing evidence and the ideal objects *in potentia* which are characteristically solicited by both textual and literary criticism.

At this point it may be worth offering for consideration two linked assumptions which might usefully govern discussions of the relationship between textual criticism and literary interpretation of the York cycle, and by extension other early dramatic texts—though as we shall see the second of these assumptions implies that in this field at least textual and literary studies are, for many important purposes, coextensive. First, I think it must be granted that textual criticism should here be taken in a wide sense, in that it cannot be divorced from detailed codicological understanding of the primary document (the Register) and extensive recourse to the use of external evidence drawn from contemporary civic records. This creates a situation which contrasts with the notion of textual criticism as traditionally practised in relation, for example, to classical and biblical materials, where the *donnée* is more likely to consist simply of diplomatic transcriptions from the primary sources, and editorial activity goes forward essentially in the spheres of *recensio*, *examinatio*, and *emendatio*.[22] In studying the text of the York cycle the manuscript should not be regarded simply as a source of readings, but needs to be perceived—because of the means whereby it was compiled and the uses to which it was subsequently put—as standing in a complex and dynamic relationship to the text which it contains. But if, in dealing with the early English drama, textual criticism must on the one hand arise out of detailed knowledge of the exact physical nature of the primary sources, then on the other it must also form part of the literary critic's approach. The second assumption, therefore, is that textual criticism in the more extended sense urged above is a continuing activity integral with rather than prior to the interpretation of the texts. The literary critic should be furnished with, and has a duty to be possessed of all the codicological, philological, and external documentary evidence

---

[22] An extended theoretical discussion of the relationship (or more precisely the current lack of it) between the traditional practice of textual criticism and the physical analysis of primary materials is given by G. Thomas Tanselle in "Classical, Biblical, and Medieval Textual Criticism and Modern Editing," *Studies in Bibliography* 36 (1983): 21-68, especially at 30-31 and 35 ff.

that might at any point bear upon the interpretative enterprise, which otherwise runs the risk of being inherently flawed.[23]

Both of these formulations will probably be considered, in different quarters, as as unpalatable as they are radical. But at the same time they should nevertheless be seen as an index of the distance that the study of the early drama has advanced in the last decade or so and of the scholarly sophistication of the developments which have taken place. Making a few honorable exceptions, Ian Lancashire in 1977 drew a generally lamentable picture of the editorial field in the early drama, giving a justifiable demonstration of the exiguous and often faulty foundations upon which an altogether more substantial edifice of literary criticism had been erected.[24] But in the same context he also suggested an agenda for scholarly activity aimed at putting all students in possession of a similar range of information to that urged as necessary above— facsimiles of the manuscripts, critical editions, authoritative collections of documentary material bearing upon the plays, and subsidiary facilities such as concordances. To these may be added the recent development of quasi-archaeological investigations of the surviving physical settings known to have been used for specific performances of medieval plays, notably at York.[25] The integrated study of this body of material ought to form the point of departure for critical commentary, analysis of dramaturgy, and the study of literary language, versification, sources, and authorship, areas where almost hopeless confusion and misapprehension have often hitherto prevailed. Lancashire's suggestion that these matters might best be pursued in the first instance through the further editing of groups of plays and sub-cycles (a medieval series parallel to the Arden Shakespeare or Revels Plays format) has recently been endorsed by Alexandra Johnston in a retrospect of what has been achieved in relation to the York and Chester cycles since Lancashire wrote.[26]

---

[23] The position taken here is related to that urged at more length recently by Jerome McGann, basically "that textual criticism is a pursuit incumbent upon anyone who works with and teaches literary products"; see "The Monks and the Giants: Textual and Bibliographical Studies and the Interpretation of Literary Texts," in *Textual Criticism and Literary Interpretation*, ed. Jerome J. McGann (Chicago: The University of Chicago Press, 1985), 180-99 (187).

[24] Ian Lancashire, "Medieval Drama," in *Editing Medieval Texts, English, French, and Latin, Written in England*, ed. A. G. Rigg (New York: Garland Publishing Inc., 1977), 58-85.

[25] See, for example, the following topograhical studies of the processional route through the streets of York, both of which have significant interpretative consequences in relation to the plays: Meg Twycross, " 'Places to Hear the Play': Pageant Stations at York, 1398-1572," *Records of Early English Drama: Newsletter*, 1978: 2, pp. 10-33; Eileen White, "Places for Hearing the Corpus Christi Play in York," *Medieval English Theatre* 9 (1987): 23-63.

[26] Alexandra F. Johnston, "The *York Cycle* and the *Chester Cycle*: What Do the

As far as the York cycle is concerned, Lancashire's agenda has now been largely fulfilled, and authoritative material on Chester is now also abundant. The documentary records for York were published in 1979, a critical edition of the register in 1982, with a facsimile of it in 1983, and a concordance based on the text of the 1982 critical edition was issued in 1986.[27] Taken together, these works provide for the first time an adequately comprehensive basis for the literary study of the cycle,[28] though as I have suggested above, the quality of such studies will frequently be conditioned by the critics' success in assimilating the lessons learned in the actual process of assembling the codicological, textual, and documentary evidence.

For example, much criticism of the Corpus Christi plays in general has taken a convenient and straightforward synchronic approach to the concept of the cycle, the coherence in relationship of the parts to one another, and the nature of the unity of the whole. Recent work on the York Register and related documents suggests that criticism in this area will henceforth have to be informed by locally contingent and therefore altogether less tidy considerations of a diachronic complexion. A significant point of departure for the critic should be the evidence suggesting that the full text of the York cycle was only brought together between the two covers of the Register at a date roughly halfway through its documented career in performance. There is general agreement that the Register was compiled at some time between 1463 and 1477, but there are bare documentary references to Corpus Christi pageants in York a century earlier (1376), and adequate grounds for assuming the existence of an extensive cycle as early as the 1390s. The well-known York civic document known as the *Ordo Paginarum* of 1415 describes in remarkable detail a cycle of Corpus Christi plays similar in a great many respects to what was registered half a century or so later, but it also reveals significant differences, and was itself heavily revised and altered over the years.[29] Critics interested in the cycle form should

---

Records Tell Us?" in *Editing Early English Drama: Special Problems and New Directions*, ed. A. F. Johnston (New York: AMS Press Inc., 1987), 121–43.

[27] See notes 3, 5, and 16 above, and G. B. Kinneavy, ed., *A Concordance to* The York Plays, with a Textual Introduction by Richard Beadle (New York and London: Garland Publishing Inc., 1986).

[28] Corrections to the existing body of evidence and new information are of course to be expected. The concordance mentioned in the previous note is based on a corrected form of the text, deriving from a fresh collation of the critical edition with the Register; see Beadle, in Kinneavy, *Concordance*, xix, xxxi–xxxii. For an example of new documentary material from York see Eileen White, "The Disappearance of the York Play Texts—New Evidence for the Creed Play," *Medieval English Theatre* 5 (1983): 103–9.

[29] The early history of the cycle and the *Ordo Paginarum* are surveyed in brief in

inspect the facsimile of the York Register carefully, because the signs are that the scribe who executed the work was compiling from diverse sources and not copying from another coucher book of the sort he himself had been commissioned to produce. His exemplars were in all likelihood the booklets containing the individual plays held by the gilds as prompt copies, the "originals" referred to above. The physical layout of the text in the early part of the Register strongly suggests that the scribe had no model from which to work when he began his compilation and that he was obliged to experiment with the *mise en page* before settling on a layout which suited him. Some of the gilds, for reasons unknown, did not submit their originals, and the compiler was further obliged to estimate the length of their plays and to leave gaps for filling in later if copy came to hand. In such cases he headed the otherwise blank leaves with the name of the defaulting gild, but in the event the texts were not forthcoming, though traces of the plays attributed to these gilds are elsewhere present in the documentary records, notably the *Ordo Paginarum*. Less accountably, the scribe of the Register also left two play-length runs of leaves without headings, as if he were vaguely aware of other material eligible for inclusion in the book, though not readily identifiable at the time of writing.

Looking at "the York cycle" in the physical form of the primary document containing it, one is inclined to conclude—and this is both critically and historically a ponderable point—that the Register of 1463-1477 had no predecessor intended as a complete record of the text. The fact that the scribe who aimed to compile the complete text had to start from scratch and was only called upon to do the work after the cycle had been in existence for some decades raises significant questions that must be pursued elsewhere. What *was* there before the Register? If for a great many years there were only the gilds' originals, then the cycle concept was only properly tangible on the occasion of the annual performance, and it only assumed the literary shape in which we are now able to read most of it during the third quarter of the fifteenth century. Under such circumstances it is interesting to speculate how the coherence and unity attributed to the York cycle were originally achieved and, indeed, maintained over the years as it was revised and reorganized.[30] Other questions suggest themselves. How, in the pre-Registration era, did the civic authorities exercise control over the content of what the gilds were

---

Beadle, *The York Plays*, 19-27.

[30] In this context, Alexandra Johnston, "The *York Cycle* and the *Chester Cycle*," 128, whilst noting the poetic diversity of the York plays, evinces a justifiable surprise at the existence of "the overarching patterns of imagery that echo from one episode to another."

playing? Why did the need arise for a complete record of the text when it did? The immediate answer to the last question probably lay in the lost York Chamberlains' records or the lost minute books (House Books) of the city council for the 1460s and 1470s. It is to be expected that the decision to compile the Register was taken at the highest level, judging by the official status it enjoyed in later life. But even if the specific minute which made the order had survived, one doubts whether it would have contained any detail as to the reasoning behind it. Further research into the surviving civic archives of the period, and not necessarily those bearing directly on the drama, is perhaps the likeliest source of ideas as to why the cycle as a whole was apparently first assembled in written form at such an advanced stage in its history.

One possible straw in the wind is the settling, during the 1470s, of a long-standing dispute concerning the scheduling of the Corpus Christi play and the Corpus Christi procession. The organization of the play was a civic responsibility, whereas the Corpus Christi procession, being a liturgical observance, was in the first instance a matter for the ecclesiastical authorities, though lay people of course took part in it. Traditionally, the procession had preceded the play along the usual route through the city as far as the Minster Gates, and the two distinct events had both been concentrated on Corpus Christi day. The crowding, and the holiday atmosphere which accompanied the performance of the play, became matters for dispute, and in 1426 there was a short-lived attempt to displace the play to the day following Corpus Christi. Evidence begins to accumulate from 1468, and may be said to be firm from 1476, that the play in the end displaced the ecclesiastical procession from the Thursday to the Friday.[31] How extraordinary a development this was demands liturgiological investigation, but the practical effect was to leave the civic authorities, the gilds, and their play as the great formal and public celebration of the feast of Corpus Christi for the remainder of its existence in York.

At much the same time as the play acquired Corpus Christ day exclusively to itself, the civic authorities established, perhaps for the first time, a formal vetting process for the constituent parts of the cycle. Again in 1476, in the first of the surviving House Books, the following minute was entered:

> Ordinacio pro Ludi Corporis christi. Also it is ordeined and stablished by þe ful consent and auctoritie of þe Counsaile aforesaide, þe day and yere within writen from þis day furth perpetually to be obserued and keped: That is to saie þat yerely in þe tyme of

---

[31] See Beadle, *The York Plays*, 28–29, and references there.

Lentyn there shall be called afore the Maire for þe tyme beyng iiij of þe moste connyng, discrete and able playeres within þis Citie to serche, here and examen all þe plaiers and plaies and pagentes thurghoute all þe artificeres belonging to Corpus Christi plaie; And all suche as þay shall fynde sufficiant in personne and connyng to þe honour of þe Citie and worship of þe saide craftes for to admitte and able, and all oþer insufficiant personnes either in connyng, voice or personne to discharge, ammove and avoide.[32]

This document institutes a formal examination of all the "plaiers" (an auditioning of the actors), the "plaies" (evidently scrutiny of the text or subject matter of individual episodes), and the "pagentes" (a check on the vehicles on which the performances were mounted). Judging by the tone and wording, this was an entirely new departure in 1476, and it is interesting that it should coincide with the cycle's new-found primacy on Corpus Christi day. The fact that officially appointed persons were evidently now being called upon to scrutinize the texts being used by the gilds may well have some bearing upon the decision to compile the Register, which, though it could have been taken as early as 1463, seems to fit well with the circumstances developing in the mid-1470s.

Further study of the social, economic, and religious conditions prevailing in York during the 1470s will probably shed more light on what was plainly a turning point in the history of the cycle in 1476: What, for example, was the temperature of relations between the civic and ecclesiastical authorities around this time? Who were the most prominent and active citizens of the day, and what were their interests? What precisely can be discovered about the economic circumstances of the gilds individually and the city as a whole, given the financial burden of mounting the cycle? These and other questions, together with the physical evidence of the Register, the critical text, and the related documentary material, must be brought to bear combinatively in any consideration of how the York cycle first assumed the literary form in which we now have it.

For critical purposes, the York Register should be understood to contain as complete a text as the civic authorities were able to establish at some time between 1463 and 1477, possibly, as I have suggested, nearer the latter date than the former. The manuscript contains gaps in the sequence of plays, some accountable on internal or external evidence and some not, and it passed into obsolescence as an accurate record of the cycle's content and organization almost as soon as the compiler

---

[32] After the transcription in Johnston and Rogerson, *REED: York*, 109, with punctuation added.

ceased work upon it. Though the Register doubtless reflected in most essentials the text and arrangements as current in the 1460s–1470s, details of the compiler's work also reveal traces of earlier, different forms of the cycle and its constituent parts. At the same time, annotations and additions by later hands provide a partial record of where, though seldom precisely how, the cycle and some of the individual plays changed during their subsequent career down to the late1560s.

Though differing forms of the York cycle are therefore known to have existed in the periods both prior to and after the compilation of the Register, the basic scope as it happened to be represented in that manuscript remained fairly stable. The literary form which it seems to have assumed for the first time in the Register consisted of a group of plays on Old Testament subjects, lesser cycles on subjects surrounding the Incarnation, Ministry, Passion, and Resurrection of Christ, a group of apocryphal episodes dealing with the later life of the Virgin, and a play of the Last Judgement. The most significant disruption of this structure was the suspension on doctrinal grounds of the Marian plays between 1548 and 1554 and their complete abandonment after 1561.[33]

It should also be borne in mind that the fairly complete written record of the cycle found in the Register would not necessarily have correlated directly and in all details with the actual text used in performance of the cycle in any given year. One document in particular suggests that performance practice may have been capable of varying quite radically from the registered form of the cycle, involving the use of only a selection of the notionally complete repertoire recorded in the manuscript. In 1535 preparations for the Corpus Christi play were interrupted when the governing body of the city decided at short notice that one of the other great civic plays should be given instead. In accordance with their usual practice, gilds proposing to bring forth Corpus Christi pageants had collected "pageant silver" to defray the costs of the the production, but the civic authorities requisitioned this money and diverted it to another purpose.[34] It seems natural to suspect that the list of gilds from whom money was thus collected was restricted to those whose play would have been seen if the performance of the Corpus Christi cycle had gone ahead in 1535, and that gilds from whom no contribution was received were apparently not planning to participate. If this was indeed the case, the performance text would not have included the following plays, all but two of which were represented in the Register:

---

[33] See Beadle, *The York Plays*, 27–28, and references there.
[34] See Beadle, *The York Plays*, 28, and references there.

Plasterers	Creation of the World
Shipwrights	Building of the Ark
Fishers and Mariners	Flood
Tilethatchers	Nativity
Chandlers	Shepherds
Masons	Purification
Vintners	Marriage at Cana*
Ironmongers	Jesus in the House of Simon the Leper*
Cooks and Waterleaders	Remorse of Judas
Shearmen	Road to Calvary
Winedrawers	Christ's Appearance to Mary Magdalene
Scriveners	Incredulity of Thomas
Hostelers	Coronation of the Virgin

(* = not in the Register)

A performance text lacking these episodes would constitute a cycle very different from the near-complete registered version upon which critical investigations are necessarily based. Especially notable are the omission of the episodes dealing with Noah and the Flood and the Nativity / Shepherds, two of the ten elements in the protocycle which V. A. Kolve, in an influential argument, indicated as part of the "essential structure" of the Corpus Christi cycles generally.[35]

Empirical knowledge concerning the York cycle and other forms of early English drama is both considerably more extensive and more exact than was the case a decade or so ago, but a condition of the new knowledge has emerged in the form of additional responsibilities for editor, critic, and teacher alike. Perhaps the primary responsibility is an acknowledgement of a situation where manuscripts, the texts they contain, and the external documents which refer to those texts stand in a complex, dynamic, and evolving relationship. Alexandra Johnston has recently warned of the dangers of allowing "what is one of the most remarkable forms of English literature . . . to languish in the prison of its own complexity."[36] I fully endorse the spirit of the warning, but find the metaphor perhaps unduly pessimistic. Given that the united object of all branches of scholarly and educational activity must naturally be truth, such complexity is, rather, a challenge. Interpretation of the early drama begins not with an edited text, but in the careful cultivation of acquaintance with the primary materials on which a text may be based and its apparatus assembled.

---

[35] V. A. Kolve, *The Play Called Corpus Christi* (Stanford: Stanford University Press, 1966), 51.

[36] Johnston, "The *York Cycle* and the *Chester Cycle*," 139.

Middle English Lyrics:
Texts and Interpretation

JULIA BOFFEY

Over the years Middle English lyrics have inspired a loosely assorted and eclectic body of textual scholarship and critical writing. Transmitted and recorded in a variety of more or less casual ways, they have survived in precarious and heterodox forms which offer little possibility of systematic textual study. A major critical obstacle is posed by the generic category which accommodates their diversity, for "lyric" has in a medieval context by common agreement come to designate any short poem, and shared themes or forms are sometimes hard to find in texts whose only real similarity is their brevity. While this phenomenon is general to all medieval European lyrics, specific difficulties are occasioned for the student of Middle English by the peculiar history of the currency of the language. Since the functions fulfilled by lyrics could for many years be served by poems in Latin and French, the numbers of surviving Middle English lyrics are comparatively small.[1] Consequently—with the exception of the carol—it is difficult to isolate related categories of short poem, and the study of Middle English lyrics often seems to take place in a kind of generic no man's land, where comparative exercises are either impossible or fruitless. For reasons of organizational convenience the poems are usually edited and studied in groups whose multifariousness (sometimes whose factitiousness) tends to discourage the forging of such methodologies as may illuminate more coherent bodies of writing. Few approaches even attempt any kind of comprehensiveness: a study of religious lyrics will bring into play standards far removed from those appropriate to a discussion of secular ones; concentration on groups of poems organized according to subject, author, form, or manuscript will realign the kaleidoscopic range of texts to generate still different editorial and critical imperatives. Perhaps the

---

[1] R. H. Robbins calculates that the extant material comprises a "couple of thousand shorter Middle English poems of all types"; *Secular Lyrics of the Fourteenth and Fifteenth Centuries*, ed. R. H. Robbins, 2d ed. (Oxford: Oxford University Press, 1955), xvii.

most distinctive feature of lyric scholarship is that it has no unassailably common core of concern.[2]

Despite the rebarbative nature of the material, however, much of it is now available in print, thanks to the monumental efforts of eighteenth- and nineteenth-century enthusiasts, and to the more systematic and editorially self-conscious exertions of the past few decades.[3] Some broad historical trends can be distinguished in the variegated body of critical writing. A concern with romantic "lyricism" and the personal voice, highlighting what was felt to be the freshness and simplicity of many of the poems, has given way to more deliberate formal analysis and a search for ironies of different kinds.[4] Devotees of New Criticism and stylistics appear to have found lyrics especially congenial, and their methods have been widely influential, informing the practice of many less avowedly partisan studies.[5] While the formulation of full-scale critical methodolo-

---

[2] Some of the problems are discussed by George Kane, in *Medieval Literature* (London: Methuen, 1951), 104–81, and "A Short Essay on the Medieval Secular Lyric," *Neuphilologische Mitteilungen* 73 (1972): 110–21.

[3] See, for example, *Reliquiae Antiquae*, ed. T. Wright and J. O. Halliwell, 2 vols. (London: William Pickering, 1841–43), and some of the early publications of the Percy Society and the Camden Society; *English Lyrics of the Thirteenth Century*, ed. C. Brown (Oxford: Oxford University Press, 1932); *Religious Lyrics of the Fourteenth Century*, ed. C. Brown, rev. G. V. Smithers (Oxford: Oxford University Press, 1952); *Religious Lyrics of the Fifteenth Century*, ed. C. Brown (Oxford: Oxford University Press, 1939); *The Early English Carols*, ed. R. L. Greene, 2d ed. (Oxford: Clarendon Press, 1977); Robbins, *Secular Lyrics*; *Historical Poems of the Fourteenth and Fifteenth Centuries*, ed. R. H. Robbins (New York: Columbia University Press, 1959). Study has been further facilitated by the *The Index of Middle English Verse*, ed. C. Brown and R. H. Robbins (New York: Columbia University Press, 1943), and the *Supplement to the Index of Middle English Verse*, ed. R. H. Robbins and J. L. Cutler (Lexington, KY: Kentucky University Press, 1965) [hereafter *IMEV* and *SIMEV*].

[4] Compare, for example, E. K. Chambers, "Some Aspects of Mediaeval Lyric," *Early English Lyrics*, ed. E. K. Chambers and F. Sidgwick (London: A. H. Bullen, 1907; repr. 1966), 259–96; the discussions of *Maiden in the mor lay* by D. W. Robertson Jr., "Historical Criticism," *English Institute Essays: 1950*, ed. A. S. Downer (New York: English Institute, 1951), 3–31, and E. T. Donaldson, "Patristic Exegesis in the Criticism of Medieval Literature: The Opposition," *Critical Approaches to Medieval Literature*, ed. Dorothy Bethurum (New York: Columbia University Press, 1960), 1–26; and Daniel J. Ransom, *Poets at Play: Irony and Parody in the Harley Lyrics* (Norman, OK: Pilgrim Books, 1985).

[5] See, for example, L. Spitzer, "*Explication du texte* Applied to Three Great Middle English Poems," *Archivum Linguisticum* 3 (1951): 1–22, 137–65 (countered by R. L. Greene's remarks in *A Selection of English Carols* [Oxford: Clarendon Press, 1962], 219, 253); E. Reiss, "A Critical Approach to the Middle English Lyric," *College English* 27 (1966): 373–79 (countered by R. H. Robbins, "A Highly Critical Approach to the Middle English Lyric," *College English* 30 [1968]: 74–75), and *The Art of the Middle English Lyric* (Athens, GA: University of Georgia Press, 1972); R. D. Stevick, "The Criticism of Middle English Lyrics," *Modern Philology* 64 (1966): 103–17. Less specifically theoretical, but benefiting from some of these approaches, are Stephen Manning, *Wisdom and Number* (Lincoln, NE: University of Nebraska Press, 1962);

gies has in general been left to continental scholars, whose more extensive primary materials have a greater theoretical tractability, attempts to incorporate and synthesize some of their perspectives have enlivened the Middle English field.[6]

An important and increasingly widespread approach views lyrics as part of a larger cultural context, as means by which a society could codify and direct some of its impulses. Its adoption involves discussion of the texts not in isolation, but in relation to other forms in the fields of literature and the arts; to social and historical circumstances; and to the expectations and responses of their readers.[7] Such investigations, in proceeding beyond formal or verbal analysis, have inevitably begun to undermine the primacy of the naked text. And although their occasionally stated claim to facilitate "objective" interpretation is in the end as historically determined as any other kind of approach, the sheer bulk of information which they uncover cannot but be valuable in aiding clearer-sighted and more sensitive evaluation of the material under scrutiny. The most successful of such studies are nonetheless those which take into account the processes by which lyrics were composed and recorded, and which remain alert to those sorts of textual difficulty which can be crucial to the success or failure of any reading. To recognize the possibility for textual instability in poems like these—whose

---

Raymond Oliver, *Poems Without Names* (Berkeley, CA: University of California Press, 1970); and Patrick S. Diehl, *The Medieval European Religious Lyric* (Berkeley, CA: University of California Press, 1985).

[6] Perhaps most influential has been Paul Zumthor, *Essai de poétique médiévale* (Paris: Editions du Seuil, 1972); see also his "Style and Expressive Register in Medieval Poetry," *Literary Style: A Symposium*, ed. Seymour Chatman (London and New York: Oxford University Press, 1971), 263-75. The range of current approaches to lyrics in different European vernaculars is illustrated in *The Interpretation of Medieval Lyric*, ed. W. H. T. Jackson (London: Macmillan, 1980), to which Jackson contributes a useful introduction, and (more generally) in *Lyric Poetry: Beyond New Criticism*, ed. Chaviva Hošek and Patricia Parker (Ithaca, NY, and London: Cornell University Press, 1985).

[7] The devotional and homiletic background has been explored by Rosemary Woolf, *English Religious Lyric in the Middle Ages* (Oxford: Clarendon Press, 1968); Douglas Gray, *Themes and Images in the Medieval Religious Lyric* (London: Routledge & Kegan Paul, 1972); and Siegfried Wenzel, *Preachers, Poets, and the Early English Lyric* (Princeton: Princeton University Press, 1986); music by J. E. Stevens, *Music and Poetry in the Early Tudor Court*, 2d ed. (Cambridge: Cambridge University Press, 1979) and *Words and Music in the Middle Ages: Song, Narrative, Dance and Drama, 1050-1350* (Cambridge: Cambridge University Press, 1986); social context by R. F. Green, *Poets and Princepleasers: Literature and the English Court in the Late Middle Ages* (Toronto: University of Toronto Press, 1980), and Glending Olson, "Towards a Poetics of the Late Medieval Court Lyric," *Vernacular Poetics in the Middle Ages*, ed. Lois Ebin, Studies in Medieval Culture, 16 (Kalamazoo, MI: Medieval Institute Publications, 1984), 227-48; reception (as evident from manuscript context) by Julia Boffey, *Manuscripts of English Courtly Love Lyrics in the Later Middle Ages* (Cambridge: D. S. Brewer, 1985).

genesis is usually obscure, whose circulation must often have been oral
rather than written, and whose uses extended far beyond the bounds of
"literature"–seems a virtual necessity.[8]

Detailed commentary on the textual history of a lyric, just like
discussion of its recreated "contexts," cannot of course be supplied in
any economical way within the confines of the conventional modern
printed edition. Facsimiles, textual notes, discussions of codicology, authorship, and cultural or historical relationships are bulky adjuncts to
what are by definition extremely short texts, and their inclusion can be
contemplated only in major scholarly undertakings.[9] In general, a
reader's access is still most conveniently to the text alone–a text which
has been comprehensively prepared for modern consumption. But we
are, I think, beginning to develop some bifocal perspective which
permits us simultaneously to enjoy the surface forms of these lyrics (with
their unanchored mysteriousness), and yet to recognize the potential
elucidation to be gained from further probing. The currents of contemporary criticism and editorial scholarship cannot but discourage faith in the
unassailable integrity of the texts in isolation. Recent studies of individual
poems have illustrated the radically divergent interpretations of particular
lyrics made by uninformed and informed critical understanding and have
speculated on the relative helpfulness or validity of the various kinds of
critical approach which may be taken.[10] More recently still, Siegfried
Wenzel has illustrated the anomalous status of many lyric texts by

---

[8] Some of the difficulties which a prospective lyric editor might encounter are
suggested by C. Frey, "Transcribing and Editing *Western Wind*," *Manuscripta* 23
(1979): 108–11, and Thomas G. Duncan, "The Text and Verse-Form of 'Adam Lay
I-Bowndyn,' " *Review of English Studies*, n.s., 38 (1987): 215–21. On the problems
posed by "open texts" see G. L. Bruns, "The Originality of Texts in a Manuscript
Culture," *Comparative Literature* 32 (1980): 113–29; David F. Hult, "Lancelot's Two
Steps," *Speculum* 61 (1986): 836–58; Dan Embree and Elizabeth Urquhart, "*The
Simonie*: The Case for a Parallel-Text Edition," in *Manuscripts and Texts: Editorial
Problems in Later Middle English Literature*, ed. D. A. Pearsall (Cambridge: D. S.
Brewer, 1987), 49–59, and Sharon L. Jansen Jaech, " 'The Marvels of Merlin' and the
Authority of Tradition," *Studies in Medieval and Renaissance History* 8 (1986): 35–
73. The broader theoretical implications of the "instability" of such texts are aired in
the essays collected in *Littérature* 41 (1981), and by Paul Zumthor, "The Text and the
Voice," *New Literary History* 16 (1984–85): 67–92.

[9] As, for instance, in Greene, *Carols*, or in *A Variorum Edition of The Works of
Geoffrey Chaucer: Volume V, The Minor Poems, Part One*, ed. G. B. Pace and Alfred
David (Norman, OK: Pilgrim Books, 1982).

[10] R. H. Robbins, "The Middle English Court Love Lyric," in *The Interpretation of
Medieval Lyric Poetry*, ed. Jackson, 205–32; J. A. Burrow, "Poems Without Contexts:
The Poems of Bodl. Rawl. D.913," *Essays in Criticism* 29 (1979): 6–32, and reprinted
in his *Essays on Middle English Literature* (Oxford: Oxford University Press, 1984),
1–26; Thomas C. Moser, Jr., " 'And I Mon Waxe Wod': The Middle English 'Foweles
in the Frith,' " *PMLA* 102 (1987): 326–37.

exposing the history of misapprehension concerning a poem conventionally known as "How Christ Shall Come," which turns out on detailed inspection to be *"not a lyrical 'poem' at all,* but the formal division of a Latin sermon put into English rhyming lines."[11] Thorough investigation of the textual relationships of any lyric, insofar as they can be recovered, is a demonstrably essential prelude to analysis of its matter and form.

In the face of these difficulties about the constitution of lyric texts, and about appropriate methods for assessing them, I should like to turn to some examples whose peculiar features perhaps prove more revealing than does a theoretical discussion. R. H. Robbins incorporates in the "courtly" section of his anthology of secular lyrics editions of two short and rather similar poems, entitled "A Pitiless Mistress" and "A Sovereign Mistress," which appear in print otherwise only in unannotated transcriptions published by Bernhard Fehr in 1901.[12] They survive in a unique copy in British Library, Sloane MS. 1212, copied onto the recto and verso of one of a few singly-mounted parchment leaves which now enclose a paper copy of Hoccleve's *Regement of Princes.*[13] I reproduce them here as diplomatically as possible, expanding contractions according to conventional practice, and keeping the layout and punctuation of the manuscript:

fol.1r   Mercy me graunt / off þat I me compleyne   1
        to ȝow my lifis soueraigne plesaunz
        and ese ȝoure seruaunt of the inportabyl peyne
        þat I suffre in ȝour obeysaunz
        and lete ȝoure femenygne nature dissolue þe cheyne 5
        þat me bonde : thorgh oo look of ȝoure eyen tweyne
        A þan to this fyne entende shal my compleynt
        syth ȝow like noȝt my peynys to remedy
        nor at my request to graunte me mercy
        In ȝoure seruyce to deye : and þat I neuere repent   10
        ffor ȝow to obeye and serue : entendith my besy cure
        tyl my lyfe relese his ryȝt : with outyn forfeture
        A lady nature : what meved the
        or passand beaute in hir face to steyne

[11] S. Wenzel, "Poets, Preachers, and the Plight of Literary Critics," *Speculum* 60 (1985): 343–63.
[12] Robbins, *Secular Lyrics,* 141–43; B. Fehr, "Weitere Beiträge zur englischen Lyrik," *Archiv* 107 (1901): 48–61.
[13] M. C. Seymour, "The Manuscripts of Hoccleve's *Regiment of Princes,*" *Transactions of the Edinburgh Bibliographical Society* 4 (1955–71; published 1974): 253–97 (274).

Whose herte deuoyde of mercy and pite   15
on me to rewe : euer*e* hath disdeyne

† ───

But sith hope hath ʒiuen me hardinesse
to lofe ʒow best . and neuer*e* to repent
Whilis þat I lyfe with al faythfulnesse
to drede and ser*ue* þough daunger*e* neu*er* assent   20
and here vp on knowith wele myn entent
how I haue vowed ffully in my mynde
to be ʒour*e* man . þough I no mercy fynde
ffor in myn herte enprentyd is so soore
ʒoure shappe ʒoure forme : and eke ʒour gentilnes 25
ʒoure port ʒoure chere ʒoure goodnes moore and more
ʒoure womanhode : and eke ʒoure semelynes
ʒoure trouthe ʒoure faith and eke ʒoure kendenes
with alle vertewis eche sette in his degre
ther is no lack : but onely off pite   30
ʒoure sad demenyng : off wil noʒt variabyl
off look benygne : and rote off al plesaunz
and exemplary to alle þat ben stabyl
discrete : prudent : off wisdom suffisaunz
mirour of witte : ground off gouernaunz   35
so þat I shortly shall noʒt fayne
Saue up on mercy I can noʒt compleyne

───────────────────────────────────────

fol. 1v   Myn wordly ioy vp on me rewe   1
And mercyles lete me noʒt pace
ffor life or deth I wyll ʒow sewe
þough I in ʒow neuer*e* fynde grace
lete pite : daunger*e* out off ʒour*e* herte race   5
Ande mercy cruelte remewe
o bountevous lady . femenygne off face
rewe on my peynys . þat am so trewe
And shal to ʒow be . whilys I haue space
and trewely ser*ue* and wilfully obeye   10
I am so bounde vndir ʒoure lace
I may : nor wil : þough þat I deye
ffrom ʒoure seruyse : myn herte reveye
myn soueraigne lady : myn her*tis* princesse
assure me mercy : þat mon*e* my woo redresse   15
Alle other vertewis weryn present in place
saue pite and mercy þei were behynde
Whan natur*e* endewed hem in ʒoure face
I suppose þei wern*e* out of mynde

It sittyth noȝt mercy be putte to flyȝt   20
Where pite haboundith I ȝow ensure
ffor mercy seweth pite be riȝt
the one with oute oþer may noȝt endure

† ────────────────────────────────────

Allas mis gouernaunce off ȝouthe and freelte
the whe[ch is] euere redy alle wisdom to refraigne   25
hath me [. . .]paired to my lady soueraigne
ȝet on my selfe haue I noo pite
With dedely wounde þus am I slayne
now swete flour of femynyte
Wheche may noþer fade nor stayne   30
fforgete me noȝt : to ȝoure mercy I me complayne

   In the context of their period, these lyrics lay little claim to great
originality or finesse of statement. The speaker of each reiterates pleas to
a lady for mercy; vows faithful service to her; praises her manifold
virtues; and reminds her that her lack of pity constitutes the only flaw in
her otherwise perfect character. The first poem varies the pattern by
reprimanding Nature for creating such a pitiless creature, stating that
hope offers some comfort, and cataloguing the lady's virtues at flamboy-
ant length. The second deviates from the common pattern only to voice
momentary and rather odd regret for the youthful folly of falling in love
in the first place. The material and its rhetorical organization, like much
of the vocabulary and phrasing, are the stuff of numerous post-Chau-
cerian love petitions. But the forms of the poems are more unusual. The
first concludes with three rhyme royal stanzas, but for its preceding
sixteen lines follows an irregular pattern of rhymes which does not
naturally divide into uniform stanzas at all (the central couplet in lines 8
and 9 marks the mid-point of what might have been intended as a
roughly symmetrical, "mirrored" rhyme sequence: *ababaacd/dceefafa*).
The second is organized in an idiosyncratic pattern which verges at times
on rhyme royal and ballade stanzas, but which (apart from lines 9 to 14)
does not quite match the pattern of either. Robbins, venturing the first
step towards interpretation of the pieces as he edited them, in fact set
them out in groups of lines which approximate as nearly as possible to
ballade and rhyme royal stanzas—the two forms which feature so
numerously elsewhere in this section of his anthology. Fehr remained
more faithful to the manuscript in transcribing the lines without a break.
   Scribal lines drawn between and within the poems, which go
unremarked by both editors, in fact seem to indicate some quite specific
points of division. These occur between lines 16 and 17 and at the end
of the material on fol. 1r, and between lines 23 and 24 on fol. 1v. Small
ink crosses draw further attention to the first and last of them. Problems
of interpretation therefore begin to arise from the mere physical layout

of these lines. Are we dealing with two poems, or with four? (It must be admitted that the discrete sections make as much sense apart as they do together—perhaps more.) Do we comment on the enhancement of conventional material by skilful and innovative adaptation of familiar stanza forms, or rather condemn clumsily mishandled platitudes? The contents of the rest of the manuscript are not helpful in presenting any relevant *usus scribendi*. Although both the parchment and paper sections appear to have been copied by the same one scribe, he supplied no further lines or crosses, using elsewhere only conventional marginal signs to indicate stanza divisions. What he understood by the portions of text which we categorize as lyrics is unfathomable.

Although the Sloane manuscript is the single witness to the existence of this material, the *Index of Middle English Verse* and its *Supplement* record connections which may be crucial to our comprehension of its form and nature. The portion of text between the first two scribal lines (fol. 1r, lines 17–37), as first noted by H. N. MacCracken, is identified as part of Lydgate's *Temple of Glass* (lines 736–54 and 762–63), and adapts sentiments uttered there in the third person by the lover about his lady ("Hir shap, hir fourme . . .") to suit the purposes of direct address ("ȝour shappe ȝoure forme . . .").[14] The textual integrity of what seemed to be two lyrics is further dented by this discovery. What speculation does it provoke? The easiest explanation of the appearance of the Lydgatian material here is that the anonymous author of the lines occupying the first part of the recto of the leaf knew that *The Temple of Glass* contained stanzas relevant to his purpose, and so appropriated them, after a sixteen-line introduction of his own composition. Another possibility, in view of the scribal line which divides the Lydgate stanzas from the rest of the piece, is that the extract was intended to be read independently, and was copied because of some whim of the scribe or manuscript-compiler. It may even represent a pragmatic and untaxing way of filling otherwise empty manuscript space. And we cannot discount two further hypotheses: that the lines represent an existing lyric which Lydgate used in *The Temple of Glass*, or that they survive as a trial run from some preliminary stage of the longer composition.

To compare the extract with complete texts of the *Temple* (which survives in seven fifteenth-century manuscripts)[15] is suggestive. None

---

[14] H. N. MacCracken, "Additional Light on *The Temple of Glass*," *PMLA* 23 (1908): 128–40. All line references to the poem are to the edition of J. Norton-Smith, *John Lydgate: Poems* (Oxford: Clarendon Press, 1966), 67–112, although *Lydgate's Temple of Glass*, ed. J. Schick, EETS, e.s. 60 (London: Oxford University Press, 1891), should be consulted for selective collation of the different MS readings.

[15] Several of these are available in facsimile: J. Norton-Smith, intro., *Bodleian MS Fairfax 16* (London: Scolar Press, 1979); M. B. Parkes and R. Beadle, intro., *Geoffrey*

of the variants is especially informative, but, significantly, in some of the manuscripts (Bodleian Library, Oxford, MSS Fairfax 16 and Bodley 638) the poem is set out in a manner which highlights its incorporation of inset lyric sections: rubrics draw attention to "Supplicacio mulieris amantis," "Supplicacio amantis," and so on. In another (Magdalene College, Cambridge, Pepys 2006) such annotation has been supplied by a later hand. Scribes and readers were obviously aware of the semi-lyric status of parts of the poem. In their introduction to the facsimile of Cambridge, University Library MS. Gg.4.27, Richard Beadle and Malcolm Parkes note occasional, more randomly positioned marginal annotation, and suggest that this may record the activities of readers who used the poem as quarry for verses of their own, perhaps like Sir John Paston, who may have gone to his copy when he needed some handy love poems.[16] In fact, several more of the manuscripts include marks of this kind, sometimes indicating obvious lyric sections, and sometimes more inexplicably placed. In three (Bodley 638, Tanner 346, and Pepys 2006) some marginal sign highlights the beginning of the portion of text extracted in Sloane 1212; in a fourth (Fairfax 16) its second stanza is singled out. In addition, part of the Sloane extract appears as a separate lyric in the mid-sixteenth-century Bannatyne manuscript (here, as in the *Temple*, as commentary on the lady, rather than direct address).[17] That this section enjoyed some potential independent status which made it recognizable to readers of certain *Temple of Glass* manuscripts is no doubt related to the history of its inclusion in MS. Sloane 1212, and may suggest that the *Temple* was itself either made up from or regarded as an agglomeration of separable units.

Questions now inevitably arise over the status of the lines which surround the extract in MS. Sloane 1212: perhaps they too duplicate material which appears elsewhere. MacCracken indeed described the first sixteen-line portion as "made up of phrases borrowed from Lydgate's *Temple of Glas*," characterizing the remainder as "two tries at a love-ballade, made of Lydgatian phrases." This view was promoted by the

---

Chaucer: Poetical Works. A Facsimile of Cambridge, University Library, MS Gg.4.27, 3 vols. (Cambridge: D. S. Brewer, 1979-80); P. R. Robinson, intro., *Bodleian MS Tanner 346* (Norman, OK, and Cambridge: Pilgrim Books, 1980), and *MS Bodley 638* (Norman, OK: Pilgrim Books, 1980); A. S. G. Edwards, intro., *MS Pepys 2006, Magdalene College, Cambridge* (Norman, OK: Pilgrim Books, 1985). Remaining MSS are BL Addit. 16165, Longleat 258, and BL Addit. 38179 (an eighteenth-century transcription of the text in Pepys 2006).

[16] Parkes and Beadle, *CUL MS Gg.4.27*, 3:65. For the Paston reference, see *The Paston Letters*, ed. J. Gairdner, intro. Roger Virgoe (Gloucester: Alan Sutton, 1986), no. 798, p. 135.

[17] Denton Fox and W. A. Ringler, intro., *The Bannatyne Manuscript: National Library of Scotland, Advocates' MS 1.1.6* (London: Scolar Press, 1980), fol. 220v.

Index and *Supplement*, along with Robbins's editions and the *Manual*,[18] and confirmed by Ethel Seaton, for whom the "first" poem was a "cento of lines from the *Temple* ingeniously fitted together," and the "second" was "at first sight original, but actually a mosaic of small borrowings."[19] Closer inspection forces some consideration of what exactly constitutes "borrowing." If—perhaps for reasons convenient for some other argument—one is determined to find Lydgatian influence in these lines, then a little evidence can be mustered: lines 1 and 6 on fol. 1r recall lines 334 and 574 of the *Temple*; the "second" piece partly echoes the poem known as *Supplicacio Amantis* which follows the *Temple* in two of its manuscripts.[20] But I can find little duplication of lines or substantial phrases, and to classify as "borrowing" the duplication of ideas and vocabulary which occur almost invariably in any fifteenth-century love poem of the Chaucerian tradition seems to stretch a point. Many of the ideas and phrases are not hard to locate elsewhere: pleas to the mistress for "mercy"; characterization of the lover as her "servant"; descriptions of his "peyn," "dedely wounde," "wo" and "besy cure"; of her as his "soueraigne" or "bounteuous lady," or "swete flour"; and of her "femenygne nature," "beaute," "daungere" and "disdeyne." Just how small is a "small borrowing"? As small as single words? It is reasonable enough to concede that portions of this material may well be adapted from as yet unidentified sources elsewhere, but it is hard to make a case for the *Temple* as the single, direct source of sections outside the obvious extract.

Whatever the exact nature of the allusions and echoes here, the obvious dependence of at least part of the material on *The Temple of Glass* turns it into something rather different from the tidied, independent poems which might catch the eye of the casual browser through Robbins's anthology. To what extent does the surrounding manuscript context illuminate our sense of its status? In its present position in MS. Sloane 1212 the single "lyric" leaf is immediately followed by another parchment leaf on which appear lines 98–162 of *The Temple of Glass* itself. The third leaf bears a fragment of Lydgate's *Defence of Holy Church* (lines 1–58), and the fourth a portion of the *Temple*-related *Supplicacio Amantis* (lines 439–505). At the end of the copy of Hoccleve's *Regement* which forms the main body of the manuscript come two further parchment singletons with a fragment of an otherwise

---

[18] MacCracken, "Additional Light," 128. A. Renoir and C. David Benson, "John Lydgate," in *A Manual of the Writings in Middle English, 1050–1500, volume 6*, ed. A. E. Hartung (New Haven: Archon Books, 1980), 2071–175 (2160).

[19] E. Seaton, *Sir Richard Roos, Lancastrian Poet* (London: Rupert Hart-Davis, 1961), 376.

[20] In CUL Gg.4.27 and BL Addit. 16165; ed. Schick, *The Temple of Glass*, 59–67.

unidentified verse epistle, and Lydgate's *Ballade in Commendation of Our Lady*. If the leaves from the outset formed part of one single manuscript—and the consistency of layout and scribal labor would seem to indicate that they did—then this was probably a Lydgate anthology of some fairly comprehensive kind. That the "borrowed" portion actually accompanied a copy of *The Temple of Glass* seems significant, if not in any sense explicable: if the compiler of the manuscript included it in the knowledge that it came from the longer poem, he must presumably have been untroubled by the fact that readers might locate what we would now castigate as an act of plagiarism. In practice, the contents of the rest of the manuscript offer a context in which open allusiveness, to texts both in the manuscript and outside it, seems entirely at home. The *Ballade in Commendation of Our Lady* incorporates a substantial quotation from *Troilus and Criseyde*,[21] while the fragmentary unidentified epistle recalls both *The Knight's Tale* (also echoed in the second "lyric" portion) and *The Temple of Glass*.[22] The *Supplicacio Amantis* illustrates the network of self-referentiality even more clearly, for it fulfils the promise made in the concluding section of the *Temple* (lines 1378–83) that its narrator will proceed to write something in praise of women, and contains a further invitation to prolong the process by promising in its own conclusion a forthcoming "balade" and "dyte" (not supplied in either of the fuller surviving texts). The "lyric" material may represent extensions of this process by which one poem answers, anticipates, or spawns another; it may even have been intended to constitute the promised *Supplicacio* accompaniments.

Establishing that this "lyric" material may not divide neatly into two poems; that a section of it duplicates a portion of a longer poem; and that it contributes in its single manuscript to a whole network of Chaucerian and Lydgatian allusion undermines significantly its status in a modern edition as two tidy texts: a responsible editor surely needs to call these features to our attention (as Robbins indeed signals the connection with *The Temple of Glass* in the notes at the end of his anthology), and a responsible critic would need to acknowledge them before proceeding with any more extensive interpretation. Other evidence in MS. Sloane 1212 leads us on from the forms and authorship of the texts to questions concerning their original functions and audience, matters crucial to the informed interpretation which historically minded critics would seek. As

---

[21] Lines 5–7 (in Norton-Smith, *Lydgate*, 25–29) echo *Troilus*, book 5, lines 1849–55. All references to Chaucer's works are to the text of *The Riverside Chaucer*, ed. L. D. Benson (Boston, MA.: Houghton Mifflin Co., 1987).

[22] It names one "Eger de ffememye," cf. *The Knight's Tale*, lines 866, 877; and associates "Pallas" and "Venus," cf. *Temple*, lines 247–49. On fol. 1v, line 21 appears to echo *The Knight's Tale*, line 3089.

MacCracken noted, the second of the lyrics is surrounded by marginal annotation comprised of family names and what appear to be family mottoes. Along the top of the leaf run "le Roy," "Vne sanz plus," "pur ma soueraigne," and "lucas." Down the left-hand margin are "ffortune allas"; "Scales" and "Ver elle tout bien"; "Morley" and "Ele est mon cure"; "ffelbrigge" and "sanz mwer"; "Normanvile" and "ʒouris for euer." Down the right-hand margin are "Mercy ma soueraigne joie," "ʒouris allone," "ʒow beste," "Noon bettir," "Soueraigne," "ʒouris for euir," "jeo nose dire," "humblement magre," "sanz mwer," and "lucas." Along the foot of the page are "ffortune humblement attendaunt *pur* ma soueraigne / Vne sanz plus *pur* le roy," "obeysaunz & plesaunz," and "jeo nose." Several more appear on the other parchment leaves: at the foot of fol. 3v "ʒourys allone wᵗ outyn otheris parte" and "mon cuer ma dite q*ue* serra ieoyous"; at the foot of fol. 4r "humblement magre" (again); at the foot of fol. 101r "Mercy ma soueraigne joie" and "fortune fa (?) mou lucas"; at the foot of fol. 101v a design incorporates the name "lucas" and the word "mercy."

The association of the phrases with personal names leads us into the murky depths of social history and postulates some set of circumstances for which circulation or performance of the texts must have been appropriate. Do the names indicate individual "lovers" involved in some social game such as the "Ragman's Roll" which can be reconstructed from a poem in Bodleian MS. Fairfax 16, in which female contestants apparently pulled strings to win themselves randomly assorted stanzas of insult or praise?[23] Documentary evidence can confirm for us that Scales, Felbrigg, and Morley families flourished in East Anglia throughout the fifteenth century and can indicate connections both between them and with members of a Lucas family (Normanviles are harder to incorporate within the circle, because geographically more remote, but they nonetheless existed at an appropriate time).[24] But the nature of the involvement of all these families in the copying and circulation of the "lyrics" in Sloane MS. 1212 can hardly be guessed at. The "Lucas" whose name features so prominently in all parts of the manuscript has often been taken to be its scribe, but even this identification is problematical: the inscription at the end of *The Regement of Princes* which has been read as "Lucas edi[t]ur" properly speaking reads more inscrutably as "lucas endure 27," and along with the other inscriptions which include

---

[23] A. Freudenberger, *Ragman Roll* (Erlangen: Friedrich-Alexanders-Universität, 1909), 2–17; see also Green, *Poets and Princepleasers*, 116 (Green here suggests that the Sloane 1212 material "may represent the product of some kind of literary game").

[24] See MacCracken, "Additional Light," and Boffey, *Manuscripts of Courtly Love Lyrics*, 120–21.

this name, could just as well refer to the manuscript's patron or destinataire.[25]

To extrapolate from the sketchy evidence of the manuscript and concoct theories about its original readership is to risk stumbling in the mist of error. Acting on the quite arbitrary suggestion of E. J. L. Scott that "Lucas" must have been the Thomas Lucas who was secretary to Jasper Tudor, duke of Bedford,[26] one might be tempted to identify some royal significance in phrases like "Vne sanz plus *pur* le roy"–Jasper Tudor was after all the son of Catherine of Valois (by her second marriage to Owen Tudor), and so half-brother of Henry VI and uncle of Henry VII–and the coincidence that Lucas appears also to have copied *The Regement of Princes* might be seen to confirm the connection. To reject it simply on the grounds that "le roy" was probably a suitable match for a "lady soueraigne" seems almost churlishly cynical.

The use to which MacCracken put his theories about the East Anglian provenance of the manuscript has its own allure. Convinced (reasonably enough) that some specific historical circumstance inspired the composition of *The Temple of Glass*, and seeking some significant local occasion for which it might have been appropriate, he chose the marriage of William Paston to Agnes Berry in 1420. Roughly summarized, his justification hinged on the duplication of the motto "de mieulx en mieulx," connected in later centuries with the Paston family, with the phrase which in some manuscripts of the *Temple* functions as the lady's motto;[27] and on the likelihood that the Pastons knew the Scales, Felbriggs, *et alia*, whose names appear in Sloane 1212. The impulse to comprehend the manuscript and to read *The Temple of Glass* in this way is one which we might well share–how else do the annotations, and the peculiar specificity of the lovers' predicament in Lydgate's poem, make sense?–but the detail of the case is less compelling. Quite apart from the unsuitability of the *Temple* as a marriage poem, its textual history, as definitively reconstructed by John Norton-Smith,[28] is exactly the reverse of MacCracken's hypothesis, with the fragmentary text in Sloane 1212 as one of the witnesses to its very earliest (possibly even unfinished) state, in which the lady's motto is "humblement magre" and not "de mieulx en mieulx."

---

[25] Of commentators on the MS, only Seaton (*Sir Richard Roos*, 376) notes the inscription verbatim, without attempting to amend it.

[26] E. J. L. Scott, *Index to the Sloane Manuscripts in the British Museum* (London: British Museum, 1904), 324.

[27] In Fairfax 16 and Bodley 638 "de mieulx en mieulx" appears at line 310; in Tanner 346 at lines 310 and 530.

[28] J. Norton-Smith, "Lydgate's Changes in *The Temple of Glass*," *Medium Aevum* 27 (1958): 167–72.

The significance of the mottoes which surround the texts is likely to be irrecoverable. They do not appear to be mottoes in the heraldic sense,[29] but rather to be elegant phrases of all-purpose applicability to anyone concerned with the cultivation of courtly feeling: statements of loyalty and devotion and pleas for mercy such as pepper almost any fifteenth-century love lyric (that they express religious devotion is a possibility, but I think a distant one). In practice, their selection and sometimes their phrasing seems to tie together the lyric fragments (and other contents of the manuscript) with *The Temple of Glass* again. All the mottoes fit the case of the petitioning lover who laments, pleads the extent of his service, and timorously begs for mercy, as do both the lover of the *Temple* and the speaker of the lyric pieces on fol. 1. The phrase "Humblement magre," here isolated as a motto, actually appears in the version of the *Temple* to which the longer fragment in MS. Sloane 1212 is affiliated, embroidered on the lady's clothes (line 310), and restated in her promise to execute Venus's command (line 530). In both the mottoes and the lyric petitions, the "soueraigne" lady is promised "obeysaunz" and "plesaunz" and their equivalents. Essentially the phrases act as synopses (sometimes elegantly translated) of the matter of both the independent lyric appeals and the similar stanzas which would have been inset in the missing portions of the text of the *Temple*. In the absence of more conclusive information about any personal application they may have had, and about the early use and circulation of MS. Sloane 1212, we can hazard few guesses at the social or biographical significance attached to the composition and preservation of any of the poems in the manuscript.

The deconstructive and intertextual tendencies by which this analysis has been overtaken are of practical as well as fashionable relevance to the field of lyrics. In formulating any kind of approach to these poems it is as well to be aware firstly that texts which appear to be independent lyrics may duplicate material which exists in some other manifestation, and secondly that they may act as appendages of some kind to more substantial works. Both of these features affect the extent to which lyrics can properly be edited or interpreted in isolation. Both also involve information which may not be easily perceived or available and whose existence may not even be suspected until prolonged research or some act of serendipity brings it to light. Just as the relationship of the synoptic "How Christ Shall Come" to the sermon which it summarizes passed unnoticed by those who ignored its manuscript surroundings,[30] so

---

[29] None of them appears in *Elvin's Handbook of Mottoes*, revised with supplement and index by R. Pinches (London: Heraldry Today, 1971).

[30] See above, n. 12.

identification of the numerous surviving extracts from *The Fall of Princes* which enjoy the status of independent lyrics has depended upon the degree of familiarity with Lydgate's works enjoyed by those encountering them: in BL MS. Arundel 26, a collection of historical material unlikely to be perused by a Lydgate scholar, such an extract is sandwiched between details of an expedition against the Turks and a description of the burial of the earl of Salisbury.[31]

The range of procedures by which these anomalous poems took shape poses interesting textual and interpretetive questions, and largely awaits investigation.[32] What kind of evidence, for instance, can help to determine whether "extract-in-context" preceded or followed the recording of "extract" alone? It is not inconceivable that some pieces which appear to be extracts might in fact have been working drafts, or merely existing independent poems which were put to enterprising new use. The evident currency of a song beginning "Princesse of youthe" and cited by Skelton in *The Garland of Laurel* and *The Bouge of Court* has persuaded commentators that the stanza of *The Temple of Glass* which it begins (at line 253) must have achieved independent status, but it is in fact impossible to determine whether the text originated with Lydgate, or whether he himself incorporated in his poem some existing formula.[33] The relationship between his *Pageant of Knowledge* and the two ballade stanzas ascribed in several manuscripts to "Halsham," which are incorporated within it, is similarly perplexing.[34] The role of manuscript *ordinatio* in inspiring extracts is also worthy of investigation. Texts which circulated in a relatively fixed form, and in which standardized rubrication signalled noteworthy or isolable sections (such as the summarizing envoys to *The Fall of Princes*), perhaps themselves stimulated the processes by which excerpts became current.

A significant factor here is of course the nature of some texts, both verse and prose, in which particular portions were expressly designed to

---

[31] For identification of this and other extracts, see A. S. G. Edwards, "Selections from *The Fall of Princes*: A Checklist," *Library*, 5th series, 26 (1971): 337-42. Comparable instances concerning other texts are noted by R. L. Greene, " 'The Port of Peace': Not Death but God," *MLN* 69 (1954): 307-9, and Curt F. Buhler, "A Middle-English Stanza on 'The Commonwealth and the Need for Wisdom,' " *English Language Notes* 2 (1964-65): 4-5.

[32] The fullest survey to date remains R. H. Robbins, "A New Lydgate Fragment," *English Language Notes* 5 (1967-68): 243-47.

[33] D. Fallows, "Words and Music in Two English Songs of the Mid-Fifteenth Century," *Early Music* 5 (1977): 38-43, and Boffey, *Manuscripts of Courtly Love Lyrics*, 98.

[34] Helen Pennock South, "The Question of Halsham," *PMLA* 50 (1935): 362-71, and A. S. G. Edwards, "Lydgate's *Tyed with a Line* and 'The Question of Halsham,' " *English Studies* 51 (1970): 527-29.

be extracted. Siegfried Wenzel has summarized the variously structural, reiterative, evidential, and mnemonic potential of lyrics incorporated in treatises like the *Fasciculus morum* and the *Speculum christiani*, of which several enjoyed a flourishing independent circulation.[35] Other semi-dramatic lyric portions of longer texts, particularly those conceived for devotional purposes, in which the speaker recreates and meditates upon some key scene, may also have served for independent retention as memory aids or focusing devices; the present-day currency of the *Coventry Carol*, lifted from its context in the Shearmen and Tailors' play, demonstrates the kind of use which such a lyric might fulfil.[36] Once again, the relative priority of lyric and lyric-in-context is usually obscure. Of the two carols in the Coventry pageant, for example, variants of the shepherds' song ("As I rode this enderes night . . .") survive in two other sources, indicating currency outside and perhaps previous to the dramatic context, whereas the mothers' lament, in R. L. Greene's words, "may have been written expressly for use in the shearmen and tailors' play,"[37] and only later (in this case, much later) have come into circulation outside it.

Isolable lyrics incorporated within longer secular narratives constitute a rather different category from those in instructive, hortatory, or devotional works, tending to be less specific in meaning, and embodying mnemonic functions only to the extent that they can suggest to the reader something of the experience of reading the longer text.[38] Part of the appeal of the first "song" to be highlighted in *Troilus and Criseyde*, which speculates inconclusively on the contradictory symptoms of lovesickness, was perhaps its all-purpose applicability: it is independently extant in several manuscripts.[39] But other equally generalizing and equally isolable love lyrics in this poem do not survive in extracted form—if anything, they seem rather to have been ignored in favor of less

---

[35] Siegfried Wenzel, *Verses in Sermons: "Fasciculus Morum" and its English Poems* (Cambridge, MA.: Medieval Academy of America, 1978).

[36] *Two Coventry Corpus Christi Plays*, ed. H. Craig, EETS, e.s. 87 (London: Oxford University Press, 1952), 32, and Greene, *Carols*, 59–60.

[37] Greene, *Carols*, 368.

[38] An exception might be made here for poems incorporated in historical texts, such as the virelai discussed by Robbins in "The Middle English Court Love Lyric," or verses preserved in chronicles such as those mentioned by V. J. Scattergood, *Politics and Poetry in the Fifteenth Century* (London: Blandford Press, 1971), 23.

[39] Book 1, lines 406 ff. *SIMEV* 1422.1, in CUL Gg.4.12, NLS Adv.1.1.6, and (unnoted in the *SIMEV* entry) in San Marino, Huntington Library EL 26.A.13; see R. Hanna III, "*The Index of Middle English Verse* and Huntington Library Collections: A Checklist of Addenda," *Proceedings of the Bibliographical Society of America* 74 (1980): 235–58. A copy apparently also existed in the burned BL Cotton Otho A.XVIII; see G. B. Pace, "Otho A.XVIII," *Speculum* 26 (1951): 306–16.

obviously discrete sections of the narrative, such as some of Pandarus's extended platitudes: gnomic and proverbial passages, like the stanza on the evils of prosperity in Walton's translation of Boethius, seem to have had an enduring appeal.[40] But to survey the nature of the extracts taken from *Troilus and Criseyde* is to gain an acute sense of the sheer variety of the processes at issue. Troilus's song and Pandarus's stanzas on the whetstone and on heedless speech survive as discrete "lyrics." But the last of these also appears in a composite poem where it is joined with stanzas from *The Fall of Princes*.[41] And in two manuscripts from the first half of the sixteenth century individual lines and groups of lines from different parts of the poem are combined to make ingenious new pieces.[42]

This brings us to the crucial question of consistency of meaning. Do these extracts, lifted from their context (and, conversely, do existing lyrics newly embedded in some kind of narrative framework) convey an identical sense in their different settings? In the case of the *Temple of Glass* extract in MS. Sloane 1212, the answer is probably "yes, approximately." Despite the changes of pronoun which mean that the lady is spoken to rather than of, the extract preserves the stanzas in the form of lover's petition. To cite a further Lydgatian example, the "Oracio ad prothomartyrem Albanum" incorporated in the Talbot Hours (Fitzwilliam Museum, Cambridge, MS. 40-1950), which constitutes a disordered version of the prayer which concludes Lydgate's *Saint Albon and Saint Amphibalus*, does not distort the sense of the text as it more frequently appears.[43] But the same is not quite true of another Lydgatian lyric in the Bannatyne manuscript, which is comprised of stanzas from *The Complaint of the Black Knight*: here, reordered and without their narrative framework, the stanzas are given a distinctly antifeminist thrust.[44] And as Lee Patterson has demonstrated, the use of Troilus's song in the *Disce mori*, while on one level preserving its sense and playing on its capacity to recall the larger narrative context, imposes a dogmatically restrictive interpretation.[45]

---

[40] *IMEV* and *SIMEV* 3327; book 1, lines 631-37 in Trinity College, Cambridge, R.3.20, and Huntington EL.26.A.13; book 3, lines 302-22 in TCC R.4.20. The Walton stanza is *IMEV* 2820; see note 31 for further extracts from this text.

[41] *IMEV* and *SIMEV* 3535, in CUL Ff.1.6.

[42] BL Addit. 17492, and Bodl. Rawl.c.813; *SIMEV* 848.5, 1418.5, 1926.5, 2577.5.

[43] *SIMEV* 2388.5; see *Saint Albon and Saint Amphibalus, by John Lydgate,* ed. George F. Reinecke (New York and London: Garland, 1985), xvi.

[44] *SIMEV* 3911.5.

[45] Lee W. Patterson, "Ambiguity and Interpretation: A Fifteenth-Century Reading of *Troilus and Criseyde*," *Speculum* 54 (1979): 297-330, and reprinted in his *Negotiating the Past: The Historical Understanding of Medieval Literature* (Madison, WI: University of Wisconsin Press, 1987), 115-53.

Thorough investigation of the network of relationships which enmesh lyrics surviving in both independent and intercalated versions (such as is currently under scrutiny in connection with the writings of some early French poets)[46] can have wider ramifications than its small-scale focus might suggest. It can for instance extend our understanding of contemporary notions of textual integrity and fixity of meaning, of authorial propriertorship, and of the processes of composition, while also shedding light on the reception and circulation of particular texts.[47] Similarly, the concentration of extracts and composite poems in particular manuscripts, or in connection with the works of particular authors, can be suggestive. The identification of these hybrid pieces is of course only one aspect of the exploration of the larger *terra incognita* of lyric sources: just as some Middle English lyrics are related to longer Middle English poems, so others are connected with sermons, or with parts of the liturgy, or (in a different kind of association) are translations from another language.[48] Obviously such connections impinge on the status of the poems as independent texts and ought properly to feature in any discussion of them. It is disquieting and yet also exhilarating to speculate on the number of lyrics whose textual and other relations remain concealed and perhaps rich in potential to modify if not completely undermine prevailing interpretations.

---

[46] See, for example, some of the essays in *Perspectives Médiévales* 3 (1977); and Sylvia Huot, *From Song to Book: The Poetics of Writing in Old French Lyric and Lyrical Narrative Poetry* (Ithaca, NY: Cornell University Press, 1987).

[47] As, for example, Fox and Ringler, *The Bannatyne MS*, and R. C. Harrier, "A Printed Source for the Devonshire Manuscript," *Review of English Studies*, n.s., 11 (1960): 54, discuss the circulation of Chaucerian poetry in the early sixteenth century.

[48] R. H. Robbins has calculated that approximately one-tenth of surviving lyrics represent translations from Latin: see "Middle English Versions of 'Christe qui lux es et dies,'" *Harvard Theological Review* 47 (1954): 55–63. On some of the relationships between English and French secular poems, see Boffey, "Richard Pynson's *Book of Fame* and *The Letter of Dido*," *Viator* 19 (1988): 339–53, and "French Lyrics and English Manuscripts: The Transmission of Some Poems in TCC MS R.3.20 and BL MS Harley 7333," *Text* 4 (1988): 135–46.

Ordinatio *in the Manuscripts of John Lydgate's* Lyf of Our Lady: Its Value for the Reader, Its Challenge for the Modern Editor

GEORGE R. KEISER

His devotion to the Virgin and his fascination with the legend and imagery associated with her inspired John Lydgate to endow *Lyf of Our Lady* with an intensity and fervor not always found in his writings. Those who have read widely, and with sympathy and sensitivity, in Lydgate's poetry agree that too little critical attention has been accorded to his remarkable achievement in what Derek Pearsall has rightly described as "an enormously prolonged Marian hymn, . . . an incomparable flowering of devotional poetry which stuns expectation."[1]

A measure of Lydgate's success is the fact that *Lyf of Our Lady* continued to stir the devotional spirits of pious readers for more than a century after its composition, apparently in the 1420s. Of the more than fifty manuscripts in which *Lyf of Our Lady* survives, two were copied circa 1600, and several others contain notes, including glosses of obsolete words, in sixteenth-century hands. In 1531 sufficient interest in the poem presumably encouraged Richard Redman to print an edition (STC 17025) based on Caxton's ?1483 printing (STC 17023). A sharp contrast to this early interest is its present neglect, for which Lydgate's reputation as a poet of dullness and prolixity must be partly responsible. Yet another possible explanation for this neglect is the fact that the only modern edition—that of J. A. Lauritis, R. A. Klinefelter, and V. F. Gallagher, published by Duquesne University in 1961—is a cumbersome volume, both in its bulk and in its presentation of the text.[2]

That this edition exists at all may be a reason for gratitude, but its inadequacies are so serious as to detract from the beauties of the poem and to inhibit the attempt to understand and appreciate its strong appeal for its early readers. Of these inadequacies the most readily apparent are misreadings of the manuscripts, inconsistent editorial practices, and

---

[1] *John Lydgate* (Charlottesville: University Press of Virginia, 1970), 285. Apparently much influenced by Pearsall is the discussion by Lois A. Ebin, *John Lydgate* (Boston: Twayne, 1985), 136–38.

[2] *Critical Edition of John Lydgate's Life of Our Lady*, Duquesne Studies, Philological Series 2 (Pittsburgh: Duquesne University; Louvain: E. Nauwelaerts, 1961); according to the preface (vii) the three editors did separate dissertations, under the direction of A. C. Baugh, before collaborating to produce the published edition.

misplaced line numbers. My concern here, however, is a different set of problems, specifically the editors' somewhat cavalier treatment of the apparatus accompanying the poem in their base-manuscript (and many others) and their failure to recognize its importance for the modern reader of the poem. To be completely fair: the Duquesne editors are not exceptional in this respect, for editors of Middle English writings quite often fail to recognize their responsibility at least to describe the nature of the apparatus found with the texts. Thus, the point I am raising in regard to editorial treatment of Lydgate's poem does have implications for editors of other Middle English writings. Deferring the consideration of the specific problems facing an editor of *Lyf of Our Lady* briefly in order to explore those wider implications will, I hope, provide a larger perspective from which to understand them.

I

Editorial treatment of *incipits*, *explicits*, rubrics, text-divisions, glosses, and other apparatus found in manuscripts is rarely explored at any length in editions of Middle English texts. Not surprisingly, given the lack of critical attention to such apparatus—either in editions or in general discussions of textual editions—and to the absence of established conventions for presenting it, editors respond (if at all) to the challenges that this apparatus offers on an *ad hoc* basis and hence with little consistency. The consequent lack of uniformity, it is true, does reflect conditions within the manuscripts (even within manuscripts of the same text), an additional fact that makes editorial decisions more difficult and perhaps encourages editors to assume, rightly in many cases, that the apparatus is largely or even wholly scribal. However, to proceed from that assumption to the conclusion that the apparatus has little or no relevance for an editor is unwise, even if the editor is not prepared to believe that a text is the creation of a community of readers.

To understand the relevance of apparatus for editors of Middle English texts, we must begin by considering the very important study, "The Influence of the Concepts of *Ordinatio* and *Compilatio* on the Development of the Book," in which M. B. Parkes examines the changes in the apparatus and hence of what he calls the *mise-en-page* in the codex from the twelfth century onwards.[3] The purpose of this apparatus, as he shows, was at first to provide access to the *auctoritates*, or inherited material, for the academic reader, but it soon came "to indicate and

---

[3] In *Medieval Learning and Literature: Essays Presented to R. W. Hunt*, ed. J. J. G. Alexander and M. T. Gibson (Oxford: Clarendon, 1976), 114–41.

emphasize the organization of the subject-matter inherent in the text, a groping towards the clearer definition of what came to be known as the *ordinatio*" (117). Refinement of the apparatus used for presenting texts was necessitated by the advances of thirteenth-century scholarship, particularly when "Vincent of Beauvais elevated *compilatio* into a literary form, [and] ... the age of the compiler had arrived" (128-29). The influence of that form on fourteenth-century English vernacular literature inevitably led to the use of apparatus for indicating *ordinatio* in such works as *The Canterbury Tales* and *Confessio Amantis*. Thus, as Parkes observes, "features of the apparatus can be found even in well-produced copies of vernacular texts" which do not presuppose an academic readership, "the most spectacular example" being the Ellesmere Manuscript (Huntington MS. El 26 C 9) of the *Canterbury Tales* (133-34).

Elsewhere Parkes and A. I. Doyle argue very persuasively that the *ordinatio* of the Ellesmere MS and its accompanying apparatus are scribal and represent a sophisticated interpretation of the *Canterbury Tales* "as a *compilatio* in that it emphasizes the role of the tales as repositories of *auctoritates–sententiae* and aphorisms on different topics which are indicated by the marginal headings."[4] However, we do have good reason to believe that in at least two instances the apparatus found in the Ellesmere and other *Canterbury Tales* manuscripts may have originated with Chaucer himself. Marginal glosses accompanying the *Man of Law's Tale* and the *Clerk's Tale* in numerous manuscripts, as Robert E. Lewis and Germaine Dempster (respectively) have shown, contain readings that must have appeared in the manuscript of the source used by Chaucer.[5] The likelihood that Chaucer himself prepared the glosses has received remarkably little notice in modern editions of the *Canterbury Tales*. In his notes to his edition Skeat included all the glosses that accompany the *Man of Law's Tale*, but only one of those found with the *Clerk's Tale*, while Manly and Rickert reproduced all of them in an appendix devoted to marginal glosses.[6] In his editions Robinson mentioned a few of the glosses almost incidentally; not until the appearance of the so-called

---

[4] "The Production of Copies of the *Canterbury Tales* and the *Confessio Amantis* in the Early Fifteenth Century," *Medieval Scribes, Manuscripts & Libraries: Essays Presented to N. R. Ker*, ed. M. B. Parkes and A. G. Watson (London: Scolar, 1978), 190.

[5] G. Dempster, "Chaucer's Manuscript of Petrarch's Version of the Griselda Story," *Modern Philology* 41 (1943): 6-16; R. E. Lewis, "Glosses to the *Man of Law's Tale* from Pope Innocent III's *De Miseria Humane Conditionis*," *Studies in Philology* 64 (1967): 1-16.

[6] W. W. Skeat, *The Works of Geoffrey Chaucer*, 2d ed. (Oxford: Clarendon, 1900), 5:145-65, 350; John M. Manly and Edith Rickert, *The Text of the Canterbury Tales* (Chicago: University of Chicago Press, 1940), 3:492-96, 505-8.

Robinson III,[7] where modern English translations of them are found in the notes, was their existence brought to the attention of those using what has been the standard edition of Chaucer's writings for generations of students. The effect of such silence is evident in a recent study by a distinguished Chaucerian, who calls attention to the presence of the *Man of Law's Tale* glosses, mostly passages from Innocent III's *De miseria*, in Paris Anglais MS. 39, describing them as "eight Latin proverbs" and attributing them to the Paris scribe ("a particularly sententious reader").[8] Modern interpreters are unlikely to reach a more accurate understanding of how these glosses, dutifully copied by generations of scribes, may have influenced early readers' perceptions of Chaucer's intentions and affected their reading of his writings if they must depend on modern editions that suppress information concerning their existence.

John Gower's *Confessio Amantis* and Thomas Hoccleve's *Regement of Princes* have fared better at the hands of past editors, who incorporate full sets of manuscript glosses, apparently of authorial origin in both instances, into their editions. George Macaulay included both the Latin verse summaries and the Latin prose glosses found in Bodleian MS. Fairfax 3, with a record of variants from other texts, while Frederick J. Furnivall scrupulously included the glosses found in British Library MS. Harley 4866, the basis for his edition of Hoccleve's poem, as well as variants from British Library MS. Royal 17.D.6. R. A. Yeager, Alastair Minnis, and Charles Runacres have explored the significance of the apparatus found with *Confessio*, especially the prose glosses, which Minnis describes as "a sporadic commentary which is probably the work of Gower himself."[9] The glosses that Hoccleve apparently provided for

---

[7] *The Riverside Chaucer*, gen. ed. Larry D. Benson (Boston: Houghton, 1987), 858–62, 880–84.

[8] Laura Kendrick, *Chaucerian Play: Comedy and Control in the Canterbury Tales* (Berkeley: University of California Press, 1988), 31. For discussion of the potential importance of glosses in the interpretation of the *Canterbury Tales* see Daniel S. Silvia, Jr., "Glosses to the *Canterbury Tales* from St. Jerome's *Epistola Adversus Jovinianum*," *Studies in Philology* 62 (1965): 28–39; Graham D. Caie, "The Significance of the Early Chaucer Manuscript Glosses (With Special Reference to the *Wife of Bath's Prologue*)," *Chaucer Review* 10 (1976): 350–60 and "The Significance of Marginal Glosses in the Earliest Manuscripts of *The Canterbury Tales*," in *Chaucer and Scriptural Tradition* (Ottawa: University of Ottawa Press, 1984), 75–88. For two more recent studies on Chaucer and glossing, the first putting forth evidence that Chaucer himself read with a careful eye to the glosses, the other concerning scribal glossing in Chaucer, see A. J. Minnis, " 'Glosynge is a Glorious Thyng': Chaucer at Work on the 'Boece,' " and T. W. Machan, "Glosses in the Manuscripts of Chaucer's 'Boece,' " in *The Medieval Boethius*, ed. A. J. Minnis (Cambridge: Brewer, 1987), 106–24 and 125–38, respectively.

[9] G. C. Macaulay, *The Complete Works of John Gower* (Oxford: Clarendon, 1901); F. J. Furnivall, *Hoccleve's Works*, vol 3, *The Regement of Princes*, EETS, e.s. 72 (London: Kegan Paul, 1897). For interpretations that make use of the glosses found in

Regement have received less attention; surprisingly, in recent studies neither of two current Hoccleve editors mentions their presence in the manuscripts.[10] Still, their existence is well enough known that acceleration of critical interest in Hoccleve will undoubtedly draw critical attention to them.

How profoundly *ordinatio* and the apparatus defining it can affect critical interpretation is nowhere more obvious than in the writings of Sir Thomas Malory. The well-known debate as to whether Malory wrote one book or eight, which raged for decades, was founded on Eugene Vinaver's argument concerning what the *incipits* and *explicits* in the Winchester MS. (BL Additional 59678) reveal about the design, structure, and intention of Malory's Arthuriad. The fervor of that debate has diminished in recent years, and a new generation of critics of Malory seems no longer to regard it as an overriding concern. Still, the editions that incorporate his argument assure that Vinaver's influence persists, even among those who regard the *Morte Darthure* as a unified work. Characteristically, modern critical studies continue to speak, usually without qualification, of Malory's text as consisting of the eight "books" of Vinaver's editions. Only in 1979, some thirty years after Vinaver published his first edition of the Winchester text, did anyone turn to the manuscript itself and re-evaluate his use of the textual evidence. Demonstrating that this use was somewhat selective and perhaps even arbitrary, Murray J. Evans has argued very forcefully that the evidence of the *incipits* and *explicits* in the Winchester volume actually supports a five-part structure at least as well as it supports the eight-book theory.[11]

A notably significant aspect of Evans's argument for five narrative units, rather than "books," is its recognition of the arrangement of tales within tales, a point that Vinaver came close to conceding when he subdivided his book 1, for example, into separate parts. If the Winchester MS.

Confessio, see R. F. Yeager, " 'Our Englisshe' and Everyone's Latin: The *Fasciculis Morum* and Gower's *Confessio Amantis*," *South Atlantic Bulletin* 46 (1981): 41–53; Alastair Minnis, " 'Moral Gower' and Medieval Literary Theory," in *Gower's* Confessio Amantis: *Responses and Reassessments*, ed. A. J. Minnis (Cambridge: Brewer, 1983), 50–78 (the quotation in my text appears on 53); Charles Runacres, "Art and Ethics in the 'Exempla' of 'Confessio Amantis,' " ibid., 107-34; A. J. Minnis and A. B. Scott with David Wallace, eds., *Medieval Literary Theory and Criticism, c. 1100–c. 1375* (Oxford: Clarendon, 1988), 379–80.

[10] M. C. Seymour, "The Manuscripts of Hoccleve's *Regiment of Princes*," *Transactions, Edinburgh Bibliographical Society* 4 (1974): 255–97; D. C. Greetham, "Normalisation of Accidentals in Middle English Texts: The Paradox of Thomas Hoccleve," *Studies in Bibliography* 38 (1985): 121–50.

[11] "The Explicits and Narrative Division in the Winchester MS: A Critique of Vinaver's Malory," *Philological Quarterly* 58 (1979): 263–81; see also Evans's "The Two Scribes in the Winchester MS: The Ninth *Explicit* and Malory's 'Hoole Book,' " *Manuscripta* 27 (1983): 38–44.

attests, as Evans argues, to a less rigid schema than Vinaver believed it did, then Caxton's division of the work into twenty-one books, separately chaptered, may be less a radical revision than an attempt to impose a more logical *ordinatio* on what he found in the copytext in order to make the parts of the work more easily accessible to readers. Indeed, it seems reasonable to assume that when he imposed a new *ordinatio* to make Malory's narrative more accessible Caxton thought of himself as extending the efforts of the Winchester scribes. Many of his chapter divisions occur at places already marked by a large capital in the manuscript,[12] and his chapter headings frequently make use of synopses of the action found in its margins. These seldom-mentioned features of the Winchester MS. imply a consciousness on the part of its scribes, not unlike that of Caxton himself, that fifteenth-century readers did not always read books from beginning to end; rather, having some familiarity with the whole compilation, they sought out specific narrative material within it to satisfy current interests.

Indeed, the sophistication of late medieval English readers, which influenced the presentation of vernacular texts by scribes and eventually printers, had been recognized and encouraged by some authors, it seems, from the mid-fourteenth century. Even before Chaucer asked those readers who might take offense at the Miller's bawdiness to "Turne over the leef and chese another tale" (A.3177), the compiler of *Contemplations of the Dread and Love of God* attempted to instruct less sophisticated readers in the use of a table of chapters:

> This shorte epystle that foloweth is dyuyded in sondry maters / & eche mater by hymselfe in sondry tytles, as this kalender sheweth. And þat thou mayst sone fynde what mater the pleaseth / these tytles ben here in the Epystle marked with dyuerse lettres in maner of a table.[13]

---

[12] F. J. Mather, "King Ponthus and the Fair Sidone," *PMLA* 12 (1897): xxvi, xxx–xxxii, calls attention to the fact that where the text of Bodleian MS. Digby 185 has illuminated capitals, the 1511 edition of *Ponthus* published by Wynkyn de Worde (STC 20108, apparently set from an earlier edition, STC 20107) supplies chapter headings. Though Mather does not do so, it is possible to infer that the headings were Wynkyn's addition, in response to current reading habits.

[13] Jeanne E. Krochalis, "*Contemplations of the Dread and Love of God*: Two Newly Identified Pennsylvania Manuscripts," *Library Chronicle* 42 (1977): 4. For very valuable comments on the consequences of lay literacy on the production of devotional writings and their transmission, see Vincent Gillespie, "*Lukynge in haly bukes*: Lectio in Some Late Medieval Spiritual Miscellanies," *Spätmittelalterliche Geistliche Literatur in der Nationalsprache*, ed. James Hogg, *Analecta Cartusiana* 106 (Salzburg: Universität Salzburg, 1984), 2:1–27; for more recent and very important remarks on the use of *ordinatio* in devotional books see Gillespie, "Vernacular Books of Religion," *Book Production and Publishing in Britain 1375–1475*, ed. Jeremy

Such a *tabula* as the author of *Contemplations* provides can be an essential element that enables a devout reader to make fuller use of devotional and meditative writings, especially when found in conjunction with such other apparatus as running titles, a hierarchy of decorated initials, headings within the text, and various marginal signifiers. One of the best-known examples of a text in which such a fully developed apparatus appears is Nicholas Love's *Myrrour of the Blessed Lyf of Jesu Christ*. This very popular translation of the pseudo-Bonaventuran *Meditationes vitae Christi*–apparently following a suggestion found in its original, that the reader divide the work and read a portion on each day of the week ("Do the same thing every week, so that these meditations become familiar to you")[14]–assigns each chapter to a particular day and canonical hour. To undertake the devotional exercises assigned a reader would almost certainly need the fully developed apparatus found in many of the manuscripts of *Myrrour*. Even if the devout reader did not observe the program of assigned meditations (and as we shall see later, Love himself did not expect the devout to be irrevocably committed to it), that reader would find the apparatus of considerable value in finding his or her way about this very lengthy work.

Though perhaps unlearned in Latin, the readers for whom Nicholas Love intended *Myrrour* had, as he recognized, a reasonably well-developed understanding of how to use books for their devotional exercises. For the purposes of this study it is necessary to recognize that these readers, who certainly included nobility and wealthy gentry,[15] cannot have been unlike those for whom Lydgate intended *Lyf of Our Lady*, which certainly drew upon the pseudo-Bonaventuran *Meditationes* and, very likely, Love's translation of it as well. An introductory rubric found in many of the extant manuscripts asserts that *Lyf of Our Lady* was written "at the excitacion and styryng of our worshipful prince Kyng harry the fifthe," and it is possible that this statement implies a royal suggestion, or even a commission, which remained unfulfilled at the time

---

Griffiths and Derek Pearsall (Cambridge: Cambridge University Press, 1989), 330–35.

[14] *Meditations on the Life of Christ*, trans. Isa Ragusa and ed. Isa Ragusa and Rosalie B. Green (Princeton: Princeton University Press, 1961), 388; V. Gillespie, "Vernacular Books of Religion," 61, observes that Love's structure is original to his version, but does not mention that the impetus for it comes from the Latin version. It might be noted that a late fourteenth-century translator of the Passion found in *Meditationes* seems to have assigned the reading of particular sections to the canonical hours, thus anticipating Love's structure; see *Privity of the Passioun*, ed C. Horstman, *Yorkshire Writers* (London: Swan Sonnenschein, 1895), 1:198–218.

[15] For a discussion of early owners of Love's treatise, see Elizabeth Salter, *Nicholas Love's "Myrrour of the Blessed Lyf of Jesu Christ," Analecta Cartusiana* 10 (Salzburg: Universität Salzburg, 1974), 16–18.

of Henry's death.[16] Such a commission fits very well with what we
know of Henry's intense devotionalism and with his commission of a
French translation of the *Meditationes.*[17]

If in the first instance Lydgate envisioned a courtly audience for *Lyf of
Our Lady*, as seems likely, then its earliest audience would consist of
readers familiar not only with Nicholas Love's *Myrrour*, but also with the
writings of Chaucer (as his praise of "my maister Chauser" in 2.1628
clearly indicates) and of Hoccleve—that is, readers familiar with works
frequently presented with a complex manuscript apparatus. Significant
corroboration for this would seem to be available from the evidence of
Huntington Library MS. HM 115, one of the earliest manuscripts in which
Lydgate's poem is preserved. Originally part of a volume dismembered in
the eighteenth century, HM 115 was copied by a hand that is also found
in a Carthusian volume mainly copied by the prolific scribe, Stephen
Doddesham, apparently during the second quarter of the fifteenth
century. Among the other contents of the original volume, all vernacular
prose works, are a life of St. Katherine of Alexander (now Harvard MS.
Richardson 44), a life of St. Jerome (St. John's, Cambridge, MS. 17) and
a double-life of St. John the Evangelist and St. John the Baptist (St. John's
MS. 16).[18] That *Lyf of Our Lady* is found in this company is significant,
first, because two of these prose lives have Lancastrian associations. A
colophon found with another text of the St. Katherine, that preserved in
Gonville and Caius MS. 390/160, asserts that it was "sent bi a discrete
maister vnto the Kyng henry v^{te}."[19] Further, the life of St. Jerome was
prepared, apparently by Symon Wynter, a Briggitine brother at Syon

---

[16] Pearsall, *John Lydgate*, 286, doubts the reliability of this rubric, observing that
"there is no internal reference, such as Lydgate invariably makes in a major poem, to
such patronage." Conceding the possibility of a royal suggestion which Henry V did
not live to see fulfilled, Pearsall prefers to believe that "it was written for reading aloud
to members of the monastic community," despite a lack of internal evidence for such
a conclusion.

[17] *Life of Our Lady*, 5–6; Jeanne E. Krochalis, "The Books and Reading of Henry
V and his Circle," *Chaucer Review* 23 (1988): 66.

[18] For current information concerning the relations of these manuscripts see *A
Handlist of Middle English in Harvard Manuscripts*, ed. Linda E. Voigts, *Harvard
Library Bulletin* 33 (1985): 64–66 and *Guide to Medieval and Renaissance
Manuscripts in the Huntington Library*, ed. C. W. Dutschke et al. (San Marino:
Huntington Library, 1989), 1:152–53. The generous source of this information is A. I.
Doyle of the Durham University Library. For the attribution of MS. Bodley 549 to
Doddesham, see Alan J. Fletcher, "The Manuscripts of John Mirk's *Manuale Sacerdo-
tia*," *Leeds Studies in English*, n.s., 19 (1988): 105–39.

[19] Auvo Kurvinen, "The Life of St. Catherine of Alexandria in Middle English Prose"
(Ph.D. diss, Oxford, 1960), 216; M. R. James, *A Descriptive Catalogue of the
Manuscripts in the Library of Gonville and Caius College* (Cambridge: Cambridge
University Press, 1908), 2:453. This text of *Lyf of Our Lady*, it must be conceded, does
not contain the colophon attributing its inspiration to Henry V.

Abbey, for Margaret Holand, duchess of Clarence, widow of Henry V's brother Thomas and, previously, of his father's half-brother, John Beaufort. Of further interest is the fact that each of the prose lives in the original volume has a program of chapter-divisions and that with each is a *tabula* in which chapter headings are set forth. As I have shown elsewhere, the program of chapter-divisions in the life of Jerome has particular importance because Symon Wynter used it in conjunction with an explanatory preface to achieve a re-interpretation of his principal source. Recommending to the duchess of Clarence and subsequent readers that they meditate on the chapters in an order different from that of the chronology, Symon Wynter devised a meditative scheme emphasizing the current devotional concern with penitential themes at the expense of the theological doctrine of Purgatory, which had been a principal concern of the author of the source a century earlier.[20]

Though it would appear that for the other prose saint's lives in the volume, *ordinatio* was of less significance than in Symon Wynter's life of Jerome, the apparatus used by scribes in presenting these texts must have had some part in the experience of their readers. Indeed, the variations within the volume are representative of a general condition, for the significance of *ordinatio* does vary from work to work. So that the modern student can reach any judgment of its significance in a particular work and make any use of it in interpreting the work, the editor of that work must acknowledge the presence of manuscript apparatus where it exists, describe it adequately, and offer some explanation of its origins. Of what value such information can be for the interpretation of Lydgate's *Lyf of Our Lady* is the subject of the next section of this study.

II

In his influential study of Lydgate, which is surely the most informed and sympathetic modern reading of that writer's *oeuvre*, Derek Pearsall praises *Lyf of Our Lady* in the language quoted at the beginning of this chapter. Yet it would be unfair to Pearsall not to notice that he does qualify his estimate of Lydgate's achievement in the poem, which he regards as a fragment and in the latter portions of which he finds "a decline in the impetus of the work." Indeed, Pearsall seems more than

---

[20] G. R. Keiser, "Patronage and Piety in Fifteenth-Century England: Margaret, Duchess of Clarence, Symon Wynter and Beinecke MS. 317," *Yale University Library Gazette* 60 (1985): 32–46 and "St. Jerome and the Brigittines: Visions of the Afterlife in Fifteenth-Century England," in *England in the Fifteenth Century*, ed. D. Williams (Woodbridge, Suffolk: Boydell, 1987), 143–52.

a little troubled by Lydgate's "throwing narrative overboard" rather than presenting a conventionally shaped "life" of the Virgin, and he describes *Lyf of Our Lady* as "a compendium of Mariolatry rather than a life, a loosely strung series of episodes which are used as the occasion for meditation, exposition, panegyric, doctrinal exegesis and lyrical rhapsody," compiled "for reading aloud to members of the monastic community."[21]

Pearsall's qualifications raise very important questions about the nature, purpose, and audience of the poem, for which we can, I believe, find answers by looking at the way in which fifteenth-century scribes presented *Lyf of Our Lady* for its readers. Though one of the most valuable aspects of Pearsall's methodology is his consideration of the Lydgate manuscripts for what they tell us about the tastes and interests of Lydgate's fifteenth-century readers, he makes surprisingly little use of the manuscripts in which *Lyf of Our Lady* is preserved. That lamentable oversight may have been encouraged by the lack of detailed information in the Duquesne edition concerning the manuscripts and about how the scribes use manuscript apparatus, specifically in the areas of book-and-chapter division and marginal glosses, which indicates how they understood the nature and purpose of the work and how they were directing its audience to use it.

The Duquesne editors present the text of *Lyf of Our Lady* as having a six-book structure, as well as a continuously numbered eighty-seven-chapter arrangement, never mentioning that these two programs of book-and chapter-divisions do not occur together in Durham MS. Cosin V.ii.16, their base-manuscript, nor for that matter in any other extant manuscript of the poem. Moreover, the editors do not clarify why the table of chapters preceding the poem in their edition has no reference to the book-structure or what, if any, relation the two programs have to each other. Their brief textual notes indicate that emendation of the chapter-numbering system has occurred in their base-text, but the editors offer no explanation and even add to the mystery by providing an unemended Roman numeral in the text in some instances, an emended Roman numeral in others, and in still others both a Roman numeral and an Arabic numeral. In the *tabula* preceding the text they provide only a consistent set of Roman numerals (running from j to lxxxvij), thereby rendering the table of little value.

---

[21] *John Lydgate*, 285–88. Pearsall also quotes from an unpublished 1957 University of London dissertation by Simon Quinlan (which I have not seen) a judgment of the work as "rather a discontinuous devotional progress from feast to feast, than a sequence of incidents with well-defined nexus" (285). By and large, Ebin (136–37) reiterates Pearsall's observations, with fewer qualifications.

In order to understand the conditions found in the edition, one needs to know that the mid-fifteenth-century scribe who copied the Cosin MS. followed a well-established practice of dividing *Lyf of Our Lady* into eighty-seven chapters; in this text, book-divisions are not marked, though somewhat larger initials appear at several places where, in other manuscripts, book-divisions occur. A later hand, apparently early in the sixteenth century, undertook to impose on the text a four-book structure, with the chapters in each book numbered separately—that is, a new *ordinatio*. In the table itself, the reviser rather crudely inserted a heading for the first book within the writing area and then used marginal notes to indicate the beginnings of the remaining three books. To establish a new system of numbering chapters independently within each of the four books, the reviser scraped away some portions of the chapter numbers; when that simple procedure did not suffice, he canceled the original numbers and replaced them. The reviser used the same techniques in the text itself and also added the revised chapter-numbers and, frequently, book-numbers as well, in the top margin.

It is unlikely that either of the two systems of book- and chapter-divisions found in the Durham MS. is authorial, for the manuscripts as a whole attest to several alternative systems, some of them obviously related, though the direction of the relation is not always clear. The eighty-seven-chapter arrangement, by far the most common, is found in sixteen manuscripts and in the two early printed editions. Three others have, respectively, seventy chapters, fifty-eight chapters, thirty-six chapters.[22] Still other manuscripts preserve a book-and-chapter program with separately numbered chapters within each book. Of these two are unclassifiable, one because it fragmentary, the other because the chapter numbering is very incomplete; of the rest three have a four-book arrangement while two have a six-book arrangement.[23]

---

[22] The manuscripts with the eighty-seven-chapter arrangement include BL Additional 19452*; BL Harley 629* (where scribal error in the table suggests that the work has 88 chapters); BL Harley 1304*; BL Harley 3952*; BL Harley 4011*; Bodl. Ashmole 39*; Bodl. Rawlinson poet. 140*; Trinity College, Cambridge, 602 (R.3.22)*; London, Society of Antiquaries 134*; National Library of Wales 21242C; Durham University, Cosin V.II.16; Longleat 15*; Rome, Venerable English College 1306; Yale University, Beinecke 218; University of Chicago 566*; University of Illinois 85. Interestingly, the manuscripts marked with an asterisk are part of textual group *d* in the stemma produced by the Duquesne editors (17). The unclassifiable manuscripts with smaller numbers of chapter-divisions include Cambridge University Library Mm.6.5 (70 chapters), BL Additional 19252 (58 chapters), Huntington HM 115 (36 chapters).

[23] The four-book arrangement appears in Hatton 73; Bodley 596; Lambeth 344; St. John's, Oxford, 56, and the six-book arrangement appears in Bodley 120 and Harley 4260. The fragmentary nature of University Library, Cambridge, Additional 3303, and the incomplete numbering in Corpus Christi, Oxford, 237, prevent us from knowing

Though we can reach only tentative conclusions about such matters, it seems likely that a program of book-divisions goes back to a very early stage of the textual tradition, indeed that it may be of authorial origin. Though only a few manuscripts preserve the six-book structure, many others preserve vestiges of it, in particular, initials and even border-pages at those places in the text where a new book should begin. In a few instances, where book-divisions are not otherwise observed in the manuscripts, a marginal notation such as "liber ij" may occur. Given the persistence of such vestiges throughout the long manuscript tradition and of Lydgate's tendency to arrange his other long works into books, it seems reasonable to suppose that a program of book-divisions in *Lyf of Our Lady* is of authorial origin.

Of the two alternative programs—the four-book and six-book structures—the latter seems more likely to have been Lydgate's own, in part because the manuscript evidence for it is more abundant than for a four-book division. The six-book arrangement also has, in some respects, a better logic governing it than the four-book arrangement. What may seem to argue against it is the fact that books 4, 5, and 6 consist, respectively, of 406, 700, and 462 lines and are thus disproportionately short in relation to Books 1, 2, and 3, which consist of 889, 1669, and 1806 lines, respectively. Concern with this apparent lack of proportion may explain a scribal decision to establish a four-book arrangement by collecting the latter three books of the six-book schema into a book 4 consisting of 1568 lines, just as it may have contributed to Pearsall's perception of "a decline in the impetus" in the latter portion of *Lyf of Our Lady*.[24] However, each of the final three books is a self-contained unit treating, respectively, the Circumcision, the Epiphany, and the Purification. It is not unreasonable to suppose that Lydgate's decision to treat each of these events as an independent unit (that is, in a separate book) reflects the influence of Nicholas Love's *Myrrour of the Blessed Lyf of Jesu Christ*, where each receives a separate chapter.

No such logic governs any of the alternative programs of chapter-

---

whether they had a four- or six-book structure. At present I can only speculate that the six-book and four-book structures are independent programs and that the six-book structure preceded and led to the eighty-seven-chapter arrangement. At a later time I hope to provide a much fuller account of the peculiarities and anomalies of *Lyf of Our Lady* manuscripts than is possible in this paper.

[24] It seems pertinent to consider that the 1568 lines of the final books, which describe the great events following from the Nativity, nearly match the 1669 lines of book 2, which describe the great event preceding the Nativity. This nice balance makes the Nativity the central event of the five described in the poem, and it remains central even if we simply consider the total number of lines in the poem, 5942, for the Nativity occurs at line 210 of book 3, the 2778th line of the whole poem, just a little less than 200 lines from the poem's numerical center.

divisions, in which chapter breaks sometimes disturb the context or even occur in mid-sentence, and it seems more likely that these programs are a scribal response, very early in the textual tradition, to a need they perceived for smaller divisions within *Lyf of Our Lady*. A survey of most of the extant manuscripts seems to indicate—most clearly from the quite different sets of chapter headings (where these exist) and from the chapter-divisions, or their absence, at several crucial places in the text— that the several alternative programs of chapter-divisions (or book-and-chapter divisions) can be classified into two general categories. As these two share a number of common points of breakage, there is a good possibility that they have a common origin—perhaps in a series of large initials found in a very early exemplar produced under Lydgate's supervision.

Whatever the origin of the programs of chapter-divisions, it is certainly significant that we find evidence of several, sometimes related, attempts to divide the work into chapters. Of at least equal significance is the great success, if manuscript witnesses are a reliable guide, of a program in which the chapter-divisions are most prolific—that is, the eighty-seven-chapter program found in sixteen manuscripts and the two early printed editions. The early readers of *Lyf of Our Lady*, it seems clear, did not come to it simply in search of yet another retelling of the familiar story of Mary's life (though they could certainly do so, if they wished). Rather, many of them came to it seeking direction for meditation on the events of that life and, emphatically, the meaning of those events. So that they might find that direction more easily the early scribes often provided not only programs of chapter-divisions, but a *tabula* containing chapter-headings and chapter-numbers at the beginning or end of the poem and within the text itself a hierarchy of scripts, red ink or decorative, colored paraphs for the better display of the chapter-headings or -numbers, as well as chapter-numbers in the top margins, to facilitate the task of finding the desired material.

That is to say, the early readers of *Lyf of Our Lady* brought to their reading of it that same spirit and attitude encouraged by Nicholas Love when he admitted that the program of reading particular passages of the *Myrrour* at particular canonical hours on particular days, which he seems to have elaborated in his translation, might not be entirely suitable:

> it semeth to me beste þat euery creature þat loueth to rede or here þis boke take the parties therof as semeth moost comfortable and sturinge to his deuocioun, som tyme oon & some tyme a-noþir, and specialy after þe tymes of þe yere and þe festes ordeined in holichirche, as þe maters be pertinent to hem (Bodleian MS. Rawlinson A.387b, f. 167b).

For sophisticated readers who would follow Nicholas Love's advice and wish to search for a favorite or, given the spiritual needs of the moment or the liturgical season, an appropriate portion of *Lyf of Our Lady* the elaborate apparatus often found in manuscripts of the work would undoubtedly be of immense value in expediting their search.[25]

Given that both *Lyf of Our Lady* and *Myrrour* are derived from *Meditationes vitae Christi* and that Lydgate probably knew and used *Myrrour*, as well as the fact that the English works were directed to similar audiences, it seems no coincidence that the manuscripts of these works sometimes bear close similarities. Notable in this regard is a group of related manuscripts of *Lyf of Our Lady* to which, in an important study of manuscript illustration, Kathleen Scott has recently called attention: Harley 629, Trinity 602 (R.3.22), and National Library of Wales 21242C, to which I would add Rawlinson poet. 140 (which contains no illustration and thus was not a part of Scott's study). All are fairly close in time (circa 1440–1470), and all are probably metropolitan or perhaps derived from a common metropolitan exemplar. All four preserve the eighty-seven-chapter arrangement and, significantly, they share many of the same features of presentation and layout.[26] In other words, in these four manuscripts we find virtually the same *ordinatio* and accompanying apparatus. While the members of this group stand apart because of the consistency that prevails among them, the other manuscripts with the eighty-seven-chapter arrangement are close enough in so many respects that we may reasonably suppose that this group represents the fullest development of a common standard to which the others in varying degrees conform. If so, then the possibility exists that use of apparatus in *Myrrour* manuscripts may have influenced the development of schema for the presentation and layout of the eighty-seven-chapter arrangement of *Lyf of Our Lady*.[27]

---

[25] Clear evidence of an interest in selected parts of *Lyf of Our Lady* is the preservation of the *Magnificat* in Gonville and Caius, Cambridge, MS. 230 and National Library of Scotland, MS. Advocates 1.1.6 and of the Debate of the Daughters of God in Huntington MS. HM 144.

[26] See Kathleen Scott, "*Caveat Lector*: Ownership and Standardization in the Illustration of Fifteenth-Century English Manuscripts," in *English Manuscript Studies 1100–1700*, ed. P. Beal and J. Griffiths (Oxford: Blackwell, 1989), 25–26. The stemma in the Duquesne edition (15) suggests that Rawlinson, Harley, and Trinity Manuscripts also share a close textual relation; the editors did not know of the existence of the manuscript now owned by the National Library of Wales. In private communication K. Scott informs me that she believes, from the illumination and hand, that Harley 629 and NLW 21242C are almost certainly metropolitan and that while the miniature and hand of Trinity 602 suggest a metropolitan origin, the use of marginal flourish to decorate the miniature makes it rather anomalous.

[27] It has been possible for me to examine only the *Myrrour* manuscripts in the collections of the Bodleian and British Libraries. Nevertheless, even among this limited number several—Arundel 112, Arundel 364, Royal 18.C.10, BL Additional 19901, Bodley

That possibility raises still further intriguing questions—specifically, whether the influence was general or specific and, in either case, whether the *ordinatio* and accompanying apparatus in this group of *Lyf of Our Lady* manuscripts may be of Carthusian origin. Though only circumstantial, sufficient evidence exists for us to conclude that there is at least a reasonable likelihood of such an origin. Of the *Myrrour* manuscripts that I have had an opportunity to examine, Rawlinson A.387b, one of those copied by the Carthusian scribe Stephen Doddesham, is without question very similar in presentation and layout to that found in the *Lyf of Our Lady* manuscripts mentioned above.[28] Among the other manuscripts Doddesham copied was Bodley 549; though primarily an anthology of Carthusian materials, this manuscript does contain a small collection of English verse offering expositions of such matters as the Pater Noster, the gifts of the Holy Ghost, and the sacraments. Appearing in mid-quire, where they interrupt a text in Doddesham's hand, these verses were copied by the scribe responsible for producing the now dismembered anthology of which Huntington MS. HM 115 was originally a part. In HM 115, which has a thirty-six-chapter arrangement, the presentation and layout are close enough to that found in the eighty-seven-chapter manuscripts to raise the possibility that the manuscript may represent an early stage in a process that led eventually to the latter.

More certain conclusions concerning the origin and development of the programs of chapter- and book-and-chapter arrangements for *Lyf of Our Lady* must await the outcome of research now in progress. Nevertheless, on the basis of the present evidence and of informed speculation based on it, we can with some confidence conclude that a knowledge of the several alternative forms of *ordinatio* and accompanying apparatus in the manuscripts of Lydgate's poem is invaluable for the interpretation of the poem. That the Duquesne editors provided so little information about it was a critical disservice to the poem, for an

---

207, Rawlinson A.387b, and Bodl e mus 35—are strikingly similar to the relevant texts of *Lyf of Our Lady*. Michael Sargent, who is engaged in producing an edition of *Myrrour*, has assured me, in private communication, that a consistent style of presentation prevails throughout the body of *Myrrour* manuscripts and seems to agree with the observation made long ago by A. I. Doyle that this consistency may "originate in the care and precision with which the author disposed his composition and its publication" (quoted from unpublished research by Doyle in Elizabeth Salter, *Nicholas Love's "Myrrour of the Blessed Lyf of Jesu Christ,"* 15).

[28] Michael Sargent assures me that the presentation of the text in Hunterian MS. T.3.15, also copied by Doddesham, is very similar to that in the Rawlinson MS. For a facsimile of a portion of fol. 15ᵛ of that text and further discussion of Doddesham's work see M. B. Parkes, *English Cursive Book Hands, 1200–1500* (Oxford: Clarendon, 1969), plate 6 (ii).

awareness of it and what it tells us about how its earliest readers read *Lyf of Our Lady* might have mitigated the harshness of such critical judgments as that of Walter Schirmer, who describes it as "not a vita and not an organic unity, . . . [but] rather a combination, swollen to epic proportions, of hymns, prayers, sermons, fragment of narrative, didactic digressions, and detailed descriptions."[29]

While Lydgate may have had no responsibility for the various programs of chapter-divisions, we have good reason to suppose that he wrote *Lyf of Our Lady* with an understanding that it would be used in conjunction with meditative exercises more often than simply read from beginning to end. The very features that incited Schirmer's unfavorable words constitute sufficient evidence for concluding that Lydgate intended to have the work serve the devotional needs of readers with varying tastes and interests. For example, when Lydgate incorporated material on the Holy Name of Jesus into his treatment of the Circumcision, he surely did so with full knowledge that the cult of the Holy Name was well established in England. Richard Rolle had promoted worship of the Holy Name early in the fourteenth century, and Walter Hilton added a chapter to *Scala perfectionis* in an apparent response to excesses of the cult. Richard Pfaff has observed that the cult "had a liturgical aspect from probably the middle of the fourteenth century"—specifically, a votive Mass, for which Robert Hallum, bishop of Salisbury, may have granted an indulgence in 1411 to its celebrants and sponsors.[30] Lydgate's awareness of the growing interest in this devotion surely accounts for the fact that his praise of the Holy Name, for which neither *Myrrour* nor *Meditationes vitae Christi* offers a precedent, runs to some 250 lines (5.155–406), while the Circumcision itself is treated in somewhat fewer lines (5.1–154).

Relevant to a consideration of the meditative reading of the poem is the citation of scriptural passages in the apparatus that often accompanies the texts of *Lyf of Our Lady*, concerning which the Duquesne edition creates a mistaken impression. Specifically, Lydgate may have composed his versions of the *Magnificat* (2.981–1060) and *Nunc dimittis* (6.141–72) with the idea that these could be used in conjunction

---

[29] *John Lydgate: A Study in the Culture of the Fifteenth Century*, trans. A. E. Keep (London: Methuen, 1952), 151.

[30] *New Liturgical Feasts in Later Medieval England* (Oxford: Clarendon, 1970), 62–63. For an English version of Richard Rolle's meditation on the Holy Name, translated from his commentary on the Psalter, see *English Prose Treatises of Richard Rolle de Hampole*, rev. ed., EETS, o.s. 20 (1921; repr. Millwood, NY: Kraus, 1974), 1–5; regarding Hilton's chapter, see Michael G. Sargent, "Walter Hilton's *Scale of Perfection*: The London Manuscript Group Reconsidered," *Medium Aevum* 52 (1983): 195–97.

with the performance of vespers and compline, respectively, where these canticles are part of the office. Here again it is necessary to recognize how the manuscript apparatus facilitates such readings: each canticle is given a separate chapter in the eighty-seven-chapter arrangement, and in most instances the original Latin verses, usually in red ink, are written at the head of the stanza devoted to its paraphrase and exposition or next to the stanza in the margin. In both instances the Duquesne edition gives only the forms of the scriptural passages found in the Cosin MS., which may have been abbreviated for a clerical readership, whose familiarity with these passages eliminated a need for more than the first few words as a reminder.[31]

At two other points in the text (3.610-37 and 1464-1582) such scriptural citations regularly appear in the manuscripts, apparently to encourage meditative reading, and once again the Duquesne editors allow their omission or abbreviation in the Cosin MS. to create a misleading impression for the student using their edition. In both instances these are well-known Old Testament passages universally accepted as prophecies of the birth of the Saviour. Very dramatically these glosses call attention to the central theme of prophecy and fulfillment. To overlook this theme is to miss an aspect of *Lyf of Our Lady* that must have given it an immense appeal in an age when scribes and readers seem never to have tired of the countless prognostications based on the significance of, say, thunder on Monday.[32] Indeed, the fascination with this theme inspired the production of such other works as the *The Mirour of Mans Saluacioune*, a poem also written "in Oure Laydis honour, hevenes souereyne qwene" (line 9) and also employing a program of chapter-divisions intended to facilitate meditative reading.[33] Perhaps it is not too extravagant to suggest that this same fascination inspired Malory, whose *Morte Darthure* is replete with prophecies and their fulfillment.

---

[31] In a working draft of his catalog of medieval manuscripts at Durham University A. I. Doyle speculates that the presence of an extract from the Martyrologium of Usuardus in Cosin MS. V.ii.16 may indicate a monastic origin.

[32] See, for example, *Religious Pieces in Prose and Verse*, rev. ed. EETS, o.s. 26 (1913; repr. New York: Greenwood, 1969), 114; *The Works of John Metham*, ed. Hardin Craig, EETS, o.s. 132 (1906; repr. Millwood, NY: Kraus, 1974), passim; and the numerous entries under "Prognostics," "Prophecies," and "Month" in Carleton Brown and R. H. Robbins, *The Index of Middle English Verse* (New York: Columbia University Press, 1943) and Robbins and J. L. Cutler, *Supplement to the Index of Middle English Verse* (Lexington: University of Kentucky Press, 1965).

[33] Ed. Avril Henry (Philadelphia: University of Pennsylvania Press, 1987); the editor emphasizes the value of *Mirour* for meditation and private prayer, as well as its typological mode which, she observes, offers a "vision of a timeless reality" (13). Kathleen Scott kindly called my attention to this remarkable work and its similarities to Lydgate's *Lyf of Our Lady*.

III

To argue, as I have, that early readers drew upon portions of *Lyf of Our Lady* in their devotional exercises is to present a partial picture and to risk overlooking the possibility that if taken as a whole, the poem does provide a satisfying emotional and aesthetic experience. It also overlooks the important possibility that a reader might return to it again and again in search of larger themes. To redress the balance of this argument, I shall bring this paper to its end with a few observations about unifying themes and the shape of the work through which they are expressed—that is, about virtues of *Lyf of Our Lady* that are too seldom acknowledged.

An attentive reader of Lydgate's poem will quickly notice that it is suffused with images of light. It opens with a description of the Virgin as

> the sterre, that bare the bright sonne
> Which holdyth the septre of Iuda in his hande
> Whose stremes been oute of Iesse ronne
> To shede hir lyght, bothe on see and lande
> Whose gladde beamys, without eclypsyng stonde
> Estwarde to vs, in the orient full shene
> With light of grace, to voiden all our tene (1.43-49).

It closes with a celebration and explication of Candlemas as a commemoration of the Purification of the Virgin, an event in which she participated—Lydgate repeatedly reminds us—not to be purified of sin, but to express her humility. In celebrating this event, Christians, humbly mindful of their exile, hold tapers which signify the light of grace that has shone upon humankind through the Virgin and that offers a hope of redemption, permitting them at the end of their exile to come

> ... where, as it is tolde,
> Seuene chaundeleris all of pure golde,
> Fresshely with light stand affore thy face (6.445-47).

Though it is predominant, the imagery of light, sun, and star is not the only unifying element in *Lyf of Our Lady*. From the Tree of Jesse, to which the first passage I quoted alludes, grow abundant images of flower and fruit, signifying that the Incarnation brings a new life to humankind through redemption and salvation. Fulfilling the prophecies and yearnings of the past, thereby bringing human history to a new fulfillment, this fructification of hope restores the dignity of mankind and points toward that final restoration in ultimate unity with God at the end of mankind's exile. The miraculous nature of this new flowering and fructification of hope is expressed through yet another structural device in the poem, the dual chronology of its composition and of its narrative. The inspiration for its composition awakens the poet's thoughtful heart from a "slombre of slouthe" during a long winter's night (1.2), and that composition occupies what seems more than a year's time. The composition of the account of Mary's early life and the Annunciation apparently having filled the intervening period, the poet begins his account of the Incarnation during early spring, "or maies dai the ferthe" (3.10), a time of rebirth signified by that event which, in deepest winter, brought the lifeless to life and which presumably inspired Lydgate to write his poem:

> And in Engady, the lusty large vynes,
> That tyme in the yere of her kynde bare,
> Gan floresshe and floure and in-stede of wynes
> With Riche Bavme her braunches to repayre (3.1247-49).

The chronologies of the narrative and of the composition of the poem converge as the poet completes his account of the Nativity in "this monyth that called is decembre" (3.1805) and writes of the Circumcision near to the beginning of January (4.1-7) and of Candlemas "In februarye —as phebus dothe retourne / The circuyt of his golden spere" (6.451-52), bringing an increase of light that heralds the coming of the fruitful spring and its promise of renewal and resurrection.

In that promise of fulfillment is the implication of a world governed by a providential order, in which the power of divine grace can lead even the sinful to salvation. While Lydgate's emphasis on chronology recognizes the impermanence of this temporal world, the poem as a whole assumes that a world so blessed and so governed does reflect the beauty and love of its Creator, and Lydgate attempts to express that beauty in a form that will move his readers to strive for ideals that will ennoble them and bring them closer to the source of all grace. With his expansive, vernacular account of the events of Mary's life preceding and immediately following the Nativity, Lydgate hoped to provide his countrymen and -women a work to which they might resort for meditation, brief or extensive, on its abundance of images and paradoxes, its exploration of sacred mysteries and favorite devotional subjects, and its presentation of an "ensaumple clere" of virtue and nobility in the life of the Virgin, who as meek maiden and mother of God, is means and mediatrix for human salvation or, as Lydgate describes her, "To lyfe eterne ... our lode sterre" (5.700).[34]

---

[34] Thanks to a fellowship awarded by the Bibliographical Society of America, I was able to undertake, in the summer of 1987, an examination of manuscripts of *Lyf of Our Lady* in British collections for a larger study, of which the present paper is an early product. I am deeply indebted to the Society for its support at an important stage in the research. Subsequently, the Bureau of General Research at Kansas State University provided some support, for which I am grateful. To Kathleen Scott and Michael Sargent, for their patient responses to my impatient requests, I am especially grateful.

Mouvance *and Interpretation in Late-Medieval Latin: The Legend of St. Cecilia in British Breviaries**

SHERRY L. REAMES

The concept of meaningful textual instability, or *mouvance*, has begun to have far-reaching effects on the way we approach medieval vernacular literature. In recent studies of Old French poems, to cite the most obvious examples, Paul Zumthor and others have dramatically revalued the work of the anonymous medieval performers and scribes who revised the texts, envisioning them as intelligent participants in an ongoing creative process, or even co-creators with the original authors.[1] Few critics of Middle English literature have wanted to shrink the distance between authors and revisers to quite this extent, but our theory of texts and textual criticism has clearly come a long way from the Lachmannian model, with its single-minded pursuit of the true, unique authorial version. Thus article after article in the present collection reminds us of the frequency with which Middle English works have actually survived in multiple manuscript traditions—or in a single tradition that is manifestly not that of the original author. Each case has its own peculiarities, and the task of the textual critic is to recognize and respond to them—not reducing the evidence to the form of a modern critical edition, as was so often done in the past, but trying to recover all the useful information that lies buried in what Derek Pearsall has called "the spoil heap of the manuscripts."[2]

To turn from Middle English to Latin texts at this juncture means confronting some new and rather enormous difficulties, but the comparisons are worth making because they can shed further light on the phenomenon of *mouvance* and its implications for the study of late-medieval literature.

---

* The research for this paper was made possible by grants from the American Council of Learned Societies and the Graduate School Research Committee of the University of Wisconsin, Madison.

[1] There is a helpful introductory article on this development in Old French studies by Mary B. Speer, "Wrestling with Change: Old French Textual Criticism and *Mouvance*," *Olifant* 7 (1980): 311–26.

[2] "Texts, Textual Criticism, and Fifteenth Century Manuscript Production," in *Fifteeth Century Studies*, ed. Robert F. Yeager (Hamden, CT: Archon Books, 1984), 121.

On the basis of current theory, one would expect medieval compilers and scribes to have been much more restrained about changing Latin works than they were about tinkering with vernacular ones. For one thing, the languages themselves were sharply differentiated in medieval people's experience. Insofar as Latin was the domain of learned literacy, with well-established rules and fixed standards of correctness, it cannot have invited scribal revision and updating as the relative orality and fluidity of the medieval vernaculars did.[3] In addition, Latin texts may have been protected against scribal change by the special prestige of Latin as the language of antiquity and *auctoritas*. Of course, not every Latin writer was considered an *auctor*—a term that united the shaping role of a father or creator with the lasting authority of a universally recognized model of beauty or wisdom, or both.[4] But medieval reverence for the *auctores* had created a strong tradition of closed recensions in Latin that had few if any parallels in the non-authorial languages.

Another important difference between vernacular texts and Latin ones is the relatively vast number of manuscripts one has to deal with in the latter case. As we shall see, the abundance of manuscript evidence in medieval Latin is a great advantage when one is studying a phenomenon like *mouvance*. But the sheer size and complexity of this manuscript tradition confront the researcher with a number of practical problems—not least among them, the question of where to start. Unlike Old French and Middle English, where most of the important manuscripts were identified and described many decades ago and the essential groundwork thus laid for systematic textual criticism, medieval Latin remains so inadequately studied and cataloged, especially for the period after 1200, that it is almost impossible to design a research project that would reach definitive conclusions.[5] One must simply start where one finds oneself and describe the part of the elephant that falls within one's reach.

---

[3] T. W. Machan gives a cogent introduction to these differences in the first section of "Editing, Orality, and Late Middle English Texts," forthcoming in *Vox Intexta: Orality and Textuality and the Middle Ages*, ed. Carol B. Pasternack and A. N. Doane (University of Wisconsin Press).

[4] On this concept see esp. A. J. Minnis, *Medieval Theory of Authorship: Scholastic Literary Attitudes in the Later Middle Ages* (London: Scolar, 1984).

[5] George Rigg surveys the current state of scholarship in the medieval Latin chapter of *Editing Medieval Texts: English, French, and Latin Written in England*, ed. A. G. Rigg (New York: Garland, 1977), 107-25. Especially interesting for our purposes is Rigg's brief closing discussion of "fluidity" in medieval Latin texts (121-22), where he cites a few examples (from satiric poetry) of texts deliberately revised by scribes.

I

The particular Latin texts I have been studying, originally for reasons that had nothing to do with the question of *mouvance*, are the accounts of St. Cecilia found in office lectionaries and breviaries—i.e., in books used for the liturgy of the daily office—written in the British Isles during the Middle English period.[6] In essence, office lectionaries consist of the lessons that were to be read at matins on each day of the church year—lessons derived from the Bible, a patristic homily, and/or a saint's legend, depending on the occasion—whereas breviaries give a synopsis of all the elements in the daily round of services. Besides the lessons, that is, a typical breviary would include at least the *incipits* of the psalms, antiphons, responsories, and prayers that made up the rest of the lengthy matins office, plus briefer listings for the other six offices celebrated each day. Since breviaries were supposed to bring together so much material and usually to be portable and relatively inexpensive as well, they tend to save space by using small writing and a variety of ingenious methods of abbreviation. Although they never quite replaced lectionaries, the surviving manuscripts suggest that they became much more widely used, especially in the fourteenth and fifteenth centuries.

There are small variations in the contents of lectionaries and breviaries that can be used, if one has sufficient expertise in such matters, to ascertain the date of a given manuscript, the particular rite or use it is following, and sometimes the exact church or monastery for which it was written. For the most part, however, these manuscripts are amazingly standardized both in general appearance and in content. Thus, for example, the matins office for a major feast is always divided into three parts, or nocturns, each of which contains a fixed number of antiphons followed by psalms and then a fixed number of lessons followed by responsories. And there is a good deal of unanimity even between different rites as to which texts are to be used on a given occasion. In the case of Cecilia, the two great English secular rites, those of Sarum and York, supplement their nine lessons with the same nine psalms and twenty-four of the same antiphons and responsories (out of twenty-seven). Monastic rites use twelve lessons instead of nine in their offices for Cecilia and other important saints, together with a larger number of psalms and choral texts;[7] but the English ones tend to include

---

[6] The most helpful general sources on such manuscripts are Pierre Salmon, *The Breviary through the Centuries*, trans. Sister David Mary (Collegeville, MN: Liturgical Press, 1962), and Andrew Hughes, *Medieval Manuscripts for Mass and Office* (Toronto: University of Toronto Press, 1982).

[7] In English monastic breviaries only the lessons of the first two nocturns (eight lessons in all) typically come from the legend of the saint, with the remaining ones

all the same psalms and a large proportion of the same antiphons and responsories that one finds in Sarum and York breviaries.

Within a given rite, of course, the standardization was more thorough-going yet. By the mid-thirteenth century or thereabouts, the liturgists of each rite had evidently compiled an official Ordinal or *Ordinarium* which prescribed not only the general design of each service, but most of the details as well—specifying, for example, just which psalms, prayers, antiphons, and responsories were to be used at each point in the service.[8] Hence all Sarum breviaries have exactly the same set of twenty-seven antiphons and responsories, in exactly the same order, in the matins office for a given saint. Breviaries of York and Hereford show equal unanimity in following their own, distinctive specifications on these matters. So do the breviaries used throughout Europe by the Dominicans, the Franciscans, and some other highly unified religious orders.[9]

In the midst of all this standardization, however, the Ordinals left one opening for variety and change in the matins office: they specified the number of lessons to be read from each kind of source, but not the length or exact content of those lessons.[10] Thus, for example, the monks at Norwich Cathedral Priory were given only a general indication of the source to use for their lessons on St. Cecilia: "Legantur duodecim lectiones de passione sacre virginis."[11] The Sarum Ordinal was a bit more specific, stipulating that the first lesson was to begin, "Beata Cecilia virgo clarissima";[12] presumably this directed readers to the *incipit* in the official Sarum lectionary. In each case there was a hint of flexibility

---

taken from an appropriate passage from the Gospels and a homily on that passage. Among the English secular rites, however, Hereford breviaries alone consistently follow the same pattern, reserving the third nocturn for biblical material. In York breviaries just one of the nine lessons (the seventh) tends to be reserved for such material, while Sarum breviaries most often take all nine lessons from saints' legends.

[8] Walter H. Frere gives a good introduction to Ordinals in *The Use of Sarum* (Cambridge: Cambridge University Press, 1898-1901), esp. 1:xi-xiii; 2:vii-ix. Some of the surviving English Ordinals have been published by the Henry Bradshaw Society, hereafter abbreviated as HBS.

[9] Except for its Cluniac and Cistercian branches, the Benedictine order was characterized by diversity, not unity, in liturgical matters. In fact, the surviving English Benedictine breviaries have so little in common that John B. Tolhurst's attempt at a critical edition gives a very misleading picture of all but one of the manuscripts (*The Monastic Breviary of Hyde Abbey, Winchester*, HBS 69, 70, 76, 78, 71, 80 [London, 1932-42]).

[10] As Salmon points out (66), this opening goes back to the Benedictine Rule, which specifies that the matins service can be abbreviated if necessary by cutting short the lessons and their responsories (but never the psalms).

[11] I quote from the *Customary of the Cathedral Priory Church of Norwich*, ed. Tolhurst (HBS 82), 193.

[12] I quote from Oxford, Corpus Christi College MS. 44, fol. 112v.

that might hardly have been noticed in another context. But the historical circumstances were such that these hints gave rise to an extraordinary amount of textual revision.

The most obvious impetus toward change in late-medieval breviaries was the need to shorten the lessons, and especially the hagiographical ones. Most traditional legends of the saints, including the *Passio S. Caeciliae*, were far too long to be read during a single service. Early in the Middle Ages, when relatively few saints were thus memorialized and most people celebrating the whole office were cloistered monks and nuns, it may have been possible to read a long legend in its entirety by just beginning it at matins on the saint's day and continuing it in the refectory, or at later services, or both. As the centuries passed, however, the calendar became much fuller and the obligation to celebrate the office became an increasingly heavy burden on groups of clergy— including canons regular, friars, ordinary parish priests, and even university students—who had other work to do.[13] Hence shortened lessons became more and more necessary.

Some official steps in this direction were taken in the thirteenth century, when the liturgists of many rites replaced their traditional collections of saints' legends with new lectionaries, compiled specifically for use at matins, that contained "choir legends"—short, self-standing lives of the saints that were readily divisible into the appropriate number of lessons.[14] The English liturgical manuscripts with which I am concerned belong in effect to the next textual generation after the new lectionaries. In most cases one can tell that their lessons on Cecilia are derived from one or another of the choir legends, rather than from their common source, the full-length *Passio S. Caeciliae*. But only a small fraction of the manuscripts I have examined (five out of forty-seven Sarum ones, to be exact, and two of ten York ones) give the relevant choir legend in its entirety.[15] The rest give sets of shorter lessons instead—a great deal shorter, in most cases.[15]

---

[13] On these developments, see Salmon, esp. 5-20 and 73-78.

[14] S. J. P. Van Dijk and Joan Hazelden Walker credit this innovation to the papal curia under Innocent III, whose liturgy was soon adopted, with revisions, by the Franciscans and a number of smaller communities (*The Origins of the Modern Roman Liturgy* [Westminster, MD: Newman Press, 1960], 126-28, 398-404).

[15] In the case of York breviaries, the standard choir legend from which the shorter versions derive is evidently the version preserved in Bodleian MS. Laud Misc. 84 and York Minster Library MS. Addit. 69. The text given in the *Breviarium ad usum insignis ecclesie Eboracensis*, ed. Stephen W. Lawley, Surtees Society 75 (Durham, 1882), based on a printed edition of 1493, is an abridgement.

For the Sarum choir legend, I have relied on the 1518 printed edition of the Sarum *Legenda* (STC 91). The *Breviarium ad usum insignis ecclesiae Sarum*, ed. Francis Procter and Christopher Wordsworth, vol. 3 (Cambridge: Cambridge University Press,

This tendency toward further and further abbreviation of the lessons is a striking and widespread phenomenon, the historical implications of which have been much debated. To some extent it presumably reflects actual attempts to shorten the solemn, public celebrations of matins that had to be held every night in monasteries, cathedrals, and other sizable churches. But two other factors appear to have been more important: the growing practice of private recitation, which permitted individuals to decide how long the lessons should be, and the sheerly practical consideration that breviaries could be made much smaller, more portable, and less expensive if the lessons were cut very short.[16]

For our purposes, what matters most about the lessons in breviaries is the range of attitudes they reflect toward a quasi-official Latin text. Basically there were four possibilities, one of which has already been suggested: the stability and completeness of the text might be prized to such an extent that the scribe would be obliged to faithfully reproduce every word of it. This is the kind of attitude that Chaucer vainly attempted to inculcate in his scribes, as Ralph Hanna has noted; and the figures given above confirm Hanna's conclusion that "the literary world of circa 1400 was not ready for authorship as Chaucer perceived it."[17] For the great majority of scribes who copied breviaries—or the book designers or prospective owners who gave them directions—such an ideal of textual perfection was obviously outweighed by more immediate, practical considerations. They chose to whittle down the lessons to a more convenient size. Interestingly enough, however, they went about this in several different ways—each reflecting a different attitude toward the text and the abbreviator's obligations to it.

The easiest way of turning long lessons into short ones—and the traditional way in liturgical manuscripts—was to give a few excerpts verbatim, omitting everything else. In its most common and old-fashioned form, this method just started at the beginning of the text, copied sequentially for the desired number of lines, and then stopped—often at a point that looks quite arbitrary to a modern observer. In the case of Cecilia's legend, for example, there are numerous breviaries whose last lesson ends somewhere in the middle of Cecilia's initial conversation with her bridegroom, Valerian.[18] One English monastic manuscript

---

1886), based on the 1531 edition, gives a text of the Cecilia legend that is virtually identical, and so do the following manuscripts: Cambridge, St. John's College, MS. F.24; Cambridge, Trinity College, MS. O.5.3; Cambridge University Library MS. Add. 3567 (just a fragment); National Library of Scotland, MS. Advocates 18.2.13B; and Lambeth Palace MS. 86.

[16] Salmon, esp. 73-74 and 78-80; Van Dijk and Walker, esp. 33, 40-44, 117-18.

[17] See above, 18.

[18] At least three British monastic manuscripts fit this description (British Library

never even gets to the conversation because it devotes the first four of its
eight lessons on Cecilia to long passages from the legend's prologue.[19]

What assumptions about the text underlie such reproductions of
fragmentary excerpts? On the one hand, the method suggests an
enormous respect for the exact readings of the source, since the scribe
copies them so faithfully, not presuming to skip or change a word.
Lessons were excerpted from the Bible in just the same way. But one
should not confuse this kind of faithfulness with the rarer and more
scholarly concern for accurate texts that gave rise to the production of
complete copies of the choir legend. Quite obviously, in fact, the
coherence of the text was not a very high priority for the people who
chose and copied these excerpts. Sometimes they seem to have treated
the text in a surprisingly automatic, unthinking way. In one fifteenth-
century Sarum breviary (to cite an extreme example) several of the
lessons on Cecilia are unintelligible as they stand because the copyist
started new lessons in the middle of syntactic units.[20] What tends to
stand out about such manuscripts is the neatness and symmetry of their
page design, to which the fragmentary excerpts contribute. Evidently
these lessons were designed less to be read than to mark the intervals
between antiphons and responsories in an aesthetically pleasing way.
Indeed, so long as the manuscripts came from traditional monastic
communities where the matins service was celebrated in choir, the
fragmentary lessons may just have been cues and their content incidental,
since the real lessons would be read aloud by the designated lector from
a different book. But as private celebrations of the office became more
common, especially among the secular clergy, the tradition of reducing
the lessons to fragmentary excerpts must have seemed less and less
functional. When attempts were finally made to reform the whole
breviary, beginning in the sixteenth century, one of the first priorities

---

MSS. Harley 4664 and Addit. 49363 and Oxford, University College MS. 101), and four
Sarum ones (British Library MS. Royal 2.A.xiv, Edinburgh University Library MS. 27,
Pierpont Morgan Library MS. M.329, and Southwark, Roman Catholic See, MS. 1).

[19] Fitzwilliam Museum MS. 369, from the Cluniac priory of Lewes.

[20] The manuscript in question is Royal 2.A.xiv. Its fifth lesson for Cecilia's office
ends, "venit nox," and the sixth begins with the rest of the thought: "In qua cum
suscepisset una cum sponso suo cubiculi secreta silentia. . . ." The eighth lesson ends
after a subordinate clause ("Si autem cognoverit quod me . . . custodias"), with the
main clause deferred to lesson nine. Here and throughout my quotations from the
manuscripts and early printed editions, I have distinguished the vowel *u* from the
consonant *v*, silently expanded the abbreviations, and modernized punctuation and
capitalization.

The same sort of automatic abbreviation was evidently practiced with regard to the
biblical lessons in many breviaries, which Salmon describes as having been reduced to
mere scraps, "meaningless remnants from the ancient *lectio continua*" rather than
deliberately selected pericopes capable of making sense by themselves (78, 84).

was to replace these fragments with lessons that made sense.[21] At least
in Britain, however, makers of secular breviaries in the late Middle Ages
had clearly begun to anticipate this reform. Among the sixty-five secular
British breviaries I have examined, in fact, only nine—seven Sarum
breviaries, one Augustinian lectionary, and one copy of the Hereford
breviary—confine their lessons on Cecilia to fragmentary excerpts from
the opening scenes.[22]

A more coherent method of abbreviating the lessons was for the
abbreviator to select the most essential parts, copying these and skipping
everything else. Although this sounds a good deal like the first method,
in practice it covers a broad range of approaches to the text. At the
conservative end, the abbreviator might simply choose a series of
verbatim excerpts that could stand on its own, conveying something like
the gist of the saint's legend. The only English manuscript I have seen
that follows this procedure is a Carmelite breviary, currently in the
Bodleian, that reproduces just three passages from Cecilia's legend: the
beginning, up to the saint's first words to Valerian (lessons 1-3); the last
two-thirds of this conversation (lessons 4-6); and the very end, recounting her execution, death, and burial (lessons 8-9).[23] Here the readings
of the original legend are clearly still being treated with great respect, but
the audience is not left hanging; in effect, the selections sum up the
legend by relating Cecilia's first important victory (the conversion of her
husband) and her final one.

A number of Continental breviaries and lectionaries also try to convey
the gist of the legend in a few large verbatim passages,[24] but the
surviving British manuscripts tend to use selective omissions in more
creative, ambitious ways. The closest approximation to the simple
Carmelite pattern occurs in a group of York breviaries that skip from
Valerian's conversation with the angel to Cecilia's execution with no
explanation or transition except "Post hec." Before and after this major
gap in the sense, however, these manuscripts use smaller omissions to
produce a highly abbreviated but continuous narrative. Regarding the
execution itself, for example, British Library MS. Additional 30511 and at

---

[21] See esp. Salmon's account of the breviary of Cardinal Quignonez, 83-88.

[22] The Sarum examples, besides those listed above in note 18, are British Library
MSS. Harley 587 and 1513 and Bodleian MS. Bodley 976. The Augustinian lectionary
is part of British Library MS. Addit. 35285; the Hereford breviary, the copy now at
Worcester Cathedral.

[23] I refer to University College MS. 9. Strangely enough, this manuscript omits the
heart of Cecilia's conversation with Valerian, her actual revelation about her angelic
protector.

[24] For example, in Bibliothèque Nationale MS. latin 3789, Vatican MS. Reg. 523, and
Archivio S. Pietro MS. A.3, also in the Vatican.

least three manuscripts in the York Minster Library have this account:

> Post hec iubet Almachius prefectus sanctam Ceciliam flammis balnearibus concremari et in ipsis decollari.[25]

> After this the prefect Almachius ordered Saint Cecilia to be burned in the heat of the baths and beheaded in the same place.

Here is the equivalent passage in the standard York choir legend, which had already been abridged in comparison with the *Passio S. Caeciliae*; the italics indicate the words and phrases that would be skipped in the more drastically abbreviated version quoted above:

> Post hec *autem* jubet Almachius sanctam Ceciliam *sibi presentari et in domo sua* flammeis balnearibus concremari. *Cumque fuisset in calore balnei inclusa die integro et nocte, quasi in loco frigido perstitit illibata. Quod cum audisset Almachius, jussit eam* in ipsis *balneis* decollari.[26]

> After this, moreover, the prefect Almachius ordered Saint Cecilia to be presented to him and to be burned in her house in the heat of the baths. But when she had been shut up for a whole day and night in the baths' heat, she remained as unharmed as if she were in a cool place. When Almachius heard this, he ordered her to be beheaded in those same baths.

The monastic breviary of Hyde Abbey, Winchester, contains a more sustained and impressive demonstration of abbreviation by selective omission. In this instance, virtually the whole Cecilia legend is retold in the space of eight moderate-sized lessons, thanks to dozens of well-chosen omissions. In its eighth and final lesson, in fact, this breviary manages to produce a fairly coherent abridgement of the whole second half of the legend by weaving together key sentences and phrases from five different parts of the *Passio*—Tiburce's baptism, Almachius's summons of Cecilia, one of his demands and one of her replies from her trial, the two attempted executions, and her burial:

> Tunc Valerianus perduxit fratrem suum ad papam Urbanum [small omission]. Qui gracias referens Deo, suscepit eum [small omission] et baptizavit [small omission], et infra septem dies Christo militem consecravit [omits eight chapters in which the *Passio* relates the

---

[25] I quote from the British Library manuscript. The York Minster manuscripts with this reading are XVI.O.23, Addit. 115, and Addit. 383.

[26] I quote from the Surtees Society edition, col. 711, which in this instance is no less complete than Laud Misc. 84 and York Minster Addit. 69; as usual, the modernized punctuation and capitalization are mine.

brothers' subsequent good deeds, arrest, trial, and execution]. Post hec Almachius prefectus [omits three chapters that give the events leading up to Cecilia's own trial] Ceciliam sibi iubet presentari, cui et dixit [omits the first one and a half chapters of the trial]: Elige tibi unum e duobus, aut sacrifica deis aut nega te Christianam esse [omits about six lines]. Quod si nolueris, dementie tue deputabis, quando sentencie subiacebis. Cecilia dixit: [omits a line] Noli me ut dementem arguere, set te ipsum qui me cogis Christum denegare [omits rest of the trial—some thirty lines]. Iratus Almachius iussit eam [small omission] in domo sua flammis balnearibus concremari. Cumque fuisset in calore balnei inclusa, et subter incendia lignorum nimia pabula ministrarent, die integro et nocte [small omission] illibata permansit, ita ut nulla pars membrorum eius saltem sudoris signo lassaretur. Quod cum audisset Almachius, iussit eam in ipsis balneis decollari [omits nine lines]. Cuius corpus sanctus Urbanus auferrens, cum diaconibus nocte sepelivit inter corpora martirum.[27]

Then Valerian took his brother to Pope Urban, who received him with thanks to God and baptized him and after seven days made him a knight for Christ. After this the prefect Almachius ordered Cecilia to be presented to him and said to her, "Choose one of these two things: either sacrifice to the gods or deny that you are a Christian. If you have not consented, you will blame it on your insanity when you undergo the sentence." Cecilia said, "Do not wish to prove that I am insane, but you yourself, who urge me to deny Christ." Enraged, Almachius ordered her to be burned in her house in the heat of the baths. But when she had been shut up in the baths' heat, and they had fed the fires underneath with great quantities of firewood, for a whole day and night she remained so unharmed that no part of her body gave up even a drop of sweat. When Almachius heard this, he ordered her to be beheaded in those same baths. Holy Urban removed her body and with his deacons buried it at night among the martyrs.

Although the Hyde Abbey breviary still confines itself to the words of the original legend, it represents a clear transition from respectful copying to the third method of abbreviation, which pragmatically edited the text and even rewrote it, when necessary, to make the narrative both brief and intelligible. In this method the scribe's obligation to conserve

---

[27] I quote from Tolhurst's edition, volume 4 (HBS 78). The comparisons with the *Passio* are based on Hippolyte Delehaye's convenient edition, published in *Étude sur le légendier romain* (Brussels: Société des Bollandistes, 1936), 194–220.

the text is effectively reinterpreted as an obligation to boil it down to its essentials, for the sake of busy contemporary readers. Today we would call the result an abstract or a summary. For some reason, this method seems not to have been used very widely in breviaries written on the Continent. Among thirty-seven French secular breviaries I have seen with abbreviated readings for Cecilia, for example, only four give abstracts or summaries of the legend; fully twenty-four, or about 65 percent, take the most conservative approach instead, just giving verbatim excerpts from the beginning. In much smaller samples of secular breviaries written in Italy and the Netherlands, the proportions are similar: one summary among eleven manuscripts and one summary among eight, respectively, with verbatim excerpts being used about six times as often.[28] In Britain, on the other hand, this third and most pragmatic method of abridging a text was obviously quite popular. If one lumps together all the British secular breviaries with abbreviated readings, in fact, one finds that well over half of them use this method; and many additional ones, as suggested above, use multiple skips to convey the gist of the legend, rather than limiting themselves to verbatim excerpts. Even York manuscripts, which tend to be the most standardized and predictable among the British secular rites, are full of the latter kind of *mouvance*. The few manuscripts that survive from the smaller rites abbreviate the legend in a number of ingenious ways, no two of them the same. For Sarum breviaries the figures are again large enough to be meaningful, and they are quite striking: fully two-thirds of the manuscripts with abbreviated readings (twenty-eight out of forty-two) give abstracts or summaries of the legend, and another sixth give versions with multiple skips.[29] Many of these Sarum abridged versions can be grouped together into families, as we shall see. But the order of the day was obviously revision, not uniformity, and a remarkably large number of people—from official and semi-official compilers down to mere copyists—seem to have participated in the process.[30]

---

[28] All my statistics exclude Dominican and Franciscan breviaries, which tend to treat the readings much more uniformly, regardless of where they were written.

[29] Three of these—Stonyhurst College MS. 44, Cambridge University Library MS. Addit. 3475, and British Library Addit. 59862—are very similar to the Hyde Abbey breviary in their creative use of skips to sum up long sections of the legend without actually changing the words.

[30] Although Salmon does not attempt to distinguish one method of abbreviation or one geographical area from another, his account of the anarchy he saw in breviary lessons is still relevant here: "From the 11th century on, the breviaries whose lessons are contained in a few lines are numerous. In this period, it seems, everyone enjoyed a great liberty in this regard. Cathedral chapters, abbeys, collegiate churches, priests, whether regular or secular, and even copyists of manuscripts—everybody hacked away [at] the texts as he pleased, without authorization or control. So true is this that it is

It will be helpful at this point to see the variety of ways in which a given passage was condensed in Sarum breviaries, and to notice the relationships among them. Consider, for example, what happened to the complicated ending of the wedding night conversation, in which Cecilia tells Valerian what he must do in order to see her angelic protector. In the standard Sarum lectionary version (or choir legend), this passage is not abbreviated at all; as in the full-length *Passio S. Caeciliae*, it consists of five speeches, running to about 170 words:

Tunc beata Cecilia dixit ei: Si consiliis meis promittas te acqui-
escere, et permittas te purificari fonte perenni, et credas unum
Deum esse in celis vivum et verum, poteris eum videre. Dixit
Valerianus ad beatam Ceciliam: Et quis me purificet ut ego angelum
videam? Respondit Cecilia: Est senior qui novit purificare homines,
ut mereantur videre angelum. Dicit ei Valerianus: Et ego ubi hunc
senem requiram? Respondit Cecilia: Vade in tertium miliarium ab
urbe, via que Appia nuncupatur, et illic invenies pauperes a
transeuntibus alimonie petentes auxilium. De his enim michi
semper cura fuit, et optime huius mei secreti sunt conscii. Hos tu
dum videris, dabis eis benedictionem meam, dicens, Cecilia me
misit ad vos, ut ostendatis michi sanctum senem Urbanum, quoniam
ad ipsum habeo eius secreta mandata que perferam. Hunc dum tu
videris, indica ei omnia verba mea. Et dum te purificaverit, induet
te vestibus novis et candidis, cum quibus mox ut ingressus fueris
istud cubiculum, videbis angelum sanctum etiam tui amatorem
effectum, et omnia que ab eo poposceris impetrabis.[31]

Then blessed Cecilia said to him, "If you promise to follow my
advice and permit yourself to be cleansed by the eternal fountain
and believe there is one God in heaven, living and true, you will be
able to see him." Valerian said to blessed Cecilia, "And who is to
cleanse me so that I can see the angel?" Cecilia answered, "There
is an old man who knows how to cleanse people so that they will
deserve to see the angel." Valerian said to her, "And where am I to
look for this old man?" Cecilia replied, "Go to the third milestone
from the city on the Appian road, and there you will find poor
people begging passers-by for alms. Truly, I have always cared for
these people, and they are well aware of this secret of mine. When

---

rare to find even in the breviaries of one and the same abbey or of one and the same church lessons of identical length. Each one made up his office book to suit himself, or almost so, abridging or lengthening the texts—especially shortening them—as seemed good to him" (note 226, p. 160).

[31] Here and throughout, my quotations from the Sarum choir legend come from the 1518 printed edition.

you see them, give them my blessing, saying, 'Cecilia has sent me to you so that you will show me the holy old man Urban, since I bring him secret instructions from her.' And when you see him, tell him all my words. And when he has cleansed you, he will clothe you in new, white garments. As soon as you return to this bedroom wearing those, you will see the holy angel, who will then love you also, and you will obtain everything you request from him."

Since the compiler(s) of the Sarum choir legend retained all the original wording in this passage, they must have considered it important. Most obviously, it provides the context for the two choral responses which always followed the third lesson in the Sarum office for Cecilia and which read, respectively, "Cecilia me misit ad vos, ut ostendatis mihi sanctum Urbanum, quia ad ipsum habeo secreta que perferam" and "Tunc Valerianus perrexit et inventis pauperibus dixit: Cecilia me misit ad vos" (Then Valerian went on and, when he found the poor people, said, "Cecilia has sent me to you"). Given the limited space available in most actual manuscripts, however, the traditional coordination between lessons and music became a luxury that had to be dispensed with.

There are at least two extant copies of the Sarum lectionary itself which significantly abbreviate the passage. The first of these, presently MS. Auct. E.1.1 in the Bodleian, simplifies Cecilia's initial speech to "Si permittas te purificari fonte perhenni, poteris eum videre" (If you permit yourself to be cleansed by the eternal fountain, you will be able to see him) and replaces everything after "mereantur videre angelum" (end of her second speech) with the following summary and transition to the next scene: "Et misit eum ad sanctum Urbanum episcopum" (And she sent him to the holy bishop Urban). The other such lectionary, now MS. Bodley 280, cuts even more words out of Cecilia's initial speech, omits the third and fourth speeches, and condenses Cecilia's last speech in a way that retains most of her closing predictions and promises—but not her message to the *pauperes*:

> Que ait: Si purgatus fueris poteris eum videre. Qui ait: Et quis me purgabit ut angelum Dei videam? Cui illa: Vade ad Urbanum episcopum. Hic te purgabit et induet te vestimentis novis, cum quibus mox ut ingressus fueris cubiculum meum videbis angelum sanctum etiam tui amatorem ef[f]ectum, et omnia que ab eo poposceris impetrabis.

She said, "If you are cleansed, you will be able to see him." He said, "And who will cleanse me so that I may see the angel?" She said to him, "Go to Bishop Urban. He will cleanse you and clothe you in new garments. As soon as you return to my bedroom wearing those, you will see the holy angel, who will then love you also, and you will obtain everything you request from him."

A large proportion of the surviving manuscripts of the Sarum breviary seem to have been derived from the abridged lectionary version just quoted. The Aberdeen Breviary has almost exactly the same text, both here and throughout the Cecilia legend, as does Bodley 280.[32] The compiler or copyist of MS. Hatton 63 in the Bodleian pruned the text a bit further, omitting the *Et* in the first line of the quote, *angelum Dei* in the second line, *etiam* in the fifth line, and all of the last clause. The person responsible for British Library MS. Royal 2.A.xii made the same omissions as Hatton and also skipped Valerian's question, inserting *ergo* after Cecilia's *Vade* instead; in addition, he made the language even simpler and more straightforward, changing *purgatus* to *baptizatus* in the first line and *purgabit* to *purificabit* in the third. Another compiler or scribe came up with a slightly different solution, giving a fuller version of Cecilia's first speech but otherwise virtually always agreeing either with Bodley 280 or with the Royal manuscript:

Que ait: Si credas unum Deum esse vivum et verum et baptizatus fueris, poteris eum videre. Vade igitur ad Urbanum episcopum. Hic te purificabit et induet vestimentis novis, cum quibus mox ut ingressus fueris cubiculum meum videbis sanctum angelum eciam tui amatorem effectum, et omnia que ab ipso poposceris impetrabis.

She said, "If you believe there is one God, living and true, and are baptized, you will be able to see him. Go therefore to Bishop Urban. He will cleanse you and clothe you in new garments. As soon as you return to my bedroom wearing those, you will see the holy angel, who will then love you also, and you will obtain everything you request from him."

The particular version just quoted was found satisfactory enough to be copied verbatim, or very nearly so, in the largest surviving group of Sarum breviaries (at least fourteen manuscripts).[33] For practical purpo-

---

[32] The Aberdeen version, compiled by Bishop Elphinstone and originally printed in 1509-10, has been republished for the Bannatyne and Maitland Clubs under the title *Breviarium Aberdonense*, 2 vols. (Edinburgh and London, 1854).

[33] The manuscripts in question are Lambeth Palace MS. 69 (from which I quote); Oxford, St. John's College MS. 179; Bodleian MSS. Laud Misc. 299 and Lat. lit. f.29; Stonyhurst College MS. 52; British Library MSS. Harley 2946, Harley 7398B, and Sloane 2466; and six manuscripts presently in Cambridge: University Library MSS. Dd.x.66 and Addit. 4500, Emmanuel College MS. 64, Fitzwilliam Museum MS. McClean 65, Peterhouse College MS. 270, St. John's College MS. F.9. Salisbury Cathedral MS. 224 has the beginning of this same abridged version, but ends abruptly before it reaches this passage.

ses, it thus displaced the choir legend as the most authoritative Sarum version of this scene—that is, the version most likely to be faithfully reproduced rather than revised or abbreviated further. And so the *mouvance* came to a stop—but only in one branch of the tradition.

In other branches of the Sarum tradition, designers and copyists found different ways of condensing this dialogue. For example, one small family of manuscripts, represented by British Library MS. Harley 587 and Edinburgh University Library MS. 26, skips the third and fourth speeches and also edits out the *pauperes*, inserting "sanctum Urbanum episcopum" after *illic invenies* and continuing at once with what Valerian is to tell Urban himself. British Library MS. Stowe 12 adopts a slightly different solution, rewriting Cecilia's final speech so that it begins, "Vade in via que Appia nuncupatur ad sanctum Urbanum, et indica ei verba mea" (Take the Appian road to holy Urban, and tell him my words). Liverpool Cathedral MS. 37, which looks like a relative of Stowe 12 with further abbreviations, cuts the first clause down to "Vade ad sanctum Urbanum episcopum." Most efficient and most distinctive of all are two extensively rewritten versions that survive in a handful of Sarum manuscripts. The first of these, found in Stonyhurst College MS. 40, sums up this passage in eighteen words:

> Cui illa: Si Christo credideris ipsum videre valebis. Misit ergo illum Cecilia ad Urbanum episcopum ut eum baptizaret.

> She said to him, "If you believe in Christ, you will be able to see him." Cecilia therefore sent him to Bishop Urban to be baptized.

The other, found in at least two Sarum breviaries from Ireland—presently Bodleian MS. Can. lit. 215 and National Library of Wales MS. 21604A, presents the entire conversation between Cecilia and Valerian in just thirty-eight words, with the last six going to the passage at hand:

> Nocte vero cum illa cubiculum cum sponso intrasset, dixit se angelum habere custodem qui ipsum perderet si eam polluto amore tangeret. Valerianus ait: Si probavero ipsum verum angelum, faciam quod fieri velis. Cecilia misit eum ad sanctum Urbanum.[34]

> At night, indeed, when she entered the bedroom with her husband, she said she had a guardian angel who would kill him if he touched her with impure love. Valerian said, "If I verify that he is really an angel, I will do what you wish." Cecilia sent him to holy Urban.

Although the kinds of textual change I have been illustrating are most obvious in Sarum breviaries, the same pragmatic methods of condensa-

---

[34] I quote from Can. lit. 215; the NLW manuscript omits *fieri*.

tion can be seen in a number of other British breviaries, including some monastic ones, and in the lectionaries with choir legends as well. For most purposes it is more reasonable to lump these manuscripts together than to separate them according to rite or extent of condensation or apparent geographical provenance; in some cases they clearly influenced each other regardless of such boundaries,[35] and they all reworked the same legends with essentially the same goals—brevity and intelligibility to a late-medieval audience being chief among them.

The most obvious result of our inquiry thus far has been the discovery that there was a wide range of ways in which late-medieval compilers and scribes could approach a quasi-official Latin text like the legend of St. Cecilia. I have enumerated four basic approaches: complete, accurate reproduction of the text; the substitution of fragmentary verbatim excerpts for the whole; abridgement by the free use of selective omissions, but not new words; and the use of both omissions and rewording to produce a summary or abstract. Quite clearly, however, these approaches make up a whole continuum of textual methods and attitudes—ranging from the faithful reproduction of an authoritative text, at one extreme, to a very pragmatic kind of editing and reworking, at the other. In terms of the implicit stance adopted by the compiler or scribe, the continuum runs from the role of a humble copyist, whose sole responsibility is to hand on the text as he received it, to that of an activist editor who can and must adapt the text to new audiences and expectations. The prevailing assumptions about medieval Latin texts and scribes would lead us to expect a preponderance of the former—and, indeed, those humbler, more conservative stances may have prevailed on the Continent even when the lessons in breviaries had to be drastically abbreviated. But in late-medieval British breviaries, at least, the need to abbreviate the lessons seems to have been widely perceived as an imperative to convey the gist of each saint's legend in as few words as possible—and the compilers and scribes responded, as we have seen, with considerable independence and ingenuity.

Was this sort of *mouvance* a great rarity in Latin? Perhaps so. As I suggested at the beginning of this paper, however, manuscripts containing late-medieval Latin are so numerous and still so little studied, in comparison with vernacular literary manuscripts, that no one is yet in a position to draw sweeping conclusions about the stability of the texts from copy to copy. And whether or not these British liturgical manu-

---

[35] Thus, for example, the lessons on Cecilia in the monastic breviary of Hyde Abbey seem to be closely related both to those in the Hereford breviary (also English, but secular) and to those in a French breviary, currently Bibliothèque St. Geneviève MS. 2626, which belonged to a community of canons regular at Rouen.

scripts turn out to represent a larger phenomenon in medieval Latin, there are good reasons to study them in much more depth and detail. When we take them together, indeed, these manuscripts offer us an extraordinary opportunity to watch a large number of late-medieval readers reacting to the same narratives—all trying to preserve the gist of the matter, as they perceived it, and pare away the words, details, sentences, even whole episodes, that were superfluous. Such a wealth of specific evidence on readers' tastes and expectations would be valuable from any period in the past. But it is especially so from the late Middle Ages—a period during which the social, collaborative phase of literary production was unusually important and is rarely well documented. With regard to the York Play, for example, Richard Beadle reminds us that the text must have evolved continuously over a very long period, but the surviving evidence shows us only a few isolated moments from this history.[36] With regard to hagiographical lessons in British breviaries, on the other hand, so much evidence is available that we can actually see the processes of collaborative revision at work.

Besides all the apparently random, unsystematic changes in these breviaries, one finds significant patterns of consensus or near-consensus on certain issues. To a very large extent, in fact, the manuscripts seem to reflect the shared values and assumptions of a sizable class of readers, as distinct from the artistic intentions of an individual. As we have seen, virtually all of the revisers agreed that the lessons needed to be brief and that the original wording was not necessarily sacrosanct; the main function of the lessons was to convey the gist of the narrative. More surprising and more suggestive is the extent to which the revisers agreed with each other when they actually defined the gist of this narrative. In fact, as we shall see, the manuscripts reveal a broad consensus about which aspects of the Cecilia legend were most essential and which aspects were ripe for cutting because they had become outdated or problematical, or both.

II

Since there is space for only a sampling of these patterns of consensus, let us focus in turn on five key sections of the legend: the very·beginning, the very end, and three much-revised passages in between.

One of the most efficient Sarum versions of the beginning is the one in Stonyhurst College MS. 40:

---

[36] See above, 114-19.

Beata Cecilia virgo clarissima Valerianum habebat sponsum, qui diem constituit nupciarum. Cantantibus igitur organis, Cecilia soli Deo decantabat, dicens: Fiat, Domine, cor meum et corpus meum immaculatum, ut non confundar.

The blessed and most noble virgin Cecilia had Valerian as her betrothed, and he set the day for the wedding. Then, while the musical instruments were singing, Cecilia sang to God alone, saying, "Lord, make my heart and body immaculate, so that I may not be overcome."

In essence, there are three components here: a brief characterization of Cecilia, her imminent wedding to Valerian, and her song to God while the instruments play. In the Sarum choir legend, which preserved the complete opening section from the *Passio*, each of these components was elaborated. Cecilia was initially characterized in terms of her secret faith, her constant prayer, and her dedication to virginity:

Beata Cecilia virgo clarissima absconditum semper evangelium Christi gerebat in pectore suo, et non diebus neque noctibus a divinis colloquiis et oratione cessabat, cum fletibus exorans ut virginitas eius ipso conservante inviolata permaneret.

The blessed and most noble virgin Cecilia always bore the gospel of Christ hidden in her breast, and did not cease either day or night from celestial conversations and prayer, beseeching Him with tears to keep her virginity inviolate.

With regard to the wedding, this version made two additional points: that Cecilia concealed a hair shirt (*cilicium*) beneath her golden garments, and that she could not reveal her true feelings because both Valerian and her own family were so intent on the marriage. Finally, after giving the content of her song, the Sarum choir legend added an account of the strenuous fasts and fervent prayers with which she reinforced her entreaties that God would preserve her purity. Clearly, the choir legend was more dramatic and suspenseful, dwelling as it did on Cecilia's anxiety and apparent helplessness at this turning point in her life. But the key difference, it seems to me, is that the choir legend invested Cecilia's virginity with larger, symbolic meanings and linked it with a set of other virtues—inward meditation on the Gospel, ceaseless prayer, asceticism, and so on—that sound very monastic; the abbreviated version, addressed to a different kind of audience, shows little interest in these dimensions of the narrative. Whereas the *Passio* and the choir legend held up the complex ideal of a life wholly consecrated to God, the abbreviated version gets on with the plot.

The abbreviator's tendency to focus on the literal level of the story rather than the original ideals and symbols is evident in many manuscripts, of course, not just one. The two Irish Sarum breviaries, for example, do not even pause to mention Cecilia's song to God at her wedding; by way of introduction to the wedding night conversation, they have only the following line: "Beata Cecilia virgo clarissima Valerianum quendam habebat sponsum." Bodley 280 and another twenty Sarum breviaries give more details about Cecilia's virtue, since they follow the choir legend faithfully for the first three or four lines; but thereafter they agree almost exactly with the Stonyhurst manuscript.[37]

Turning to the very end of the text, one finds a similar pattern of change. In its standard, full-length form, the legend ended with the following steps: Almachius's order that Cecilia be beheaded; the executioner's inability to do so completely in three blows; her three-day survival, during which she continued to encourage her followers; her final arrangements for her followers and property, including her last speech to Pope Urban on these matters; his burial of her body and consecration of her house, in accordance with her wish; and a closing formula that mentions the services held in that church, in memory of Cecilia, down to the present day. The actual moment of the saint's death, one notes, was not even mentioned. What mattered were the arrangements before it and the papal ceremonies afterward, both of which incorporated her individual witness into the institutional life of the church. In the vast majority of late-medieval English breviaries, on the other hand, the individual's death has become more important than the official arrangements and ceremonies. The fullest York breviaries include most of the steps in the original sequence, but end the text with Cecilia's burial and insert this sentence after her final speech: "Ipsa vero post hec verba spiritum celo reddidit" (After these words she yielded up her spirit to heaven).[38] The fullest Sarum versions run as far as the burial, or even the consecration of her house, with a similar addition on her death: "Et hec dicens, reddidit spiritum," or "Et his dictis, reddidit spiritum."[39] More typically, both Sarum and non-Sarum English breviaries omit the later ceremonies, taking Cecilia's death as the logical end of the legend.

---

[37] The manuscripts in question are the fifteen listed in note 33, plus the Aberdeen breviary, the Hatton and Royal manuscripts, and British Library MSS. Addit. 59862 and Sloane 1909.

[38] Versions with this ending are the Surtees Society edition, Laud Misc. 84, and York Minster Addit. 69.

[39] These endings are found in Bodley 280, Aberdeen, and Bodleian MS. Auct. E.1.1; the manuscripts and printed editions of the full-length choir legend also have the closing formula. Sarum abridgements that end with Cecilia's death include Hatton and Royal, Laud Misc. 299 and ten of the manuscripts most closely related to it, Stonyhurst 40 and 44, Stowe 12, and the Liverpool Cathedral manuscript, besides those cited specifically in the text.

And they use so many different wordings and selections of detail as to suggest that a number of different compilers reached this conclusion independently. Grolier Club MS. 3, for example, a tiny secular breviary from the fourteenth century that seems not to belong to any of the major rites, ends with Cecilia's division of her property among the faithful and then her death: "Que triduo supervivens et fideles confortans, divisit eis cuncta que habuit, et sic spiritum celo reddidit" (Living three more days and consoling the faithful, she distributed to them everything that she owned and so yielded up her spirit to heaven). The two Irish Sarum breviaries emphasize her care for the spiritual well-being of her followers and do not mention the property, but they too end the narrative with her death: "per triduum supervixit. Puellas quas nutrivit in fide Christi confirmatas, sancto Urbano tradidit commendendas et spiritum emisit" (She lived three more days. Strengthening the young women she had brought up in the faith of Christ, she committed them to the care of holy Urban and sent forth her spirit). Salisbury Cathedral MS. 152 and British Library Addit. 32427, two Sarum breviaries from western England, omit all the final arrangements, just mentioning Cecilia's three-day survival and then skipping to her death: "Et sic supervixit per triduum, et postea Domino tradidit spiritum."

Apart from the very beginning and end, the part of the text that most clearly illustrates the dominance of new conventions is the section in the middle on the martyrdom of Cecilia's husband, Valerian, and his brother, Tiburce. The original account of the brothers' arrest, trial, and execution was so long and so obviously detachable from the rest of the Cecilia legend that compilers often omitted it even when they were not abridging the rest of the text. Since Tiburce and Valerian had their own feast day and office, but not their own legend, many liturgists thought of using this account for that occasion; and the lessons for Cecilia were certainly long enough without it. But late-medieval compilers of breviaries, at least in England, tended not to be content with the discontinuity that was created when this block of the text was just removed, and they tried to fill it by summarizing what had happened to Valerian and Tiburce.

In the original version of the legend, the heroic faith of the two brothers after their conversions was illustrated in four ways: (a) their burial of martyred Christians, defying the edict of the local persecutor, Almachius; (b) a very long trial scene in which both brothers bravely stood up to Almachius, who finally ordered them executed unless they would sacrifice to his gods; (c) an episode in which they converted their jailer Maximus and his companions by their fearlessness in the face of death; and (d) the brief scene in which they silently refused to offer the required sacrifice, knelt down instead, and were executed. In their summaries of this material, several York breviaries and an unusual monastic one from Ely (Cambridge University Library MS. Ii.iv.20) mention the conversion of Maximus.[40] All but one of the same small group of breviaries place some emphasis on the brothers' works of mercy before their arrest, updating them a bit by adding some good works that late-medieval Christians could still do:

> Ceperunt ambo sanctis operibus insistere: martires Dei quos Almachius occidit sepelire, pauperes recreare, nudos vestire, ieiuniis et orationibus vacare.

> They both began to devote themselves to holy works: burying martyrs of God whom Almachius had killed, feeding the poor, clothing the naked, giving their time to fasts and prayers.[41]

With regard to the brothers' trial before Almachius, on the other hand, late-medieval British breviaries are almost unanimous in skipping over it. Only the unusual monastic manuscript from Ely, which devotes six of its eight lessons from the legend to the post-baptismal careers of Valerian and Tiburce, offers so much as a brief summary of this scene:

> ... Almachius prefectus iussit eos adduci ad se, et cum eis diutissimam sermocinacionem habens, ita permotus responsionibus eorum iussit Valerianum fustigari. Denique iussit eos duci ad ydolum Iovis. ...

> Almachius the prefect ordered them brought to him, and having a very long disputation with them, was so enraged by their responses that he ordered Valerian beaten. Finally he ordered them to be led to the idol of Jove. ...

Everywhere else, the brothers' confrontation with Almachius simply disappears, and the emphasis is shifted completely to their patient endurance of the penalties he decrees. Patience, of course, was one of the great themes of late-medieval piety, and defiance of worldly authority was not.[42] The new portrayal of the brothers' martyrdom is best illustrated in the largest group of Sarum breviary manuscripts:

> Eo tempore Almachius urbis Rome prefectus Christianos variis penis afflictos occidere fecit. Tyburcius vero et Valerianus corpora eorum

---

[40] The York versions with this detail are the same ones listed above in note 38.

[41] I quote from the Ely breviary. Laud Misc. 84 and York Minster Addit. 69 have almost exactly the same passage, and another York breviary, presently Sion College MS. L.1, has all but the last four words of it. The Surtees Society edition omits everything after *insistere*.

[42] See, for example, Richard Kieckhefer, *Unquiet Souls: Fourteenth-Century Saints and Their Religious Milieu* (Chicago: University of Chicago Press, 1984), esp. chap. 3.

sepelierunt. Unde tenti et variis penis afflicti, in carcere recludun-
tur. Ad quos veniens beata Cecilia, ait: Eya, milites Christi, abicite
opera tenebrarum et induimini arma lucis. Cum ergo coram
prefecto presentati non potuit eos cogere ut Iovi thura ponerent,
gladio eos animadverti precepit. His vero duobus fratribus ad celum
per martyrii palmam transmissis. . . .[43]

At that time Almachius, prefect of the city of Rome, tortured
Christians in various ways and had them killed. However, Tiburce
and Valerian buried their bodies. For this reason they themselves
were arrested, tortured in various ways, and cast into prison.
Coming to them, blessed Cecilia said, "Hail, knights of Christ; cast
off the works of darkness and clothe yourselves in the armor of
light." When they were brought face to face with the prefect, then,
he could not persuade them to offer incense to Jove; he ordered
them to be put to death by the sword. Truly, when these two
brothers had been conveyed to heaven with the palm of martyrdom. . . .

Here the martyrdom of Valerian and Tiburce is rather fully assimilated to
the expectations of a late-medieval audience. The martyrs' patient
endurance of suffering, underlined by the repeated reference to torture,
has replaced both the original emphasis on their fearless defiance of the
persecutor and their ability to convert his officers. Cecilia evidently
comes to visit them in prison before their trial, as angels came to comfort
and encourage the martyrs in a number of other legends;[44] in the
original version of this legend, on the other hand, she visited them in
Maximus's house, bringing priests to baptize all their new converts, and
the occasion was almost a celebration because the brothers had already
stood fast against Almachius and were on the verge of winning their
eternal crowns.

The other two parts of the legend that evidently cried out for revision,
from the perspective of the late Middle Ages, were the accounts of
Tiburce's conversion and of Cecilia's own arrest and trial. Both scenes
seem to have posed a number of problems for late-medieval readers, and
it is interesting to see how the various abbreviators attempted to resolve
them.

There are two obvious objections to the scene in which Cecilia, with

---

[43] I quote from Lambeth Palace MS. 69. Essentially the same passage occurs in the
Aberdeen breviary, Laud Misc. 299, and most of the other manuscripts closely related
to them. But Bodley 280, Hatton, Royal, and a few other manuscripts skip from
Cecilia's exhortation to "His vero," omitting the actual execution.

[44] For example, in the legends of Saints Vincent, Mark the Evangelist, and Catherine
of Alexandria. The motif may derive from the New Testament story about Peter's
deliverance from prison by an angelic messenger (Acts 12:6–11).

some help from Valerian, instructs Tiburce in the faith and gradually persuades him to seek baptism: the scene is enormously long and, except at the very beginning, is essentially a sermon rather than a dramatic dialogue. But late-medieval abbreviators also seem to have felt uncomfortable with its strong portrayal of Cecilia as a preacher. The fullest and most faithful synopsis in British breviaries is the one in the Sarum choir legend, which gives selections from the initial dialogue between Tiburce, Valerian, and Cecilia, and then this summary of the remainder of the scene:

> Cumque diligenter instruxisset eum beata Cecilia de fide Trinitatis, et unum Deum esse in tribus personis evidenter ei ostendisset, et de his que Salvator in corpore gessit sufficienter edocuisset, Tyburcius pedibus eius prostratus cum ingenti fletu et lachrymis dixit: Ego usque hodie sine causa vixi, sed iam non sit michi sine causa vivere. Et ad fratrem suum conversus, ait: Miserere mei, frater carissime. Obsecro te, perduc me ad purificationem, ut purificatus eterne vite particeps efficiar.

> After blessed Cecilia had carefully instructed him in the Trinitarian faith, clearly shown him that there is one God in three persons, and thoroughly informed him about what the Savior did during His incarnation, Tiburce fell prostrate at her feet with great weeping and said, "Until today I have lived without a purpose, but let me no longer live that way." And turning to his brother, he said, "Have mercy on me, dearest brother. I beseech you, lead me to be cleansed, that once clean I may become a sharer in eternal life."

Even this version does not convey a very adequate picture of the scope and authoritativeness of Cecilia's preaching in the *Passio*, nor of its powerful effect on Tiburce; in that version, for example, he also prostrated himself before her just after she had begun to preach, exclaiming that she seemed to speak with the tongue of an angel rather than that of a mere human being.[45] But the account in the Sarum choir legend, brief and watered-down as it is, gives far more credit to Cecilia here than the compilers of most late-medieval breviaries were willing to do.

In the majority of Sarum breviaries, Cecilia's preaching simply got left out. The abridgement in MS. Bodley 280 and the Aberdeen breviary keeps most of the steps leading up to it—Tiburce's entrance, his reaction to the scent of the invisible crowns, and a little of the early dialogue with

---

[45] In Delehaye's edition of the *Passio* this exclamation is found near the end of chap. 12.

Valerian and Cecilia—but then jumps to his baptism in one sentence: "Tunc iussu Cecilie Valerianus duxit eum ad Urbanum episcopum" (Then by Cecilia's order Valerian led him to Bishop Urban). Nor did the condensation process stop here. In at least fifteen other Sarum manuscripts, including most of those already shown to be related to Bodley 280, the *iussu Cecilie* was excised from this sentence, leaving the impression that Valerian was the primary architect of Tiburce's conversion.

One might suppose that this result was just a coincidence of the abbreviation process, except that something similar seems to have happened in nearly every family of breviaries in Great Britain. Among York breviaries, even the fullest versions just describe the general tenor and effect of Cecilia's preaching—and that not in totally positive terms:

> Tunc inter dulcia colloquia Cecilia prolixiorem disputacionem introducens eum constanti animo fidem Christi perdocuit. Quid multa? Credidit Tiburtius per verba exhortacionis beate Cecilie, et a beato Urbano baptizatus est.[46]

> Then, introducing a very prolonged debate into pleasant conversation, Cecilia with an immovable spirit thoroughly taught him the faith of Christ. In brief, Tiburce believed because of the exhortations of blessed Cecilia and was baptized by blessed Urban.

In the shorter version published by the Surtees Society, Cecilia's role as Tiburce's teacher is further deemphasized:

> Tunc sancta Cecilia Tyburtium constanti animo fidem Christi perdocuit. Credidit Tyburtius, et a beato Urbano baptisatus est.

> Then holy Cecilia with an immovable spirit thoroughly taught Tiburce the faith of Christ. Tiburce believed and was baptized by blessed Urban.

And a number of surviving York breviary manuscripts simply skip this episode, saying nothing at all about how Tiburce was converted.[47]

Outside the main Sarum and York traditions, one encounters the same pattern. At least one of the surviving English monastic breviaries, the unusual one from Ely, continues the older tradition of giving Cecilia all the credit for the conversions of Valerian and Tiburce:[48]

---

[46] I quote from Bodleian MS. Laud Misc. 84. The same passage is found in York Minster Addit. 69 and Sion College L.1.

[47] Manuscripts that omit the entire episode include British Library Addit. 30511 and York Minster MSS. XVI.O.23, Addit. 115, and Addit. 383.

[48] The older tradition is clearly expressed, for example, in Usuard's martyrology (ninth century): "Romae, natalis sanctae Caeciliae virginis, quae sponsum suum

Cecilia ... habebat sponsum, quem cum fratre suo Tyburcio per verba exortacionis sue ad fidem Christi convertit.

Cecilia had a bridegroom and with her exhortations converted him, together with his brother Tiburce, to the faith of Christ.

But in the Grolier Club manuscript, representing a still-unidentified secular rite, Cecilia and Valerian share the credit for Tiburce's conversion:

Post hec Tiburcius per exortacionem Cecilie et Valeriani ad fidem conversus a sancto Urbano baptizatus est.

Afterwards Tiburce, converted to the faith by the exhortation of Cecilia and Valerian, was baptized by holy Urban.

And elsewhere in these minor and relatively independent textual traditions, Cecilia's role as Tiburce's teacher tends to vanish entirely. The small Sarum family represented by Stowe 12 and the Liverpool Cathedral manuscript, for example, gives a summary account of Tiburce's conversion that attributes everything to Valerian:

Cumque Valerianus rei geste ordinem ei exposuisset, Tyburcius cum omni alacritate flecti cepit ad credendum et ait: Miserere me[i], frater karissime, et perduc me ad purificacionem ut eterne vite particeps efficiar.

When Valerian had explained the course of events to him, Tiburce with great eagerness began to turn toward belief and said, "Have mercy on me, dearest brother, and lead me to be cleansed so that I may become a sharer in eternal life."

Stonyhurst 40 gives a completely independent account that has the same result:

... venit Tiburcius, Valeriani frater, qui dixit se in odoris fragrancia innovatum. Cui Valerianus: Me interpellante sensisti odorem, cuius aspectu gaudebis si Christo credideris baptizatus. Et statim baptizatus est.

Tiburce, Valerian's brother, came and said he was renewed by the sweet scent (of the invisible crowns of flowers). Valerian told him,

---

Valerianum et fratrem ejus Tiburtium ad credendum Christo ac martyrium perdocuit, et ipsa deinde martyrizata est ..." (*Acta Sanctorum*, jun., vi, 628) (At Rome, the birthday of the virgin Saint Cecilia, who thoroughly taught her bridegroom Valerian and his brother Tiburce to believe in Christ and to undergo martyrdom, and was herself finally martyred . . .).

"Through my intercession you have perceived the scent of what
you will rejoice to see if you believe in Christ and are baptized."
And at once he was baptized.

The two Irish Sarum breviaries leave out the whole scene, suggesting by
their selectivity that Tiburce's conversion was brought about solely by
divine intervention, in accordance with the angel's promise to Valerian:

> Valerianus rogavit angelum pro fratre suo Tyburcio ut particeps fieri
> mereretur corone repromisse, quod ei concessum est et angelus ad
> celos migravit. Tyburcius vero a sancto Urbano baptizatus est.

> Valerian asked the angel that his brother Tiburce might deserve to
> share in the promised crown. This was granted to him, and the
> angel departed to heaven. And in fact Tiburce was baptized by holy
> Urban.

If late-medieval British abbreviators favored martyrs who suffered
patiently and if they resisted the idea of a female saint as an authoritative
teacher, even in private, one would not expect them to like the dramatic
trial scene in which Cecilia publicly defies and ridicules the Roman
persecutor, Almachius. And apparently they did not. Out of all the
liturgical abridgements that have come down to us, only the Sarum choir
legend and a few of its close relatives retain very much of the combative
dialogue from the trial.[49] Nine other manuscripts, at least four of them
either early or monastic (or both), give a brief selection of Almachius's
demands and Cecilia's undaunted replies.[50] One additional early
manuscript, the unusual monastic one from Ely, summarizes the trial in
a way that at least suggests the length and argumentative tone of the
original scene:

> [Almachius] cum ea longam disputacionem habuit, ut ydolis
> sacrificare consentiret. Ipsa vero fide armata sermonibus eum
> confutans, pro Domini nomine martyrizata est.

> Almachius had a long argument with her, in order to persuade her
> to sacrifice to the idols. But armed with faith and refuting him with
> her words, she was martyred for the name of the Lord.

---

[49] The Sarum choir legend itself has four lengthy exchanges between Cecilia and
Almachius. Most of the same material appears in Bodleian MS. Auct. E.1.1; a somewhat
different selection, in British Library MS. Addit. 32427 and Salisbury Cathedral MS. 152.

[50] These manuscripts are the Exeter Cathedral lectionary; the Hyde Abbey breviary
and another Benedictine version, Bodleian MS. Rawlinson C.489; Bodley 547 and John
Rylands MS. 354, both probably Augustinian and dating from the thirteenth century;
and (with very short excerpts) Stonyhurst 40 and the three Sarum versions with skips
that were enumerated above in note 29.

From the remaining manuscripts—the majority—one would be hard put to tell that there had been any trial. Bodley 280, the Aberdeen breviary, and all the Sarum manuscripts related to them say only that Almachius orders Cecilia executed because she refuses to sacrifice ("cum sacrificare nollet" or "cum sacrificare contempneret"). The Grolier Club manuscript has a very similar reading: "Quam quia diis sacrificare recusabat, iussit in balneo bulliente concremari" (Since she refused to sacrifice to the gods, he ordered her to be burned in a boiling bath). Stowe 12 says the same thing in different words: "cepit eam Almachius compellere ut ydolis sacrificaret, sed eam nullatenus a proposito fidei potuit dimoveri" (Almachius began to force her to sacrifice to the idols, but could not budge her at all from the precept of the faith). The Liverpool Cathedral manuscript starts to give a similar summary but omits the last clause, calling our attention to how formulaic and dispensable it is when Almachius is about to condemn her to death. And York breviaries say nothing whatever about Cecilia's trial. The fullest copies move from the execution of Valerian and Tiburce to Almachius's summons to Cecilia, and then skip directly to her sentencing, as we have already seen; the copies with shorter lessons even leave out the summons.[51]

Since this trial scene was originally the climax of the legend, to omit or greatly weaken it has major consequences for the portrayal of Cecilia—especially in versions of the text which had done the same thing to her instruction of Tiburce. The traditional image of this saint as a strong and fruitful virgin, who taught with authority and overcame persecution with courage, is splendidly summed up in the little homily that the Exeter Cathedral lectionary prescribes for reading in the chapterhouse on her feast day:

Sancta Cecilia virgo, cuius hodie natalicia celebramus, mori pro Domino non potuisset in corpore, si prius a terrenis desideriis mortua non fuisset in mente. Erectus namque in virtutis culmine eius animus tormenta derisit, premia calcavit. Ante armatos reges et presides ducta stetit, feriente robustior, iudicante sublimior. Quid inter hec, nos barbari et debiles dicimus, qui ire ad regna celestia puellas per ferrum videmus, quos ira superat, superbia inflat, ambicio perturbat, luxuria inquinat?[52]

The holy virgin Cecilia, whose birthday we celebrate today, could not have died in body for the Lord if she had not first been dead to

---

[51] See above in the text at notes 26 and 25, respectively.

[52] I quote from the third volume of the *Exeter Ordinale*, ed. from Exeter Cathedral MSS. 3504 and 3505 by J. N. Dalton, HBS 63 (London, 1926), 428.

worldly desires in her mind. For, elevated on the summit of virtue, her spirit laughed at tortures and spurned rewards. Led before armed kings and governors, she stood fast, mightier than the one wielding the sword, more exalted than the one pronouncing judgment. Meanwhile, what do we say, we uncivilized and feeble ones, who see girls ascend to the heavenly kingdom by the sword while we ourselves are overcome by anger, puffed up by pride, agitated by ambition, stained by licentiousness?

The same tradition is reflected in a number of the old antiphons and responses for Cecilia's office. Among the choral texts prescribed by the Sarum Ordinal, in fact, an unusually prominent one—used four times during matins, as a whole or in part—is the following: "Cilicio Cecilia membra domabat, Deum gemitibus exorabat, Almachium exuperabat, Tiburtium et Valerianum ad coronas vocabat" (Cecilia tamed her flesh with a hairshirt, entreated God successfully with her lamentations, conquered Almachius, summoned Tiburce and Valerian to crowns). Also worth citing is a pair of responsories used later in the service: "O beata Cecilia, que duos fratres convertisti, Almachium iudicem superasti, Urbanum episcopum in vultu angelico demonstrasti" (O blessed Cecilia, who converted two brothers, overcame the judge Almachius, revealed Bishop Urban in the countenance of an angel), and "Beata es, virgo, et gloriosa, et benedictus sermo oris tui" (Blessed and glorious are you, virgin, and blessed is the discourse of your mouth).[53]

These texts presumably continued to be read or sung between the lessons in Cecilia's office, whether or not they still corresponded to anything in the lessons' content. And here and there one finds a stubbornly independent breviary in which something has been done to restore the image of a strong Cecilia, compensating for the loss of the trial scene and instruction of Tiburce. Thus Stonyhurst MS. 40 revises the end of the legend in a way that emphasizes the defeat of her would-be executioner and adds a vivid last image of her heroism and fruitfulness as a teacher:

Ictibus tribus caput sanctum non potuit amputare. Sed sacro cruore suo cruentatam dereliquit confusus, que per triduum vivens multos ad Christum convertebat et sic fine felici dulciter obdormivit.

He could not cut off her sacred head with three strokes but, confounded, left her stained with her sacred blood. Living for three

---

[53] All three of these choral texts are also found in York and Hereford breviaries and in most English monastic ones as well.

days, she converted many to Christ, and so with a blessed end went peacefully to sleep.

The two Irish Sarum breviaries emphasize her heroism and fruitfulness at an earlier point in the narrative, giving a tiny but effective excerpt to summarize her trial and also including a summary of the preceding scene, in which Almachius sent officers to arrest her and she converted them, along with a large number of bystanders:

> Cum vero comprehensa esset beata Cecilia, apparitores et alios promiscui sexus amplius quam quadringentos ad fidem convertebat. Sistitur ergo coram Almachio, qui eam nimis terrebat ut Christum negaret. Respondit Cecilia: Vitam potes viventibus tollere, sed illam mortuis dare n[on] potes.

> Indeed, when blessed Cecilia was arrested, she converted to the faith both the officers and over 400 other people of both sexes. Therefore she was brought face to face with Almachius, who made great threats to get her to deny Christ. Cecilia answered, "You can take away life from the living, but you cannot give it to the dead."

Most stubbornly independent of all in its portrayal of Cecilia is the so-called Bute breviary, a fifteenth-century Sarum manuscript from Scotland. Like the Irish manuscripts—and unlike virtually every English one except the Exeter Cathedral lectionary and the full-length Sarum choir legend—this version includes a summary of the scene in which the saint converts Almachius's officers:

> Sancta vero Cecilia postquam ab apparitoribus fuerat comprehensa, eos ad Christi fidem convertebat. Et baptizati erant in domo ejus promiscui sexus amplius quam quadring[e]nti.[54]

> Indeed, after holy Cecilia had been arrested by the officers, she converted them to the faith of Christ. And over 400 people of both sexes were baptized in her house.

In this version the trial scene is, if anything, more bowdlerized than usual, with Cecilia said only to have confessed her faith ("Jussu postea Almachii cum se Christianam esse confiteretur, flammis traditur concremanda" [Afterwards, at the order of Almachius, since she confessed that she was a Christian she was committed to the flames to be burned]). But at the very end she is portrayed as taking charge of everything, including

---

[54] I quote from the published edition, entitled *Breviarium Bothanum, sive portiforium secundum usum ecclesiae cujusdam in Scotia*, ed. W. D. Macray (London: Longmans, Green, and Co., 1900), 650.

the consecration of her house, with no apparent need for Urban or any other member of the clergy:

> ... eam dereliquit sem[i]viventem. Que confirmavit Christianos in fide, et domum illius in ecclesiam consecravit, et post triduum beata virgo spiritum Deo commendavit.[55]

> He left her half-dead, and she strengthened Christians in the faith and consecrated her house as a church. After three days the blessed virgin committed her spirit to God.

The strong and independent female saint of the Bute, Irish, and Stonyhurst breviaries looks so revolutionary in our era that it is important to re-emphasize that the revolution in late-medieval English breviaries was apparently going the other way. Just as they updated other conventions and resolved other problems in the legend, in effect making the way smooth for contemporary audiences, so the abbreviators tended to produce a tamed, domesticated, decorous version of the female hero herself. Indeed, one would hesitate to call her a hero at all on the basis of many of these breviaries, since they do not allow her to do anything except convert her own husband in the privacy of their bedroom, eventually refuse the persecutor's order to sacrifice, and somehow acquire a group of female followers whom she commits to the pope when she dies.

The handful of examples discussed in this paper do not permit us to draw any hard-and-fast conclusions about Latin liturgical manuscripts, of course—or even about late-medieval British ones. But it is not too early to formulate some working hypotheses about the meaning of what we have seen. (1) The evidence turned up so far almost certainly represents just the tip of the iceberg. If a relatively obscure and uncontroversial legend like Cecilia's was prone to this much *mouvance* in British breviaries, it is only reasonable to suppose that many other saints' legends were being rewritten at the same time. And surely such rewriting cannot have been confined to British breviaries, even if (as my preliminary research suggests) it was most common there. (2) The particular revisions seen in the Cecilia legend suggest that the traditional breviary lessons about the saints were undergoing some momentous alterations in the late Middle Ages. The very nature of the legend seems to be changing, as a literal reading displaces a symbolic one; horizontal gaps in the narrative are

---

[55] The idea that Cecilia consecrated her own house evidently had some currency in the late Middle Ages, since John Wyclif cites it as a fact in one of his Latin controversial works; see S. L. Reames, "A Recent Discovery concerning the Sources of Chaucer's 'Second Nun's Tale,' " *Modern Philology* 87 (1990): 344.

carefully filled while allegorical possibilities are pruned away. The implicit use of the legend also changes. Whereas the traditional lessons were evidently designed for worship and individual meditation, with music and poetic language serving to enhance their effect, the abbreviated ones might best be described as plot summaries—most useful, one would think, to a busy churchman who just needed to be reminded of the story. At the same time, the content of the saint's example is apparently being revised and updated—brought into closer line, that is, with the values and expectations of the revisers' own culture. (3) Of course, further research may significantly modify our understanding of the patterns of change discussed in this paper. We can be sure, however, that the research is worth doing. A good deal of cultural history is preserved in these manuscripts—unnoticed until now because the scholars in the field were only looking for the original, authorial versions. Since the versions by anonymous scribes and revisers can obviously be illuminating too, we need to start paying attention to them in medieval Latin studies, as well as in the vernaculars.

General Index

Index of Manuscripts

Medieval Literature: Texts and Interpretation is a collection of nine original essays on late Middle English literature, all of which focus on the interrelations between textual and interpretive studies. Employing neither the exclusively empirical approach of much traditional textual criticism nor the almost exclusively theoretical approach of recent schools, these critics claim a middle ground—a criticism that is both empirical and theoretical.

The authors discuss such topics as the effect of editorial decisions on literary history, the interpretive information latent in medieval manuscripts, and the nature of medieval literary texts. All the major genres—romance, drama, the lyric—and the major writers—Chaucer, Langland, Lydgate—are examined in these essays.

This collection is the first to bring together these issues in one volume and will define a coherent interpretive approach. The contributors are leading authorities in the field: Richard Beadle, Julia Boffey, Charlotte Brewer, A. S. G. Edwards, Ralph Hanna III, George R. Keiser, Derek Pearsall, and Sherry L. Reames.

Tim William Machan, Associate Professor of English at Marquette University, is the author of *Techniques of Translation: Chaucer's "Boece"* (1985). He has edited the Old Norse *Vafþrúðnismál* (1989) and has published articles in *Chaucer Review, Studies in the Age of Chaucer,* and *Studies in Bibliography.*

mRts

medieval & Renaissance texts & studies
is the publishing program of the
Center for Medieval and Early Renaissance Studies
at the State University of New York at Binghamton.

mRts emphasizes books that are needed —
texts, translations, and major research tools.

mRts aims to publish the highest quality scholarship
in attractive and durable format at modest cost.